AN INTRODUCTION TO THERMAL PHYSICS

By

Dr. Baikunth Pandey

M.Sc., Ph.D.

Principal

Rajendra College

Chapra (Bihar)

DPH

DISCOVERY PUBLISHING HOUSE PVT. LTD.

NEW DELHI-110 002

Published by:
Tilak Wasan

DISCOVERY PUBLISHING HOUSE PVT. LTD.
4383/4B, Ansari Road, Darya Ganj
New Delhi-110 002 (India)
Phone : +91-11-23279245, 43596064-65
Fax : +91-11-23253475
E-mail : discoverypublishinghouse@gmail.com
sales@discoverypublishinggroup.com
parul.wasan@gmail.com
web : www.discoverypublishinggroup.com

First Edition: **2014**

ISBN: 978-93-5056-404-2

An Introduction to Thermal Physics

Printed at:
Dynamic Printers
Delhi

Preface

Thermal physics is crucial to much of modern physics, chemistry and engineering. Thermal physics, generally speaking, is the study of the statistical nature of physical systems from an energetic perspective. Heat, energy and temperature pervade our lives. We give notice to hot and cold in deciding what we wear during the day, at night and when we go to bed. We think about the topic when deciding how many covers, if any at all, we will wrap in or sleep under at night in order to maintain the right temperature. Many of us have heating and cooling systems in our homes, schools and work places that control the temperature during the day and night to keep us as comfortable as possible without spending too much money.

The temperature of an object is a property of the object that determines how hot or cold the body is. It depends on the amount of thermal energy absorbed by the object and also the nature of the object and its mass. The temperature of two objects determines the direction of the transfer of thermal energy between them. Although both objects will give out heat energy there will be a net transfer of thermal energy from the hot object to the cold object. This transfer may be by radiation or by conduction through the intervening material between them.

We must therefore consider the change in temperature of a body to be related to the change in the heat content of that body. During the last century two men, Rumford and Joule, proposed that heat was related to energy, indeed that heat was itself a form of energy. Davy showed that even cold objects like blocks of ice could be melted if they were rubbed together. In 1843 Joule performed his classic paddle wheel experiment, in which water was heated by friction from a rotating paddle wheel driven by the loss of potential energy from a falling mass.

The usual textbook statement of the zeroth law of thermodynamics is that if two systems are each in thermal equilibrium with a third system, then they are also in thermal equilibrium with each other. This statement is taken to justify a statement that all three systems have the same temperature, but, by itself, it does not justify the idea of temperature as a numerical scale for a concept of hotness which exists on a one-dimensional manifold with a sense of greater hotness. Sometimes the zeroth law is stated to provide the latter justification. For suitable systems, an empirical temperature scale may be defined by the variation of one of the other state variables, such as pressure, when all other coordinates are fixed. The second law of thermodynamics is used to define an absolute thermodynamic temperature scale for systems in thermal equilibrium.

This book will help the readers to build a strong foundational knowledge of the major topics in thermal physics. Students, specialists within the field, and researchers in related fields will appreciate the unified presentation and extensive references.

—Author

Contents

1

Introduction

HEAT AND TEMPERATURE

Heat, energy and temperature pervade our lives. Just think about it. We give concentration to hot and cold in deciding what we wear during the day, at night and when we go to bed. We think about the topic when deciding how many covers, if any at all, we will wrap in or sleep under at night in order to maintain the right temperature. Many of us have heating and cooling systems in our homes, schools and work places that control the temperature during the day and night to keep us as comfortable as possible without spending too much money. We install fans or use portable fans in our homes to keep us comfortable. Most of us have cars equipped with heating and air conditioning systems; some may even have meters in their cars that register the indoor and outdoor temperatures. Many of us watch and listen to weather reports, especially the forecasted temperatures, with great interest so that we can make decisions about what to wear and what to do on the following day.

Our bodies are highly sensitive to hot and cold. We learn very early in life through the University of Pain that we shouldn't touch a hot pot on the stove or a hot light bulb in a lamp. It is a remarkable lesson that makes an impression for a lifetime. In that same university, we learn that we should be careful about mouthing or tasting hot foods. We learn how to use our hands to feel the heat that emanates from such foods and we learn how to blow gently on the food to help cool it down. Those of us with either poor genes or poor dental care (or both) know the pain of cold ice cream hitting a nerve in a tooth cavity. And we all have vivid memories of Mom and Dad sticking a thermometer under our tongue (or elsewhere) to get our body temperature to see if we had a fever. We all know the experience of perspiring-our bodies built-in mechanism of cooling us down when temperatures begin to rise. Our bodies have a narrow range of temperatures that they can maintain. Any departure from this range can result in major consequences, including death. Energy topics have become topics of national and global interests. Politicians and scholars debate topics associated with energy supplies, energy alternatives and the impact of our energy dependencies upon the environment. Global warming is a hot topic in both national and global circles. As the price of octane gasoline rises at the pump, our interest in energy efficient transportation becomes heightened. Scientists search passionately for alternative fuels which will be cost effective and environmentally friendly. We often hear of an energy crisis or even an energy shortage. Meanwhile, scientists preach about the law of *conservation of energy*, leaving the public confused about how there can be a shortage of something that is *conserved*.

TEMPERATURE

We all have *a* feel for what temperature is. We even have a shared language that we use to qualitatively describe temperature. The water in the shower or bathtub feels hot or cold or warm. The weather outside is chilly or steamy. We certainly have a good feel for how one temperature is qualitatively different than another temperature. We may not always agree on whether the room temperature is too hot or too cold or just right. But we will likely all agree that we possess built-in thermometers for making qualitative judgments about relative temperatures.

How a Thermometer Works?

Today, there are a variety of types of thermometers. The type that most of us are familiar with from science class is the type that consists of a liquid encased in a narrow glass column. Older thermometers of this type used liquid mercury. In response to our understanding of the health concerns associated with mercury exposure, these types of thermometers usually use some type of liquid alcohol. These liquid thermometers are based on the principal of thermal expansion. When a substance gets hotter, it expands to a greater volume. Nearly all substances exhibit this behaviour of thermal expansion. It is the basis of the design and operation of thermometers.

As the temperature of the liquid in a thermometer increases, its volume increases. The liquid is enclosed in a tall, narrow glass (or plastic) column with a constant cross-sectional area. The increase in volume is thus due to a change in height of the liquid within the column. The increase in volume, and thus in the height of the liquid column, is proportional to the increase in temperature. Suppose that a 10-degree increase in temperature causes a 1-cm increase in the column's height. Then a 20-degree increase in temperature will cause a 2-cm increase in the column's height. And a 30-degree increase in temperature will causes 3-cm increase in the column's height. The relationship between the temperature and the column's height is linear over the small temperature range for which the thermometer is used. This linear relationship makes the calibration of a thermometer a relatively easy task.

The calibration of any measuring tool involves the placement of divisions or marks upon the tool to measure a quantity accurately in comparison to known standards. Any measuring tool-even a meter stick-must be calibrated. The tool needs divisions or markings; for instance, a meter stick typically has markings every 1-cm apart or every 1-mm apart. These markings must be accurately placed and the accuracy of their placement can only be judged when comparing it to another object known to have an accurate length.

A thermometer is calibrated by using two objects of known temperatures. The typical process involves using the freezing point and the boiling point of water. Water is known to freeze at 0°C and to boil at 100°C at an atmospheric pressure of 1 atm. By placing a thermometer in mixture of ice water and allowing the thermometer liquid to reach a stable height, the 0-degree mark can be placed upon the thermometer. Similarly, by placing the thermometer in boiling water (at 1 atm of pressure) and allowing the liquid level to reach a stable height, the 100-degree mark can be placed upon the thermometer. With these two markings placed upon the thermometer, 100 equally spaced divisions can be placed between them to represent the 1-degree marks. Since there is a linear relationship between the temperature and the height of the liquid, the divisions between 0 degree and 100 degree can be equally spaced. With a calibrated thermometer, accurate measurements can be made of the temperature of any object within the temperature range for which it has been calibrated.

Temperature Scales

The thermometer calibration process results in what is known as a centigrade thermometer. A centigrade thermometer has 100 divisions or intervals between the normal freezing point and the normal boiling point of water. Today, the centigrade scale is known as the Celsius scale, named after the Swedish astronomer Anders Celsius who is credited with its development. The Celsius scale is the most widely accepted temperature scale used throughout the world. It is the standard unit of temperature measurement in nearly all countries, the most notable exception being the United States. Using this scale, a temperature of 28° Celsius is abbreviated as 28°C. Usually slow to adopt the metric system and other accepted units of measurements, the United States more commonly uses the Fahrenheit temperature scale. A thermometer can be calibrated using the Fahrenheit scale in a similar manner. The difference is that the normal freezing point of water is designated as 32 degrees and the normal boiling point of water is designated as 212 degrees in the Fahrenheit scale. As such, there are 180 divisions or intervals between these two temperatures when using the Fahrenheit scale. The Fahrenheit scale is named in honour of German physicist Daniel Fahrenheit. A temperature of 76° Fahrenheit is abbreviated as

76°F. In most countries throughout the world, the Fahrenheit scale has been replaced by the use of the Celsius scale.

Temperatures expressed by the Fahrenheit scale can be converted to the Celsius scale equivalent using the equation below:

$$°C = (°F - 32°)/1.8$$

Similarly, temperatures expressed by the Celsius scale can be converted to the Fahrenheit scale equivalent using the equation below:

$$°F = 1.8 \bullet °C + 32°$$

The Kelvin Temperature Scale

The Celsius and Fahrenheit scales are the most widely used temperature scales, there are several other scales that have been used throughout history. For example, there is the Rankine scale, the Newton scale and the Romer scale, all of which are rarely used. Finally, there is the Kelvin temperature scale, which is the standard metric system of temperature measurement and perhaps the most widely used temperature scale used among scientists. The Kelvin temperature scale is similar to the Celsius temperature scale in the sense that there are 100 equal degree increments between the normal freezing point and the normal boiling point of water. However, the zero-degree mark on the Kelvin temperature scale is 273.15 units cooler than it is on the Celsius scale. So a temperature of 0 Kelvin is equivalent to a temperature of –273.15 °C. Observe that the degree symbol is not used with this system. So a temperature of 300 units above 0 Kelvin is referred to as 300 Kelvin and not 300 degree Kelvin; such a temperature is abbreviated as 300 K.

Conversions between Celsius temperatures and Kelvin temperatures and *vice versa* can be performed using one of the two equations below.

$$°C = K - 273.15°$$

$$K = °C + 273.15$$

The zero point on the Kelvin scale is known as absolute zero. It is the lowest temperature that can be achieved. The concept of an absolute temperature minimum was promoted by Scottish physicist William Thomson (a.k.a. Lord Kelvin) in 1848. Thomson theorized based on thermodynamic principles that the lowest temperature which could be achieved was –273°C. Prior to Thomson, experimentalists such as Robert Boyle (late 17th century) were well aware of the observation that the volume (and even the pressure) of a sample of gas was dependent upon its temperature.

Measurements of the variations of pressure and volume with changes in the temperature could be made and plotted. Plots of volume vs. temperature (at constant pressure) and pressure vs. temperature (at constant volume) reflected the same conclusion-the volume and the pressure of a gas reduces to zero at a temperature of -273°C.

Since these are the lowest values of volume and pressure that are possible, it is reasonable to conclude that -273°C was the lowest temperature that was possible.

Absolute Zero

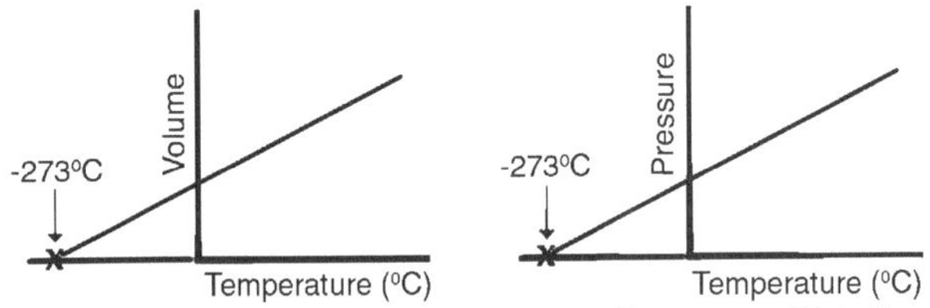

A Volume vs. Temperature and a Pressure vs. Temperature Plot will each havean x-Intercept of -273 C. The Volume and the Pressure of a Gas Seem to Reduce to 0 at a Very Specific Temperature (Assuming the Gas Remains as a gas).

Thomson referred to this minimum lowest temperature as *absolute zero* and argued that a temperature scale be adopted that had absolute zero as the lowest value on the scale. Today, that temperature scale bears his name. Scientists and engineers have been able to cool matter down to temperatures close to –273.15°C, but never below it. In the process of cooling matter to temperatures close to absolute zero, a variety of unusual properties have been observed. These properties include superconductivity, superfluidity and a state of matter known as a Bose-Einstein condensate.

THERMOMETERS AS SPEEDOMETERS

The process of calibrating a thermometer was explained and the variety of commonly used temperature scales were described. Finally, the concept of an absolute lowest temperature was discussed. But in the end, the fundamental definition of temperature was not given. Temperature was only defined in practical terms-the reading on a thermometer. Now we have to answer the more fundamental question: what is the reading on a thermometer the reflection of? What is temperature a measure of? It is at this point that we can use a more sophisticated definition of temperature. Temperature is a measure of the average kinetic energy of the particles within a sample of matter. Previously, kinetic energy was defined as the energy of motion. An object, or a particle, that is moving has kinetic energy. There are three common forms of kinetic energy-vibrational kinetic energy, rotational kinetic energy and translational kinetic energy. Up to this point of the learning, we have associated kinetic energy with the movement of an object (or particle) from one location to another. This is referred to as translational kinetic energy. A ball moving through space has translational kinetic energy. An object can also have vibrational kinetic energy; this is the energy of motion possessed by an object that is oscillating or vibrating about a fixed position. A mass attached to a spring has vibrational kinetic energy. Such a mass is not permanently displaced from its position like a ball moving through space. Finally an object can have rotational kinetic energy; this is the energy associated with an object that is rotating about an imaginary axis of rotation. A spinning top isn't moving through space and isn't vibrating about a fixed position, but there is still kinetic energy associated with its motion about an axis of rotation. This form of kinetic energy is called rotational kinetic energy.

A sample of matter consists of particles that can be vibrating, rotating and moving through the space of its container. So at the particle level, a sample of matter possesses kinetic energy. A warm cup of water on a countertop may appear to be as still as can be; yet it still has kinetic energy. At the particle level, there are atoms and molecules that are vibrating, rotating and moving through the space of its container. Stick a thermometer in the cup of water and you will see the evidence that the water possesses kinetic energy. The water's temperature, as reflected by the thermometer's reading, is a measure of the average amount of kinetic energy possessed by the water molecules.

The temperature of an object increases, the particles that compose the object begin to move faster. They either vibrate more rapidly, rotate with greater frequency or move through space with a greater speed. Increasing the temperature causes an increase in the particle speed. So as a sample of water in a pot is heated, its molecules begin to move with greater speed and this greater speed is reflected by a higher thermometer reading. Similarly, if a sample of water is placed in the freezer, its molecules begin to move slower (with a lower speed) and this is reflected by a lower thermometer reading. It is in this sense that a thermometer can be thought of as a speedometer.

At the onset of this page, temperature was defined as a measure of the average amount of kinetic energy possessed by an object. But what exactly is meant by *average* kinetic energy? In any sample of matter, particles are moving. Consider the sample of helium gas inside of a helium-filled balloon. The predominant motion of the helium atoms is translational motion. The helium atoms move through the space of the balloon from one location to another. As they do, they encounter collisions with one another and with the balloon walls. These collisions result in changes in speed and direction. As a result, there is not a single speed at which the helium atoms move, but a range of speeds. Being that there is a range of speeds with which the helium atoms move, there is a range of kinetic energies possessed by these particles. This is often referred to as a Boltzmann speed distribution and is represented graphically by the diagram below:

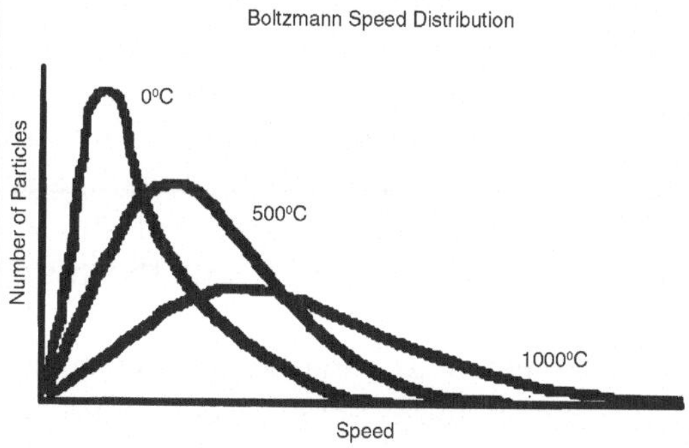

For Any Given Temperature, Then is a distribution of Speeds With Which Particles Within the Sample Can Move. As the Temperature is increased, There is a greater Percentage of Particles Moving at the Higher Speeds.

The macroscopic description of matter-a thermometer reading-is tied to a particulate description of matter-the speed with which particles move. Now we have to probe the question: what is the relationship between temperature and heat? What is heat? Is temperature the same thing as heat? Is temperature in any way related to heat? What is the cause of heat?

Concept of Heat and Energy

Consider a very hot mug of coffee on the countertop of your kitchen. We will say that the cup of coffee has a temperature of 80°C and that the surroundings (countertop, air in the kitchen, etc.) has a temperature of 26°C. What do you suppose will happen in this situation? We suspect that you know that the cup of coffee will gradually cool down over time. At 80°C, you wouldn't dare drink the coffee. Even the coffee mug will likely be too hot to touch. But over time, both the coffee mug and the coffee will cool down. Soon it will be at a drinkable temperature. And if you resist the temptation to drink the coffee, it will eventually reach room temperature. The coffee cools from 80°C to about 26°C. So what is happening over the course of time to cause the coffee to cool down? The answer to this question can be both macroscopic and particulate in nature.

On the macroscopic level, we would say that the coffee and the mug are transferring heat to the surroundings. This transfer of heat occurs from the hot coffee and hot mug to the surrounding air. The fact that the coffee lowers its temperature is a sign that the average kinetic energy of its particles is decreasing. The coffee is losing energy. The mug is also lowering its temperature; the average kinetic energy of its particles is also decreasing. The mug is also losing energy. The energy that is lost by the coffee and the mug is being transferred to the colder surroundings. We refer to this transfer of energy from the coffee and the mug to the surrounding air and countertop as heat. In this sense, heat is simply the transfer of energy from a hot object to a colder object.

Now let's consider a different scenario-that of a cold can of pop placed on the same kitchen counter. We will say that the pop and the can which contains it has a temperature of 5°C and that the surroundings (countertop, air in the kitchen, etc.) has a temperature of 26°C. What will happen to the cold can of pop over the course of time? The cold pop and the container will both warm up to room temperature. But what is happening to cause these colder-than-room-temperature objects to increase their temperature? Is the cold escaping from the pop and its container? No! There is no such thing as *the cold escaping* or *leaking*. Rather, our explanation is very similar to the explanation used to explain why the coffee cools down. There is a heat transfer.

Over time, the pop and the container increase their temperature. The temperature rises from 5°C to nearly 26°C. This increase in temperature is a sign that the average kinetic energy of the particles within the pop and the container is increasing.

In order for the particles within the pop and the container to increase their kinetic energy, they must be gaining energy from somewhere. But from where? Energy is being transferred from the surroundings (countertop, air in the kitchen, etc.) in the form of heat. Just as in the case of the cooling coffee mug, energy is being transferred from the higher temperature objects to the lower temperature object. Once more, this is known as heat-the transfer of energy from the higher temperature object to a lower temperature object.

An object decreases its temperature by releasing energy in the form of heat to its surroundings. And an object increases its temperature by gaining energy in the form of heat from its surroundings. Both the warming up and the cooling down of objects works in the same way-by heat transfer from the higher temperature object to the lower temperature object. So now we can meaningfully re-state the definition of temperature. Temperature is a measure of the ability of a substance, or more generally of any physical system, to transfer heat energy to another physical system. The higher the temperature of an object is, the greater the tendency of that object to transfer heat. The lower the temperature of an object is, the greater the tendency of that object to be on the receiving end of the heat transfer.

The fact that the volume of air in the room is so large and that the energy quickly diffuses away from the surface of the mug and of the means that the temperature change of the air in the kitchen will be abnormally small. In fact, it will be *negligibly small*. There would have to be a lot more heat transfer before there is a noticeable temperature change.

THERMAL EQUILIBRIUM

The countertop and the air in the kitchen were referred to as the surroundings. It is common in physics discussions of this type to use a mental framework of a system and the surroundings. The coffee mug (and the coffee) would be regarded as the system and everything else in the universe would be regarded as the surroundings. To keep it simple, we often narrow the scope of the surroundings from the rest of the universe to simply those objects that are immediately surrounding the system.

Suppose that a small metal cup of hot water is placed inside of a larger Styrofoam cup of cold water. Let's suppose that the temperature of the hot water is initially 70°C and that the temperature of the cold water in the outer cup is initially 5°C. And let's suppose that both cups are equipped with thermometers (or temperature probes) that measure the temperature of the water in each cup over the course of time. What do you suppose will happen?

Before you read on, think about the question and commit to some form of answer. When the cold water is done warming and the hot water is done cooling, will their temperatures be the same or different? Will the cold water warm up to a lower temperature than the temperature that the hot water cools down to? Or as the warming and cooling occurs, will their temperatures cross each other?

The hot water cooled down to approximately 30°C and the cold water warmed up to approximately the same temperature. Heat is transferred from the high temperature object (inner can of hot water) to the low temperature object (outer can of cold water). If we designate the inner cup of hot water as the system, then we can say that there is a flow of water from the system to the surroundings. As long as there is a temperature difference between the system and the surroundings, there is a heat flow between them. The heat flow is more rapid at first as depicted by the steeper slopes of the lines. Over time, the temperature difference between system and surroundings decreases and the rate of heat transfer decreases. This is denoted by the gentler slope of the two lines. Eventually, the system and the surroundings reach the same temperature and the heat transfer ceases. It is at this point, that the two objects are said to have reached thermal equilibrium.

We learned that a difference in electric potential between two locations causes a flow of charge along a conducting path between those locations. As long as an electric potential difference is maintained, a flow of charge will exist. A temperature difference between two locations will cause a flow of heat along a (thermally) conducting path between those two locations. As long as the temperature difference is maintained, a flow of heat will occur. This flow of heat continues until the two objects reach the same temperature. Once their temperatures become equal, they are said to be at thermal equilibrium and the flow of heat no longer takes place.

This principle is sometimes referred to as the zeroeth law of thermodynamics. This principle became formalized into a law after the first, second and third laws of thermodynamics had already been discovered. But because the law seemed more fundamental than the previously discovered three, it was titled the zeroeth law. All objects are governed by this law-this tendency towards thermal equilibrium. It represents a daily challenge for those who wish to control the temperature of their bodies, their food, their drinks and their homes. We use ice and insulation to try to keep our cold drinks cold and we use insulation and ongoing pulses of microwave energy to keep our hot drinks hot. We equip our vehicles, our homes and our office buildings equipped with air conditioners and fans in order to keep them cool during the warm summer months. And we equip these same vehicles and buildings with furnaces and heaters in order to keep them warm during the cold winter months. Whenever any of these systems are at a different temperature as the surroundings and not perfectly insulated from the surroundings (an ideal situation), heat will flow. This heat flow will continue until the system and surroundings have achieved equal temperatures. Because these systems have a considerably smaller volume than the surroundings, there will be a more noticeable and substantial change in temperature of these systems.

THE CALORIC THEORY

Scientists have long pondered the nature of heat. Well into the mid-19th century, the most accepted notion of heat was one that associated it with a fluid known as caloric. Noted chemist Antoine Lavoisier reasoned that there were two forms of caloric-the kind that was latent or stored in combustible materials and the kind that was sensible and observable through a temperature change. For Lavoisier and his followers, the burning of fuel resulted in the release of this latent heat to the surroundings where it was observed to cause a temperature change of the surroundings. To Lavoisier and his followers, the heat was always present-either in latent form or in sensible form. If a hot kettle of water cooled down to room temperature, it was explained by the flow of caloric from the hot water to the surroundings.

According to caloric theory, heat was material in nature. It was a physical substance. It was stuff. Like all stuff in Lavoisier's world, caloric was a conserved substance. Similar to our modern view of heat, the calorist view was that if caloric was released by one object, then it was gained by another object. The total amount of caloric never changed; it was simply transferred from one object to another and transformed from one type (latent) to another type (sensible). But unlike our modern view of heat, caloric was an actual physical substance-a fluid that could flow from one object to another. And unlike our modern view, heat was always present in one form or another. Finally, in the modern view, heat is present only when there is an energy transfer. It is senseless to speak of the heat as still existing once the two objects have come to thermal equilibrium. Heat is not something contained in an object; rather it is something transferred between objects. The heat no longer exists when the transfer ceases.

The caloric theory, it was the most accepted view up until the mid 19th century. One of the first challenges to the caloric theory was from Anglo-American scientist Benjamin Thompson (a.k.a., Count Rumford). Thompson was one of the primary scientists appointed to the task of boring out the barrels of cannons for the British government. Thompson was amazed by the high temperatures reached by the cannons and by the shavings that were shed from the cannons during the boring process. In one experiment, he immersed the cannon in a tank of water during the boring process and observed that the heat generated by the boring process was capable of boiling the surrounding water within a few hours. Thompson demonstrated that this heat generation occurred in the absence of any chemical or physical change in the cannon's composition. He attributed the generation of heat to friction between the cannon and the boring tool and argued that it could not have been the result of the flow of fluid into the water. Thompson published a paper in 1798 that challenged the view that heat was a fluid that was conserved. He advocated a mechanical view of heat, suggesting that its origin was related to the motion of atoms and not the transfer of a fluid.

English physicist James Prescott Joule took up where Thompson left off, delivering several fateful blows to the caloric theory through a collection of experiments. Joule, for whom the standard metric unit of energy is now named, performed experiments in which he experimentally related the amount of mechanical work to the amount of heat transferred from the mechanical system. In one experiment, Joule allowed falling weights to turn a paddle wheel that was submerged in a reservoir of water. A drawing of the apparatus is depicted at the right. The falling weights did work on the paddle wheel, which in turn heated the water. Joule measured both the amount of mechanical work done and the amount of heat gained by the water. Similar experiments demonstrating that heat could be generated by an electric current dealt a further blow to the thought that heat was a fluid that was contained within substances and was always conserved.

In chemical reactions, a portion of this energy can be released to the surroundings in the form of heat. However, this internal energy is not a material substance or a fluid contained by the object. It is simply the potential energy stored in the bonds that hold particles within the object together. Heat or thermal energy is the form this energy possesses when it is being transferred between systems and surroundings. There is nothing material about heat. It is neither a substance nor a fluid that is conserved. Heat is a form of energy that can be transferred from one object to another or even created at the expense of the loss of other forms of energy.

The temperature is a measure of the ability of a substance, or more generally of any physical system, to transfer heat energy to another physical system. If two objects-or if a system and its surroundings-have a different temperature, then they have a different ability to transfer heat. Over time, there will be a flow of energy from the hotter object to the cooler object. This flow of energy is referred to as heat. The heat flow causes the hotter object to cool down and the colder object to warm up. The flow of heat will continue until they reach the same temperature. At this point, the two objects have established a thermal equilibrium with each other.

METHODS OF HEAT TRANSFER

Temperature is a measure of the average amount of kinetic energy possessed by the particles in a sample of matter. The more the particles vibrate, translate and rotate, the greater the temperature of the object. You have hopefully adopted an understanding of heat as a flow of energy from a higher temperature object to a lower temperature object. It is the temperature difference between the two neighbouring objects that causes this heat transfer. The heat transfer continues until the two objects have reached thermal equilibrium and are at the same temperature. The discussion of heat transfer has been structured around some everyday examples such as the cooling of a hot mug of coffee and the warming of a cold can of pop. Finally, we have explored a thought experiment in which a metal can containing hot water is placed within a Styrofoam cup containing cold water. Heat is transferred from the hot water to the cold water until both samples have the same temperature.

A Particulate View of Transmission

Heat is transferred from the hot water to the cold water until both samples have the same temperature. In this instance, the transfer of heat from the hot water through the metal can to the cold water is sometimes referred to as conduction. Conductive heat flow involves the transfer of heat from one location to another in the absence of any material flow. There is nothing physical or material moving from the hot water to the cold water. Only energy is transferred from the hot water to the cold water. Other than the loss of energy, there is nothing else escaping from the hot water. And other than the gain of energy, there is nothing else entering the cold water.

We have to think about matter as consisting of tiny particles atoms, molecules and ions. These particles are in constant motion; this gives them kinetic energy. These particles move throughout the space of a container, colliding with each other and with the walls of their container. This is known as translational kinetic energy and is the main form of kinetic energy for gases and liquids. But these particles can also vibrate about a fixed position. This gives the particles vibrational kinetic energy and is the main form of kinetic energy for solids. To put it more simply, matter consists of little wigglers and little bangers. The wigglers are those particles vibrating about a fixed position. They possess vibrational kinetic energy. The bangers are those particles that move through the container with translational kinetic energy and collide with the container walls.

The container walls represent the perimeters of a sample of matter. Just as the *perimeter of your property* (as in real estate property) is the furthest extension of the property, so the perimeter of an object is the furthest extension of the particles within a sample of matter. At the perimeter, the *little bangers* are colliding with particles of another substance-the particles of the container or even the surrounding air. Even the wigglers that are fixed in a position along the perimeter are doing some banging. Being at the perimeter, their wiggling results in collisions with the particles that are next to them; these are the particles of the container or of the surrounding air.

At this perimeter or boundary, the collisions of the little bangers and wigglers are elastic collisions in which the total amount of kinetic energy of all colliding particles is conserved. The net effect of these elastic collisions is that there is a transfer of kinetic energy across the boundary to the particles on the opposite side. The more energetic particles will lose a little kinetic energy and the less energetic particles will gain a little kinetic energy. Temperature is a measure of the average amount of kinetic energy possessed by the particles in a sample of matter. So on average, there are more particles in the higher temperature object with greater kinetic energy than there are in the lower temperature object.

So when we average all the collisions together and apply the principles associated with elastic collisions to the particles within a sample of matter, it is logical to conclude that the higher temperature object will lose some kinetic energy and the lower temperature object will gain some kinetic energy. The collisions of our little bangers and wigglers will continue to transfer energy until the temperatures of the two objects are identical. When this state of thermal equilibrium has been reached, the average kinetic energy of both objects' particles is equal. At thermal equilibrium, there are an equal number of collisions resulting in an energy gain as there are collisions resulting in an energy loss. On average, there is no net energy transfer resulting from the collisions of particles at the perimeter.

At the macroscopic level, heat is the transfer of energy from the high temperature object to the low temperature object. At the particulate level, heat flow can be explained in terms of the net effect of the collisions of a whole bunch of little bangers. Warming and cooling is the macroscopic result of this particle-level phenomenon. Now let's apply this particle view to the scenario of the metal can with the hot water positioned inside of a Styrofoam cup containing cold water. On average, the particles with the greatest kinetic energy are the particles of the hot water. Being a fluid, those particles move about with translational kinetic energy and bang upon the particles of the metal can. As the hot water particles bang upon the particles of the metal can, they transfer energy to the metal can. This warms the metal can up. Most metals are good thermal conductors so they warm up quite quickly throughout the bulk of the can.

The can assumes nearly the same temperature as the hot water. Being a solid, the metal can consists of little wigglers. The wigglers at the outer perimeter of the metal can *bang upon* particles in the cold water. The collisions between the particles of the metal can and the particles of the cold water result in the transfer of energy to the cold water. This slowly warms the cold water up. The interaction between the particles of the hot water, the metal can and the cold water results in a transfer of energy outward from the hot water to the cold water. The average kinetic energy of the hot water particles gradually decreases; the average kinetic energy of the cold-water particles gradually increases; and eventually, thermal equilibrium would be reached at the point that the particles of the hot water and the cold water have the same average kinetic energy. At the macroscopic level, one would observe a decrease in temperature of the hot water and an increase in temperature of the cold water.

The mechanism in which heat is transferred from one object to another object through particle collisions is known as conduction. In conduction, there is no net transfer of physical stuff between the objects. Nothing material moves across the boundary. The changes in temperature are wholly explained as the result of the gains and losses of kinetic energy during collisions.

Transmission Through the Bulk of an Object

The heat transfers from one object to another through conduction. But how does it transfer through the bulk of an object? For instance, suppose we pull a ceramic coffee mug out of the cupboard and place it on the countertop. The mug is at room temperature-maybe at 26°C. Then suppose we fill the ceramic coffee mug with hot coffee at a temperature of 80°C. The mug quickly warms up. Energy first flows into the particles at the boundary between the hot coffee and the ceramic mug. But then it flows through the bulk of the ceramic to all parts of the ceramic mug. How does heat conduction occur in the ceramic itself?

The mechanism of heat transfer through the bulk of the ceramic mug is described in a similar manner as it before. The ceramic mug consists of a collection of orderly arranged wigglers. These are particles that wiggle about a fixed position. As the ceramic particles at the boundary between the hot coffee and the mug warm up, they attain a kinetic energy that is much higher than their neighbours. As they wiggle more vigorously, they bang into their neighbours and increase their vibrational kinetic energy. These particles in turn begin to wiggle more vigorously and their collisions with their neighbours increase their vibrational kinetic energy. The process of energy transfer by means of the little bangers continues from the particles at the inside of the mug (in contact with the coffee particles) to the outside of the mug (in contact with the surrounding air). Soon the entire coffee mug is warm and your hand feels it.

This device of conduction by particle-to-particle interaction is very common in ceramic materials such as a coffee mug. Does it work the same in metal objects? For instance, you likely have noticed the high temperatures attained by the metal handle of a skillet when placed upon a stovetop. The burners on the stove transfer heat to the metal skillet. If the handle of the skillet is metallic, it too attains a high temperature, certainly high enough to cause a bad burn. The transfer of heat from the skillet to the skillet handle occurs by conduction. But in metals, the conduction mechanism is slightly more complicated. In a manner similar to electrical conductivity, thermal conductivity in metals occurs by the movement of free electrons. Outer shell electrons of metal atoms are shared among atoms and are free to move throughout the bulk of the metal. These electrons carry the energy from the skillet to the skillet handle. The details of this mechanism of thermal conduction in metals are considerably more complex. The main point to grasp is that heat transfer through metals occurs without any movement of atoms from the skillet to the skillet handle. This qualifies the heat transfer as being categorized as thermal conduction.

HEAT MOVE BY CONVECTION

The model of heat transfer through the ceramic coffee mug and the metal skillet involved conduction. The ceramic of the coffee mug and the metal of the skillet are both solids. Heat transfer through solids occurs by conduction. This is primarily due to the fact that solids have orderly arrangements of particles that are fixed in place. Liquids and gases are not very good conductors of heat. In fact, they are considered good thermal insulators. Heat typically does not flow through liquids and gases by means of conduction. Liquids and gases are fluids; their particles are not fixed in place; they move about the bulk of the sample of matter. The model used for explaining heat transfer through the bulk of liquids and gases involves convection. Convection is the process of heat transfer from one location to the next by the movement of fluids. The moving fluid carries energy with it. The fluid flows from a high temperature location to a low temperature location.

To understand convection in fluids, let's consider the heat transfer through the water that is being heated in a pot on a stove. Of course the source of the heat is the stove burner. The metal pot that holds the water is heated by the stove burner.

As the metal becomes hot, it begins to conduct heat to the water. The water at the boundary with the metal pan becomes hot. Fluids expand when heated and become less dense. So as the water at the bottom of the pot becomes hot, its density decreases. Differences in water density between the bottom of the pot and the top of the pot results in the gradual formation of circulation currents. Hot water begins to rise to the top of the pot displacing the colder water that was originally there. And the colder water that was present at the top of the pot moves towards the bottom of the pot where it is heated and begins to rise. These circulation currents slowly develop over time, providing the pathway for heated water to transfer energy from the bottom of the pot to the surface.

Convection also explains how an electric heater placed on the floor of a cold room warms up the air in the room. Air present near the coils of the heater warm up. As the air warms up, it expands, becomes less dense and begins to rise. As the hot air rises, it pushes some of the cold air near the top of the room out of the way. The cold air moves towards the bottom of the room to replace the hot air that has risen. As the colder air approaches the heater at the bottom of the room, it becomes warmed by the heater and begins to rise. Once more, convection currents are slowly formed. Air travels along these pathways, carrying energy with it from the heater throughout the room.

Convection is the main method of heat transfer in fluids such as water and air. It is often said that heat rises in these situations. The more appropriate explanation is to say that heated fluid rises. For instance, as the heated air rises from the heater on a floor, it carries more energetic particles with it. As the more energetic particles of the heated air mix with the cooler air near the ceiling, the average kinetic energy of the air near the top of the room increases. This increase in the average kinetic energy corresponds to an increase in temperature. The net result of the rising hot fluid is the transfer of heat from one location to another location. The convection method of heat transfer always involves the transfer of heat by the movement of matter. This is not to be confused with the caloric theory. In caloric theory, heat was the fluid and the fluid that moved was the heat. Our model of convection considers heat to be energy transfer that is simply the result of the movement of more energetic particles.

The two examples of convection — heating water in a pot and heating air in a room-are examples of natural convection. The driving force of the circulation of fluid is natural-differences in density between two locations as the result of fluid being heated at some source. Natural convection is common in nature. The earth's oceans and atmosphere are heated by natural convection. In contrast to natural convection, forced convection involves fluid being forced from one location to another by fans, pumps and other devices. Many home heating systems involve force air heating. Air is heated at a furnace and blown by fans through ductwork and released into rooms at vent locations. This is an example of forced convection. The movement of the fluid from the hot location (near the furnace) to the cool location (the rooms throughout the house) is driven or forced by a fan. Some ovens are forced convection ovens; they have fans that blow heated air from a heat source into the oven. Some fireplaces enhance the heating ability of the fire by blowing heated air from the fireplace unit into the adjacent room. This is another example of forced convection.

HEAT TRANSFER BY RADIATION

A final method of heat transfer involves radiation. Radiation is the transfer of heat by means of electromagnetic waves. To radiate means to send out or spread from a central location. Whether it is light, sound, waves, rays, flower petals, wheel spokes or pain, if something radiates then it protrudes or spreads outward from an origin. The transfer of heat by radiation involves the carrying of energy from an origin to the space surrounding it. The energy is carried by electromagnetic waves and does not involve the movement or the interaction of matter. Thermal radiation can occur through matter or through a region of space that is void of matter (*i.e.*, a vacuum). In fact, the heat received on Earth from the sun is the result of electromagnetic waves travelling through the void of space between the Earth and the sun.

All objects radiate energy in the form of electromagnetic waves. The rate at which this energy is released is proportional to the Kelvin temperature (T) raised to the fourth power.

Radiation rate = $k \bullet T^4$

The hotter the object, the more it radiates. The sun obviously radiates off more energy than a hot mug of coffee. The temperature also affects the wavelength and frequency of the radiated waves. Objects at typical room temperatures radiate energy as infrared waves. Being invisible to the human eye, we do not see this form of radiation. An infrared camera is capable of detecting such radiation. Perhaps you have seen thermal photographs or videos of the radiation surrounding a person or animal or a hot mug of coffee or the Earth. The energy radiated from an object is usually a collection or range of wavelengths. This is usually referred to as an emission spectrum. As the temperature of an object increases, the wavelengths within the spectra of the emitted radiation also decrease. Hotter objects tend to emit shorter wavelength, higher frequency radiation. The coils of an electric toaster are considerably hotter than room temperature and emit electromagnetic radiation in the visible spectrum. Fortunately, this provides a convenient warning to its users that the coils are hot.

The tungsten filament of an incandescent light bulb emits electromagnetic radiation in the visible (and beyond) range. This radiation not only allows us to see, it also warms the glass bulb that contains the filament. Put your hand near the bulb (without touching it) and you will feel the radiation from the bulb as well.

Thermal radiation is a form of heat transfer because the electromagnetic radiation emitted from the source carries energy away from the source to surrounding (or distant) objects. This energy is absorbed by those objects, causing the average kinetic energy of their particles to increase and causing the temperatures to rise. In this sense, energy is transferred from one location to another by means of electromagnetic radiation. The image at the right was taken by a thermal imaging camera. The camera detects the radiation emitted by objects and represents it by means of a colour photograph. The *hotter* colours represent areas of objects that are emitting thermal radiation at a more intense rate.

RATES OF HEAT TRANSFER

The three main methods of heat transfer-conduction, convection and radiation. Now we will investigate the topic of the rate of heat transfer. This topic is of great importance because of the frequent need to either increase or decrease the rate at which heat flows between two locations. For instance, those of us who live in colder winter climates are in constant pursuit of methods of keeping our homes warm without spending too much money. Heat escapes from higher temperature homes to the lower temperature outdoors through walls, ceilings, windows and doors. We make efforts to reduce this heat loss by adding better insulation to walls and attics, caulking windows and doors, and buying high efficiency windows and doors.

As another example, consider electricity generation. Household electricity is most frequently manufactured by using fossil fuels or nuclear fuels. The method involves generating heat in a reactor. The heat is transferred to water and the water carries the heat to a steam turbine (or other type of electrical generator) where the electricity is produced. The challenge is to efficiently transfer the heat to the water and to the steam turbine with as little loss as possible. Attention must be given to increasing heat transfer rates in the reactor and in the turbine and decreasing heat transfer rates in the pipes between the reactor and the turbine.

The variables affecting the rate of heat transfer, we will look at a mathematical equation that expresses the dependence of rate upon these variables.

Temperature Difference

In conduction, heat is transferred from a hot temperature location to a cold temperature location. The transfer of heat will continue as long as there is a difference in temperature between the two locations. Once the two locations have reached the same temperature, thermal equilibrium is established and the heat transfer stops. The transfer of heat for a situation involving a metal can containing high temperature water that was placed within a Styrofoam cup containing low temperature water. If the two water samples are equipped with temperature probes that record changes in temperature with respect to time, then the following graphs are produced.

The slope of the line represents the rate at which the temperature of each individual sample of water is changing. The temperature is changing because of the heat transfer from the hot to the cold water. The hot water is losing energy, so its slope is negative. The cold water is gaining energy, so its slope is positive.

The rate at which temperature changes is proportional to the rate at which heat is transferred. The temperature of a sample changes more rapidly if heat is transferred at a high rate and less rapidly if heat is transferred at a low rate. When the two samples reach thermal equilibrium, there is no more heat transfer and the slope is zero.

So we can think of the slopes as being a measure of the rate of heat transfer. Over the course of time, the rate of heat transfer is decreasing. Initially heat is being transferred at a high rate as reflected by the steeper slopes. And as time progresses, the slopes of the lines are becoming less steep and more gently sloped.

The rate of heat transfer is high, the hot water has a temperature of 70°C and the cold water has a temperature of 5°C. The two containers have a 65°C difference in temperature. As the hot water begins to cool and the cold water begins to warm, the difference in their temperatures decrease and the rate of heat transfer decreases. As thermal equilibrium is approached, their temperatures are approaching the same value. With the temperature difference approaching zero, the rate of heat transfer approaches zero. In conclusion, the rate of conductive heat transfer between two locations is affected by the temperature difference between the two locations.

Material Transfer

The first variable that we have identified as affecting the rate of conductive heat transfer is the temperature difference between the two locations. The second variable of importance is the materials involved in the transfer. A metal can containing high temperature water was placed within a Styrofoam cup containing low temperature water.

The heat was transferred from water through the metal to water. The materials of importance were water, metal and water. What would happen if the heat were transferred from hot water through glass to cold water? What would happen if the heat were transferred from hot water through Styrofoam to cold water? Answer: the rate of heat transfer would be different. Replacing the inner metal can with a glass jar or a Styrofoam cup would change the rate of heat transfer. The rate of heat transfer depends on the material through which heat is transferred.

The effect of a material upon heat transfer rates is often expressed in terms of a number known as the heat transfer coefficient. Heat transfer coefficients are numerical values that are determined by experiment. The higher that the coefficient is for a particular material, the more rapidly that heat will be transferred through that material. Materials with relatively high heat transfer coefficients are referred to as thermal conductors. Materials with relatively low heat transfer coefficients are referred to as thermal insulators. The table below lists heat transfer coefficients (k) for a variety of materials, in units of W/m/°C.

Material	*k*	*Material*	*k*
Aluminum	237	Sand	0.06
Brass	110	Cellulose	0.039
Copper	398	Glass wool	0.040
Gold	315	Cotton wool	0.029
Cast Iron	55	Sheep's wool	0.038
Lead	35.2	Cellulose	0.039
Silver	427	Expanded Polystyrene	0.03
Zinc	113	Wood	0.13
Polyethylene (HDPE)	0.5	Acetone	0.16
Polyvinyl chloride (PVC)	0.19	Water	0.58
Dense Brick	1.6	Air	0.024
Concrete (Low Density)	0.2	Argon	0.016
Concrete (High Density)	1.5	Helium	0.142
Ice	2.18	Oxygen	0.024
Porcelain	1.05	Nitrogen	0.024

As is apparent from the table, heat is generally transferred by conduction at considerably higher rates through solids (coloured red) in comparison to liquids (blue) and gases (green). Heat transfer occurs at the highest rates for metals (first eight items in left-hand column) because the mechanism of conduction includes mobile electrons.

Several of the solids in the right-hand column have very low heat transfer coefficients and are considered insulators. The structure of these solids is characterized by pockets of trapped air interspersed between fibres of the solid. Since air is a great insulator, the pockets of air interspersed between these solid fibres gives these solids low heat transfer coefficients. One of these solid insulators is expanded polystyrene, the material used in Styrofoam products. Such Styrofoam products are made by blowing an inert gas at high pressure into the polystyrene before being injected into the mold. The gas causes the polystyrene to expand, leaving air filled pockets that contribute to the insulating ability of the finished product. Styrofoam is used in coolers, pop can insulators, thermos jugs, and even foam boards for household insulation. Another solid insulator is cellulose. Cellulose insulation is used to insulate attics and walls in homes. It insulates homes from heat loss as well as sound penetration. It is often blown into attics as *loose fill cellulose insulation*. It is also applied as *fibreglass batts* to fill the spacing between 2x4 studs of the exterior (and sometimes interior) walls of homes.

Area Transfer

Another variable that affects the rate of conductive heat transfer is the area through which heat is being transferred. For instance, heat transfer through windows of homes is dependent upon the size of the window. More heat will be lost from a home through a larger window than through a smaller window of the same composition and thickness. More heat will be lost from a home through a larger roof than through a smaller roof with the same insulation characteristics. Each individual particle on the surface of an object is involved in the heat conduction process. An object with a wider area has more surface particles working to conduct heat. As such, the rate of heat transfer is directly proportional to the surface area through which the heat is being conducted.

Thickness or Distance of Heat Transfer

A final variable that affects the rate of conductive heat transfer is the distance that the heat must be conducted. Heat escaping through a Styrofoam cup will escape more rapidly through a thin-walled cup than through a thick-walled cup. The rate of heat transfer is inversely proportional to the thickness of the cup. A similar statement can be made for heat being conducted through a layer of cellulose insulation in the wall of a home. The thicker that the insulation is, the lower the rate of heat transfer. Those of us who live in colder winter climates know this principle quite well. We are told to dress in layers before going outside. This increases the thickness of the materials through which heat is transferred, as well as trapping pockets of air (with high insulation ability) between the individual layers.

A Mathematical Equation of Heat Transfer

So far we have learned of four variables that affect the rate of heat transfer between two locations. The variables are the temperature difference between the two locations, the material present between the two locations, the area through which the heat will be transferred, and the distance it must be transferred. As is often the case in physics, the mathematical relationship between these variables and the rate of heat transfer can be expressed in the form of an equation. Let's consider the transfer of heat through a glass window from the inside of a home with a temperature of T_1 to the outside of a home with a temperature of T_2. The window has a surface area A and a thickness d. The coefficient of heat transfer of the window glass is k. The equation relating the heat transfer rate to these variables is

$$\text{Rate} = k \bullet A \bullet (T_1 - T_2)/d$$

The units on the rate of heat transfer are Joule/second, also known as a Watt. This equation is applicable to any situation in which heat is transferred in the same direction across a flat rectangular wall. It applies to conduction through windows, flat walls, slopes roofs (without any curvature), etc. A slightly different equation applies to conduction through curved walls such as the walls of cans, cups, glasses and pipes.

MEASURING THE QUANTITY OF HEAT

Heat gains or losses result in changes in temperature, changes in state or the performance of work. Heat is a transfer of energy. When gained or lost by an object, there will be corresponding energy changes within that object. A change in temperature is associated with changes in the average kinetic energy of the particles within the object. A change in state is associated with changes in the internal potential energy possessed by the object. And when work is done, there is an overall transfer of energy to the object upon which the work is done.

PRECISE HEAT CAPACITY

Suppose that several objects composed of different materials are heated in the same manner. Will the objects warm up at equal rates? The answer: most likely not. Different materials would warm up at different rates because each material has its own specific heat capacity. The specific heat capacity refers to the amount of heat required to cause a unit of mass (say a gram or a kilogram) to change its temperature by 1°C. Specific heat capacities of various materials are often listed in textbooks. Standard metric units are Joules/kilogram/Kelvin (J/kg/K). More commonly used units are J/g/°C.

The specific heat capacity of solid aluminum (0.904 J/g/°C) is different than the specific heat capacity of solid iron (0.449 J/g/°C). This means that it would require more heat to increase the temperature of a given mass of aluminum by 1°C compared to the amount of heat required to increase the temperature of the same mass of iron by 1°C. In fact, it would take about twice as much heat to increase the temperature of a sample of aluminum a given amount compared to the same temperature change of the same amount of iron. This is because the specific heat capacity of aluminum is nearly twice the value of iron.

Heat capacities are listed on a per gram or per kilogram basis. Occasionally, the value is listed on a *per mole* basis, in which case it is called the molar heat capacity. The fact that they are listed on a per amount basis is an indication that the quantity of heat required to raise the temperature of a substance depends on how much substance there is. Any person who has boiled a pot of water on a stove, undoubtedly know this truth. Water boils at 100°C at sea level and at slightly lowered temperatures at higher elevations. To bring a pot of water to a boil, its temperature must first be raised to 100°C. This temperature change is achieved by the absorption of heat from the stove burner.

One quickly notices that it takes considerably more time to bring a full pot of water to a boil than to bring a half-full of water to a boil. This is because the full pot of water must absorb more heat to result in the same temperature change. In fact, it requires twice as much heat to cause the same temperature change in twice the mass of water.

Specific heat capacities are also listed on a per K or a per °C basis. The fact that the specific heat capacity is listed on a per degree basis is an indication that the quantity of heat required to raise a given mass of substance to a specific temperature depends upon the change in temperature required to reach that final temperature. In other words, it is not the final temperature that is of importance, it is the overall temperature change.

It takes more heat to change the temperature of water from 20°C to 100°C (a change of 80°C) than to increase the temperature of the same amount of water from 60°C to 100°C (a change of 40°C). In fact, it requires twice as much heat to change the temperature of a given mass of water by 80°C compared to the change of 40°C. A person who wishes to bring water to a boil on a stovetop more quickly should begin with warm tap water instead of cold tap water.

The term specific heat capacity is somewhat of a *misnomer*. The term implies that substances have a capacity to contain heat. Heat is not something that is contained in an object. Heat is something that is transferred to or from an object. Objects contain energy in a variety of forms. When that energy is transferred to other objects of different temperatures, we refer to transferred energy as heat or thermal energy. While it's not likely to catch on, a more appropriate term would be specific energy capacity.

CONNECTING THE QUANTITY OF HEAT TO THE TEMPERATURE CHANGE

Specific heat capacities provide a means of mathematically relating the amount of thermal energy gained (or lost) by a sample of any substance to the sample's mass and its resulting temperature change. The relationship between these four quantities is often expressed by the following equation.

$$Q = m.C.\Delta T$$

where Q is the quantity of heat transferred to or from the object, m is the mass of the object, C is the specific heat capacity of the material the object is composed of, and ΔT is the resulting temperature change of the object.

As in all situations in science, a *delta* (Δ) value for any quantity is calculated by subtracting the initial value of the quantity from the final value of the quantity. In this case, ΔT is equal to $T_{final}-T_{initial}$. When using the above equation, the Q value can turn out to be either positive or negative. As always, a positive and a negative result from a calculation has physical significance. A positive Q value indicates that the object gained thermal energy from its surroundings; this would correspond to an increase in temperature and a positive ΔT value. A negative Q value indicates that the object released thermal energy to its surroundings; this would correspond to a decrease in temperature and a negative ΔT value.

Knowing any three of these four quantities allows an individual to calculate the fourth quantity. A common task in many physics classes involves solving problems associated with the relationships between these four quantities.

Heat and Changes of State

The accompanying equation relates the heat gained or lost by an object to the resulting temperature changes of that object.

As we have learned, sometimes heat is gained or lost but there is no temperature change. This is the case when the substance is undergoing a state change. So now we must investigate the mathematics related to changes in state and the quantity of heat.

The various state changes that could be observed for a sample of matter. The table below lists several state changes and identifies the name commonly associated with each process.

Process	Change of State
Melting	Solid to Liquid
Freezing	Liquid to Solid
Vapourization	Liquid to Gas
Condensation	Gas to Liquid
Sublimation	Solid to Gas

Deposition Gas to Solid

In the case of melting, boiling and sublimation, energy would have to be added to the sample of matter in order to cause the change of state. Such state changes are referred to as being endothermic. Freezing, condensation and deposition are exothermic; energy is released by the sample of matter when these state changes occur. So one might notice that a sample of ice (solid water) undergoes melting when it is placed on or near a burner. Heat is transferred from the burner to the sample of ice; energy is gained by the ice causing the change of state. But how much energy would be required to cause such a change of state? Is there a mathematical formula that might help in determining the answer to this question? There most certainly is.

The amount of energy required to change the state of a sample of matter depends on three things. It depends upon what the substance is, on how much substance is undergoing the state change, and upon what state change that is occurring. For instance, it requires a different amount of energy to melt ice (solid water) compared to melting iron. And it requires a different amount of energy to melt ice (solid water) as it does to vaporize the same amount of liquid water. And finally, it requires a different amount of energy to melt 10.0 grams of ice compared to melting 100.0 grams of ice. The substance, the process and the amount of substance are the three variables that affect the amount of energy required to cause a specific change in state. Use the widget below to investigate the effect of the substance and the process upon the energy change. The values for the specific heat of fusion and the specific heat of vaporization are reported on a *per amount* basis. For instance, the specific heat of fusion of water is 333 J/gram. It takes 333 J of energy to melt 1.0 gram of ice. It takes 10 times as much energy - 3330 J - to melt 10.0 grams of ice. Reasoning in this manner leads to the following formulae relating the quantity of heat to the mass of the substance and the heat of fusion and vaporization.

For melting and freezing: $Q = m.\Delta H_{fusion}$

For vapouurization and condensation: $Q = m.\Delta H_{vapourization}$

where Q represents the quantity of energy gained or released during the process, m represents the mass of the sample, ΔH_{fusion} represents the specific heat of fusion (on a per gram basis) and $\Delta H_{vapourization}$ represents the specific heat of vaporization (on a per gram basis).

Similar to the discussion regarding

$$Q = m.C.\Delta T,$$

the values of Q can be either positive or negative. Values of Q are positive for the melting and vaporization process; this is consistent with the fact that the sample of matter must gain energy in order to melt or vaporize. Values of Q are negative for the freezing and condensation process; this is consistent with the fact that the sample of matter must lose energy in order to freeze or condense.

HEATING AND COOLING CURVES

The heating curve showed how the temperature of water increased over the course of time as a sample of water in its solid state (*i.e.*, ice) was heated. We learned that the addition of heat to the sample of water could cause either changes in temperature or changes in state. At the melting point of water, the addition of heat causes a transformation of the water from the solid state to the liquid state. And at the boiling point of water, the addition of heat causes a transformation of the water from the liquid state to the gaseous state. These changes in state occurred without any changes in temperature. However, the addition of heat to a sample of water that is not at any phase change temperatures will result in a change in temperature.

The sample of water is undergoing melting; the solid is changing to a liquid. The sample of water is undergoing boiling; the liquid is changing to a gas. The quantity of heat transferred to the water is related to the mass of the sample and the temperature change by the formula $Q = m.C.\Delta T$. And the quantity of heat transferred to the water is related to the mass of the sample and the heat of fusion and vaporization by the formulae

$$Q = m.\Delta H_{fusion} \text{ and } Q = m.\Delta H_{vapourization}.$$

So now we will make an effort to calculate the quantity of heat required to change 50.0 grams of water from the solid state at -20.0°C to the gaseous state at 120.0°C. The calculation will require five steps.

While the specific heat capacity of a substance varies with temperature, we will use the following values of specific heat in our calculations:

Solid Water: C = 2.00 J/g/°C
Liquid Water: C = 4.18 J/g/°C
Gaseous Water: C = 2.01 J/g/°C

Finally, we will use the previously reported values of;

ΔH_{fusion} (333 J/g) and $\Delta H_{vapourization}$ (2.23 kJ/g).

DIFFERENCE BETWEEN HEAT AND TEMPERATURE

Knowing the difference between heat and temperature is important. It can lead to a clearer understanding of energy. We will define both terms and hopefully reach an understanding of how they are related, but not identical ideas.

INITIAL DEFINITIONS

Temperature is a number. That number is related to energy, but it is not energy itself. Temperature is a number that is related to the average kinetic energy of the molecules of a substance. It does not say that temperature is kinetic energy, nor does it state exactly what is the relation between temperature and kinetic energy.

Here is the relation: If temperature is measured in Kelvin degrees, then its value is directly proportional to the average kinetic energy of the molecules of a substance. Note that temperature is not energy, it is a number proportional to a type of energy.

Heat, on the other hand, is actual energy measured in Joules or other energy units. Heat is a measurement of some of the energy in a substance. When you add heat to a substance, you are adding energy to the substance. This added heat (energy) is usually expressed as an increase in the kinetic energies of the molecules of the substance. If the heat (energy) is used to change the state of the substance, say by melting it, then the added energy is used to break the bonds between the molecules rather than changing their kinetic energy.

AGAIN, ABOUT TEMPERATURE

So, temperature is not energy. It is, though, a number that relates to a type of energy possessed by the molecules of a substance. Temperature directly relates to the kinetic energy of the molecules. Temperature can be measured in a variety of units. If you measure it in degrees Kelvin, then the temperature value is directly proportional to the average kinetic energy of the molecules in the substance. Notice we did not say that temperature *is* the kinetic energy. We said it is a number, if in degrees Kelvin, that is proportional to the average kinetic energy of the molecules of a substance. That means if you double the Kelvin temperature of a substance, you double the average kinetic energy of its molecules.

When the average kinetic energy of the molecules goes up (a rise in temperature), the average speed of the molecules increases. A change in average kinetic energy is not directly proportional to a change in average speed.

MORE ABOUT HEAT

Heat is energy. When you add heat to a substance, you are adding energy. When heat (energy) goes into a substance one of two things can happen:

- The substance can experience a rise in temperature. The heat (the added energy) can be realised as an increase in the average kinetic energy of the molecules. The molecules now, on average, have more kinetic energy. This increase in average kinetic energy is registered as a number called temperature that changes proportionally with it. Note that this increase in the average kinetic energy of the molecules means that they will now, on average, be travelling faster than before the heat arrived.
- The substance can change state. For example, if the substance is ice, it can melt into water. Perhaps surprisingly, this change does not cause a rise in temperature. At the exact moment before melting, the average kinetic energy of the ice molecules is the same as the average kinetic energy of the water molecules at the exact moment after melting. That is, the melting ice and the just melted water are at the same temperature. Although heat (energy) is absorbed by this change of state, the absorbed energy is not used to change the average kinetic energy of the molecules, and thus proportionally change the temperature. The energy is used to change the bonding between the molecules. Changing the manner in which the molecules bond to one another can require an absorbtion of energy (heat) as in the case of melting, or require a release of energy (heat) as in the case of freezing.

So, when heat comes into a substance, energy comes into a substance. That energy can be used to increase the kinetic energy of the molecules, which means an increase in their temperature which means an increase in their speed. Or at certain temperatures the added heat could be used to break the bonds between the molecules causing a change in state that is not accompanied by a change in temperature.

THE DIFFERENCE BETWEEN TEMPERATURE AND HEAT

There is a fundamental difference between temperature and heat. Heat is the amount of energy in a system. The SI units for heat are Joules. A Joule is a Newton times a meter. A Newton is a kilogram-meter per second squared. Heat is transferred through radiation, conduction and convection. The amount that molecules are vibrating, rotating or moving is a direct function of the heat content. Energy is transported by conduction as molecules vibrate, rotate and/or collide into each other. Heat is moved along similar to dominos knocking down their neighbours in a chain reaction. An increase of electromagnetic radiation into a system causes the molecules to vibrate, rotate and/or move faster. With convection, higher energy molecules are mixed with lower energy molecules. When higher energy molecules are mixed with lower energy molecules the molecular motion will come into equilibrium over time. The faster moving molecules will slow down and the slow moving molecules will speed up.

Temperature is the MEASURE of the AVERAGE molecular motions in a system and simply has units of (degrees F, degrees C, or K). Notice that one primary difference between heat and temperature is that heat has units of Joules and temperature has units of (degrees F, degrees C, or K). Another primary difference is that energy can be transported without the temperature of a substance changing (*e.g.* latent heat, ice water remains at the freezing point even as energy is brought into the ice water to melt more ice). But, as a general statement (ignoring latent heat), as heat energy increases, the temperature will increase. If molecules increase in vibration, rotation or forward motion and pass that energy to neighbouring molecules, the measured temperature of the system will increase.

STATES OF MATTER

The simplest way to describe a state of matter is that it indicates how much heat is contained within the molecules of the substance. The more heat that is added, the more the molecules move and the harder it is for them to stay close together. The state of matter is dependent therefore upon both the temperature and pressure of a given substance. Plasma is actually the most abundant state of matter in the universe, because it is the state that exists inside stars that are undergoing nuclear fusion. Ball lightning is an example of plasma that manifests on the Earth.

Superfluids exist only for certain types of molecules when they are cooled to temperatures near absolute zero, when quantum effects begin to manifest.

Phase Transitions

Substances can go through a number of transitions between their states:

condensation - gas to liquid
fusion (or freezing) - liquid to solid
melting - solid to liquid
sublimation - solid to gas
vaporization - liquid or solid to gas.

As mentioned before, these transitions are governed for a given substance by the temperature and pressure. Water boils at lower temperatures on a high mountain than at sea level, due to the difference in pressure.

PHASE DIAGRAM

It is possible to make a phase diagram which outlines the changes in phase. Generally temperature is along the horizontal axis and pressure is along the vertical axis. It is sometimes convenient to create the diagram using Kelvin as the temperature scale, so that the origin will be 0 for both temperature and pressure, but this is obviously not required.

Curves representing the "Fusion curve" (liquid/solid barrier), the "Vaporization curve" (liquid/vapour barrier), and the "Sublimation curve" (solid/vapour barrier) can be seen in the diagram. The area near the origin is the Sublimation curve and it branches off to form the Fusion curve (which goes mostly upward) and the Vaporization curve (when goes mostly to the right).

Along the curves, the substance would be in a state of phase equilibrium, balanced precariously between the two states on either side.

The point at which all three curves meet is called the triple point. At this precise temperature and pressure, the substance will be in a state of equilibrium between the three states, and minor variations would cause it to shift between them.

The point at which the Vapourization curve "ends" is called the critical point. The pressure at this point is called the "critical pressure" and the temperature at this point is the "critical temperature." For pressures or temperatures (or both) above these values, essentially there is a blurry line between the liquid and gaseous states. Phase transitions between them do not take place, although the properties themselves can transition between those of liquids and those of gases. They just do not do so in a clear-cut transition, but metamorph gradually from one to another.

3D Phase Diagrams

In actuality, a phase diagram needs to be three dimensional to be fully complete, because the equations of state for a material are dependent upon temperature, pressure, and also on volume. These three values-temperature, pressure, and volume-are sometimes called the state coordinates of a material.

The standard, 2-dimensional phase diagram assumes that the volume remains relatively constant. You could also assume that, say, temperature remains constant, and would get a very different looking phase diagram.

Obviously, extending the phase diagram to include all three state coordinates can become rather complex and is generally not required for most analyses of state situations, especially in a non-ideal gas.

PRESSURE AND TEMPERATURE CIRCUMSTANCES OF STATE OF MATTER

The state or phase of a given set of matter can change depending on pressure and temperature conditions, transitioning to other phases as these conditions change to favour their existence; for example, solid transitions to liquid with an increase in temperature.

A state of matter is also characterised by phase transitions. A phase transition indicates a change in structure and can be recognized by an abrupt change in properties. A distinct state of matter can be defined as any set of states distinguished from any other set of states by a phase transition. Water can be said to have several distinct solid states. The appearance of superconductivity is associated with a phase transition, so there are superconductive states. Likewise, ferromagnetic states are demarcated by phase transitions and have distinctive properties. When the change of state occurs in stages the intermediate steps are called mesophases. Such phases have been exploited by the introduction of liquid crystal technology.

More recently, distinctions between states have been based on differences in molecular interrelationships. Solid is the state in which intermolecular attractions keep the molecules in fixed spatial relationships. Liquid is the state in which intermolecular attractions keep molecules in proximity, but do not keep the molecules in fixed relationships. Gas is the state in which molecules are comparatively separated and intermolecular attractions have relatively little effect on their respective motions. Plasma is a highly ionized gas that occurs at high temperatures. The intermolecular forces created by ionic attractions and repulsions give these compositions distinct properties, for which reason plasma is described as a fourth state of matter.

Forms of matter that are not composed of molecules and are organized by different forces can also be considered different states of matter. Superfluids (like Fermionic condensate) and the quark–gluon plasma are examples.

THE CLASSICAL STATES OF MATTER

Each of the classical states of matter, unlike plasma for example, can transition directly into any of the other classical states.

Solid Particles

The particles (ions, atoms or molecules) are packed closely together. The forces between particles are strong enough so that the particles cannot move freely but can only vibrate. As a result, a solid has a stable, definite shape, and a definite volume. Solids can only change their shape by force, as when broken or cut.

In crystalline solids, the particles (atoms, molecules, or ions) are packed in a regularly ordered, repeating pattern. There are many different crystal structures, and the same substance can have more than one structure (or solid phase). For example, iron has a body-centred cubic structure at temperatures below 912 °C, and a face-centred cubic structure between 912 and 1394 °C. Ice has fifteen known crystal structures, or fifteen solid phases, which exist at various temperatures and pressures.

Glasses and other non-crystalline, amorphous solids without long-range order are not thermal equilibrium ground states; therefore they are described below as non-classical states of matter. Solids can be transformed into liquids by melting, and liquids can be transformed into solids by freezing. Solids can also change directly into gases through the process of sublimation.

Liquid Fluid

A liquid is a nearly incompressible fluid that conforms to the shape of its container but retains a (nearly) constant volume independent of pressure. The volume is definite if the temperature and pressure are constant. When a solid is heated above its melting point, it becomes liquid, given that the pressure is higher than the triple point of the substance. Intermolecular (or interatomic or interionic) forces are still important, but the molecules have enough energy to move relative to each other and the structure is mobile. This means that the shape of a liquid is not definite but is determined by its container. The volume is usually greater than that of the corresponding solid, the most well known exception being water, H_2O. The highest temperature at which a given liquid can exist is its critical temperature.

Gas Container

A gas is a compressible fluid. Not only will a gas conform to the shape of its container but it will also expand to fill the container. In a gas, the molecules have enough kinetic energy so that the effect of intermolecular forces is small (or zero for an ideal gas), and the typical distance between neighbouring molecules is much greater than the molecular size. A gas has no definite shape or volume, but occupies the entire container in which it is confined. A liquid may be converted to a gas by heating at constant pressure to the boiling point, or else by reducing the pressure at constant temperature. At temperatures below its critical temperature, a gas is also called a vapour, and can be liquefied by compression alone without cooling. A vapour can exist in equilibrium with a liquid (or solid), in which case the gas pressure equals the vapour pressure of the liquid (or solid).

A supercritical fluid (SCF) is a gas whose temperature and pressure are above the critical temperature and critical pressure respectively. In this state, the distinction between liquid and gas disappears. A supercritical fluid has the physical properties of a gas, but its high density confers solvent properties in some cases, which leads to useful applications. For example, supercritical carbon dioxide is used to extract caffeine in the manufacture of decaffeinated coffee.

STATE SYMBOLS

In a chemical equation, the state of matter of the chemicals may be shown as (s) for solid, (l) for liquid, and (g) for gas. An aqueous solution is denoted 'aq'.

NON-CLASSICAL STATES

Glass is a non-crystalline or amorphous solid material that exhibits a glass transition when heated towards the liquid state. Glasses can be made of quite different classes of materials: inorganic networks (such as window glass, made of silicate plus additives), metallic alloys, ionic melts, aqueous solutions, molecular liquids, and polymers. Thermodynamically, a glass is in a metastable state with respect to its crystalline counterpart. The conversion rate, however, is practically zero.

Crystals with Some Degree of Disorder

A plastic crystal is a molecular solid with long-range positional order but with constituent molecules retaining rotational freedom; in an orientational glass this degree of freedom is frozen in a quenched disordered state. Similarly, in a spin glass magnetic disorder is frozen.

Liquid Crystal States

Liquid crystal states have properties intermediate between mobile liquids and ordered solids. Generally, they are able to flow like a liquid, but exhibiting long-range order. For example, the nematic phase consists of long rod-like molecules such as para-azoxyanisole, which is nematic in the temperature range 118–136 °C. In this state the molecules flow as in a liquid, but they all point in the same direction (within each domain) and cannot rotate freely.

Other types of liquid crystals are described in the main section on these states. Several types have technological importance, for example, in liquid crystal displays.

Magnetically Ordered

Transition metal atoms often have magnetic moments due to the net spin of electrons that remain unpaired and do not form chemical bonds. In some solids the magnetic moments on different atoms are ordered and can form a ferromagnet, an antiferromagnet or a ferrimagnet.

In a ferromagnet—for instance, solid iron—the magnetic moment on each atom is aligned in the same direction (within a magnetic domain). If the domains are also aligned, the solid is a permanent magnet, which is magnetic even in the absence of an external magnetic field. The magnetization disappears when the magnet is heated to the Curie point, which for iron is 768 °C. An antiferromagnet has two networks of equal and opposite magnetic moments, which cancel each other out so that the net magnetization is zero. For example, in nickel(II) oxide (NiO), half the nickel atoms have moments aligned in one direction and half in the opposite direction.

In a ferrimagnet, the two networks of magnetic moments are opposite but unequal, so that cancellation is incomplete and there is a non-zero net magnetization. An example is magnetite (Fe_3O_4), which contains Fe^{2+} and Fe^{3+} ions with different magnetic moments.

Microphase-separated

Copolymers can undergo microphase separation to form a diverse array of periodic nanostructures, as shown in the example of the styrene-butadiene-styrene block copolymer shown at right. Microphase separation can be understood by analogy to the phase separation between oil and water. Due to chemical incompatibility between the blocks, block copolymers undergo a similar phase separation. However, because the blocks are covalently bonded to each other, they cannot demix macroscopically as water and oil can, and so instead the blocks form nanometer-sized structures. Depending on the relative lengths of each block and the overall block topology of the polymer, many morphologies can be obtained, each its own phase of matter.

LOW-TEMPERATURE STATES

Superfluids

Close to absolute zero, some liquids form a second liquid state described as superfluid because it has zero viscosity (or infinite fluidity; *i.e.*, flowing without friction). This was discovered in 1937 for helium, which forms a superfluid below the lambda temperature of 2.17 K. In this state it will attempt to "climb" out of its container. It also has infinite thermal conductivity so that no temperature gradient can form in a superfluid. Placing a super fluid in a spinning container will result in quantized vortices.

These properties are explained by the theory that the common isotope helium-4 forms a Bose–Einstein condensate in the superfluid state. More recently, Fermionic condensate superfluids have been formed at even lower temperatures by the rare isotope helium-3 and by lithium-6.

Bose-Einstein Condensates

In 1924, Albert Einstein and Satyendra Nath Bose predicted the "Bose-Einstein condensate," (BEC) sometimes referred to as the fifth state of matter. In a BEC, matter stops behaving as independent particles, and collapses into a single quantum state that can be described with a single, uniform wavefunction.

In the gas phase, the Bose-Einstein condensate remained an unverified theoretical prediction for many years. In 1995 the research groups of Eric Cornell and Carl Wieman, of JILA at the University of Colorado at Boulder, produced the first such condensate experimentally. A Bose-Einstein condensate is "colder" than a solid. It may occur when atoms have very similar (or the same) quantum levels, at temperatures very close to absolute zero (–273.15 °C).

A Fermionic Condensates

A fermionic condensate is similar to the Bose-Einstein condensate but composed of fermions. The Pauli exclusion principle prevents fermions from entering the same quantum state, but a pair of fermions can behave as a boson, and multiple such pairs can then enter the same quantum state without restriction.

The Rydberg Molecules

One of the metastable states of strongly non-ideal plasma is Rydberg matter, which forms upon condensation of excited atoms. These atoms can also turn into ions and electrons if they reach a certain temperature. In April 2009, Nature reported the creation of Rydberg molecules from a Rydberg atom and a ground state atom, confirming that such a state of matter could exist. The experiment was performed using ultracold rubidium atoms.

Quantum Hall States

A quantum Hall state gives rise to quantized Hall voltage measured in the direction perpendicular to the current flow. A quantum spin Hall state is a theoretical phase that may pave the way for the development of electronic devices that dissipate less energy and generate less heat. This is a derivation of the Quantum Hall state of matter.

Strange Matter

Strange matter is a type of quark matter that may exist inside some neutron stars close to the Tolman-Oppenheimer-

Volkoff limit (approximately 2-3 solar masses). May be stable at lower energy states once formed.

HIGH-ENERGY STATES

Plasma (Ionized Gas)

Plasmas or ionized gases can exist at temperatures starting at several thousand degrees Celsius, where they consist of free charged particles, usually in equal numbers, such as ions and electrons. Plasma, like gas, is a state of matter that does not have definite shape or volume. Unlike gases, plasmas may self-generate magnetic fields and electric currents, and respond strongly and collectively to electromagnetic forces. The particles that make up plasmas have electric charges, so plasma can conduct electricity. Two examples of plasma are the charged air produced by lightning, and a star such as our own sun.

As a gas is heated, electrons begin to leave the atoms, resulting in the presence of free electrons, which are not bound to nuclei, and ions, which are chemical species that contain unequal number of electrons and protons, and therefore possess an electrical charge. The free electric charges make the plasma electrically conductive so that it responds strongly to electromagnetic fields. At very high temperatures, such as those present in stars, it is assumed that essentially all electrons are "free," and that a very high-energy plasma is essentially bare nuclei swimming in a sea of electrons. Plasma is the most common state of non-dark matter in the universe.

A plasma can be considered as a gas of highly ionized particles, but the powerful interionic forces lead to distinctly different properties, so that it is usually considered as a different phase or state of matter.

Quark-gluon Plasma

Quark-gluon plasma is a phase in which quarks become free and able to move independently (rather than being perpetually bound into particles) in a sea of gluons (subatomic particles that transmit the strong force that binds quarks together); this is similar to splitting molecules into atoms. This state may be briefly attainable in particle accelerators, and allows scientists to observe the properties of individual quarks, and not just theorize.

Weakly symmetric matter: for up to 10^{-12} seconds after the Big Bang the strong, weak and electromagnetic forces were unified. Strongly symmetric matter: for up to 10^{-36} seconds after the Big Bang the energy density of the universe was so high that the four forces of nature — strong, weak, electromagnetic, and gravitational — are thought to have been unified into one single force. As the universe expanded, the temperature and density dropped and the gravitational force separated, a process called symmetry breaking.

Quark-gluon plasma was discovered at CERN in 2000.

VERY HIGH ENERGY STATES

The gravitational singularity predicted by general relativity to exist at the center of a black hole is *not* a phase of matter; it is not a material object at all (although the mass-energy of matter contributed to its creation) but rather a property of spacetime at a location. It could be argued, of course, that all particles are properties of spacetime at a location, leaving a half-note of controversy on the subject.

OTHER PROPOSED STATES

Degenerate Matter

Under extremely high pressure, ordinary matter undergoes a transition to a series of exotic states of matter collectively known as degenerate matter. In these conditions, the structure of matter is supported by the Pauli exclusion principle. These are of great interest to astrophysicists, because these high-pressure conditions are believed to exist inside stars that have used up their nuclear fusion "fuel", such as the white dwarfs and neutron stars.

Electron-degenerate matter is found inside white dwarf stars. Electrons remain bound to atoms but are able to transfer to adjacent atoms. Neutron-degenerate matter is found in neutron stars.

Vast gravitational pressure compresses atoms so strongly that the electrons are forced to combine with protons via inverse beta-decay, resulting in a superdense conglomeration of neutrons. (Normally free neutrons outside an atomic nucleus will decay with a half life of just under 15 minutes, but in a neutron star, as in the nucleus of an atom, other effects stabilize the neutrons.)

Supersolid Material

A supersolid is a spatially ordered material (that is, a solid or crystal) with superfluid properties. Similar to a superfluid, a supersolid is able to move without friction but retains a rigid shape. Although a supersolid is a solid, it exhibits so many characteristic properties different from other solids that many argue it is another state of matter.

String-net Liquid

In a string-net liquid, atoms have apparently unstable arrangement, like a liquid, but are still consistent in overall pattern, like a solid. When in a normal solid state, the atoms of matter align themselves in a grid pattern, so that the spin of any electron is the opposite of the spin of all electrons touching it. But in a string-net liquid, atoms are arranged in some pattern that requires some electrons to have neighbours with the same spin. This gives rise to curious properties, as well as supporting some unusual proposals about the fundamental conditions of the universe itself.

Superglass

A superglass is a phase of matter characterized, at the same time, by superfluidity and a frozen amorphous structure.

Dark Matter

While dark matter is estimated to comprise 83% of the mass of matter in the universe, most of its properties remain a mystery due to the fact that it neither absorbs nor emits electromagnetic radiation, and there are many competing theories regarding what dark matter is actually made of. Thus, while it is hypothesized to exist and comprise the vast majority of matter in the universe, almost all of its properties are unknown and a matter of speculation, because it has only been observed through its gravitational effects.

THERMOMETRY PHYSICS

Measurement of temperature is called Thermometry Physics. Temperature is the thermal condition of the body which determines the direction of flow of heat, hence we can say the degree of hotness or coldness is known as temperature.

Temperature Scale

One of the fixed points in the freezing points of water is known as ice point or lower point. The other fixed point is the boiling point of water and known as steam point or upper point.

A Thermometer may be Graduated in following Scales :

- The upper and lower points of Centigrade scale are 100°C and 0°C and the fundamental interval is 100°C.
- The upper and lower points of Fahrenheit scale are 212°F and 32°F and fundamental interval is 180°.
- The upper and lower points of Reaumur scale are 80°R and 0°R and fundamental interval is 80°.
- The upper and lower points of Kelvin scale are 373 K and 273 K and the fundamental interval is 100°.
- The upper and lower points of Rankine scale are 672°Ra and 460°Ra and the fundamental interval is 212°.

Relation between different Temperature Scales :

$$C/100 = F - 32/180 = R/80$$

$$C/100 = K - 273/100 = Ra - 460/212$$

Note : The exact value of absolute zero is 273. 16K.

Triple Points of Water

A substance is found to exist in three states : solid, liquid and gas. For each substance there is a set of temperatures and pressures at which any two of the three states of the substance may coexist in equilibrium.

This temperature is called triple point of the substance.

Triple point of water has coordinates 0.0075°C temperature and 4.58 mm pressure.

Memorable Points

The temperature at which centigrade and Fahrenheit thermometers read the same is -40°C. The temperature at which Fahrenheit and Kelvin scale read the same is 574.25.

The temperature at which Fahrenheit and Reaumur scale read the same is -25.6. The temperature at which Celsius and Reaumur scale read the same is zero.

What is Temperature?

Temperature is a measure of the average kinetic energy of the particles making up the substance being examined. Temperature must not be confused with heat. Heat is the amount of vibrational energy contained in a particular mass.

Fixed Points

For any temperature scale, it is necessary to have two fixed points. These are temperatures at which particular physical properties manifest themselves e.g. melting, boiling.

Common fixed points:

- Ice point- temperature when pure water ice is in equilibrium with liquid water at standard atmospheric pressure (76mm Hg).
- Steam point - temperature when pure liquid water exists in equilibrium with water vapour at standard atmospheric pressure.
- Triple point - temperature when pure water ice, pure liquid water and pure water vapour exist in equilibrium.

Temperature scales are divided into a specific number of degrees between the two fixed points. The gap between the upper and lower fixed points is called the fundamental interval.

As a matter of historical interest, the Fahrenheit scale was founded on the following fixed points:

- Lower fixed point 0 deg.(0°F) the coldest salt mixture temperature attained
- Higher fixed point 100 deg.(100°F) horse blood temperature.

THE KELVIN (ABSOLUTE) TEMPERATURE SCALE

This scale uses the triple point of water as the upper fixed point and absolute zero (zero molecular motion) as the lower fixed point. The triple point of water is assigned the temperature 273.16K while the ice point is 273.15K and the steam point 373.15K.

By definition one degree Kelvin is: 1/273.16 (approximately 0.00366) of the difference between absolute zero and the triple point of water.

THE CELSIUS TEMPERATURE SCALE

The Celsius scale was introduced to replace the Centigrade scale. The Centigrade scale had the melting point of ice as its lower fixed point and the boiling point of water as the upper fixed point, both measured at standard atmospheric pressure. However, unlike the triple point of water, the melting point of ice cannot be measured with enough precision to make it an absolute marker.

The Celsius scale is closely related to the Kelvin scale. By definition one degree Celsius is: 1/273.16 (approximately 0.00366) of the difference between absolute zero and the triple point of water.

This is the same definition as for a degree Kelvin. So a temperature change of 1K equates to a change of 1°C.

The two scales are also defined by the equation:

$$\theta = T - 273.15$$

θ = temperature in °C

T = temperature in K

2

Thermal Concepts

TEMPERATURE SCALES

Fahrenheit temperature scale is a scale based on 32 for the freezing point of water and 212 for the boiling point of water, the interval between the two being divided into 180 parts. The 18th-century German physicist Daniel Gabriel Fahrenheit originally took as the zero of his scale the temperature of an equal ice-salt mixture and selected the values of 30 and 90 for the freezing point of water and normal body temperature, respectively; these later were revised to 32 and 96, but the final scale required an adjustment to 98.6 for the latter value.

FOUR TEMPERATURE SCALES

The most commonly used temperature scale in the US today is the Fahrenheit scale, abbreviated F. In this scale, water freezes at 32 degrees and boils at 212 degrees. (This only holds strictly when atmospheric pressure equals the average sea level pressure. At high altitudes, water boils at a lower temperature, as anyone who cooks in the mountains knows.) Another common scale is the Celsius scale. In this scale, water freezes at 0 degrees and boils at 100 degrees.

To convert between Fahrenheit and Celsius use this formula:

Fahrenheit Temperature = (Celsius Temperature) × (9/5) + 32

There are also temperature scales in which zero is absolute zero, the lowest possible temperature. (People have gotten close to absolute zero, but have never reached it. According to theory, we never will.) Absolute zero is at -273.15 Celsius, or -459.67 Fahrenheit. The Kelvin temperature scale uses the same size degree as Celsius, but has its zero set to absolute zero. To convert from Celsius to Kelvin, add 273.15 to the Celsius reading.

The Rankine temperature scale uses the same size degree as Fahrenheit, but has its zero set to absolute zero. To convert from Fahrenheit to Rankine, add 459.67 to the Fahrenheit reading. To convert from Kelvin to Rankine, multiply the Kelvin temperature by 9/5.

Here's one example of temperature comparisons: 68 Fahrenheit is the same as 20 Celsius, 293.15 Kelvin, and 527.67 Rankine. For other comparisons table below:

Fahrenheit	*Celsius*	*Kelvin*	*Comments*
212	100	373.15	water boils
32	0	273.15	water freezes
-40	-40	233.15	Fahrenheit equals Celsius
-320.42	-195.79	77.36	liquid nitrogen boils
-452.11	-268.95	4.2	liquid helium boils
-459.67	-273.15	0	absolute zero

ABSOLUTE ZERO

Absolute zero, according to current scientific thought, is the lowest temperature that could ever be. In fact, it's so low that we can never quite reach it, although research teams have come within a fraction of a degree. So if we can never get there, how do we know it's really there? The first clue to the existence of absolute zero came from the expansion and contraction of gasses. We know that hot air rises and cold air falls. Air rises when it's heated because it expands, so it's less dense than the cooler air around it. It has bouyancy, just like a piece of wood in a pond, which floats because it's less dense than the water. Air sinks when it cools because it contracts, so it's more dense than the warmer air around it. Suppose we took a certain amount of air and cooled it as much as we could. How much would it shrink?

When scientists first began studying the behaviour of heated and cooled gasses, they didn't have our modern cooling methods. They measured as best they could over the temperature range that they could reach. Then they plotted their data on graphs.

The graph of volume vs temperature for a sample of gas forms a straight line. (This assumes that you keep the pressure constant.) The lower the temperature, the smaller the volume. If you extend this line to low enough temperatures, it will eventually hit zero volume.

Scientists noticed that, for all gasses, the temperature at which the graph said they would reach zero volume was about -273 Celsius (about -460 Fahrenheit). This temperature became known as absolute zero, and is today the zero for the Kelvin and Rankine temperature scales. Nowadays, we know that gasses do not shrink to zero volume when cooled to absolute zero, because they condense into liquids at higher temperatures. However, absolute zero remains one of the basic concepts in cryognenics to this day. Although nothing can be colder than absolute zero, there are a few physical systems that can have what are called negative absolute temperatures. Oddly enough, such systems are hotter than some with positive temperatures!

TEMPERATURE

The temperature of an object is a property of the object that determines how hot or cold the body is. It depends on the amount of thermal energy absorbed by the object and also the nature of the object and its mass.

The temperature of two objects determines the direction of the transfer of thermal energy between them. Although both objects will give out heat energy there will be a net transfer of thermal energy from the hot object to the cold object. This transfer may be by radiation or by conduction through the intervening material between them.

The temperature of body A is greater than that of body B. T_1 is greater than T_2 and so there is a net flow of thermal energy from A to B. This fits in with the second law of thermodynamics which in one of its forms says that thermal energy cannot pass from one object to another object which is at a higher temperature without some work being done on the system.

Temperature Scales Measured

Temperature is measured with a thermometer but before we can take any readings we have to set up a temperature scale.

Thermodynamic or Kelvin Scale

The thermodynamic scale is the one that is used for scientific measurement. It is measured in units called kelvins (K), the temperature itself being given the letter T. It is defined using one fixed point- the triple point of water. This is the temperature where saturated water vapour, pure water and ice are all in equilibrium at a temperature of 273.16 K.

Absolute Zero

This is defined as 0 K, or –273.15 °C. This is the lowest temperature possible. In fact the third law of thermodynamics states that it is impossible to actually reach this temperature. When an object is cooled its internal energy is reduced and the temperature approaches absolute zero it becomes more and more difficult to lower the temperature further. You can think of the energy being reduced in smaller and smaller steps – the steps being rather like those of a stationary escalator as you near the bottom – they get smaller and smaller. We are always left with what is known as 'zero point energy' and so we can define absolute zero as the temperature at which substances have a minimum internal energy. The temperature in deep space is about 3 K above absolute zero and temperatures as low as 10^{-6} K have been achieved in the laboratory by sophisticated means.

Celsius Scale

The Celsius scale is now defined by $\theta = T - 273.15$.

The two fixed points on this scale are the ice point (0°C) and the steam point (100°C). The ice point and the triple point differ by 0.01 K.

Definition of a Temperature Scale

A temperature scale depends on the particular property on which it is based. In setting up a scale of temperature we must:

- Choose a property that varies with temperature,
- Assume that it varies uniformly with temperature.

If we denote the property by F, then on the Celsius scale:

$$\theta/100 = [F_q - F_0]/[F_{100} - F_0]$$

where q is the temperature to be measured and F_q its value at θ °C, F_0 its value at 0 °C and F_{100} its value at 100 °C.

Standard Temperature and Pressure (STP on NTP)

This set of conditions which is usually applied to gases is defined as a temperature of 273 K and a pressure of 760 mm of mercury (1.013×10^5 Pa). At STP 1 mole of any gas has a volume of 22.4×10^{-3} m^3.

HEAT ENERGY AND TEMPERATURE

Over the past few centuries scientists have put forward some very strange theories concerning the nature of heat. One of these was that heat was some sort of fluid that you added to a body to make it hot and removed from a body to cool it down. Whatever heat was, the result of its addition or removal was clear the temperature of the body rose or fell.

We must therefore consider the change in temperature of a body to be related to the change in the heat content of that body. During the last century two men, Rumford and Joule, proposed that heat was related to energy, indeed that heat was itself a form of energy. Davy showed that even cold objects like blocks of ice could be melted if they were rubbed together. In 1843 Joule performed his classic paddle wheel experiment, in which water was heated by friction from a rotating paddle wheel driven by the loss of potential energy from a falling mass. We can summarise their results as:

To heat up a body requires energy. This energy increases the internal energy of the body by increasing the kinetic energy of its molecules and so the temperature of the body rises.

ENERGY

This is one of those words which everybody knows, but is hard to define well. Energy is: the ability (or capacity) of a system to do work or supply (or produce) heat. Of course, there are words in there which require definitions also, but we will get to that in a moment. First some other energy-related stuff.

Association of Kinetic Energy

Kinetic energy is the energy associated with motion; the faster an object moves, the more kinetic energy it has. There is an equation which governs this:

$$K.E. = (1/2)\, mv^2$$

m means mass and v is velocity. This equation means that the general units on kinetic energy are:

$$(\text{mass})\ (\text{distance})^2\ (\text{time})^{-2}$$

Since any mass, time or distance unit could be used, it has been agreed to standardize on specific units for these three quantities and they are the kilogram, second and meter. Inserting them in the above equation gives:

$$(\text{kg})\ (\text{m})^2\ (\text{s})^{-2}$$

This unit has been given a name: Joule. This is in honour of James Prescott Joule, who in the mid-1800s did pioneering work on energy. The Joule is the standard metric (or SI) unit for all energy and it will be used on this web site. By the way, an older energy unit is still around. It is called "calorie" and it gets a bit of a mention on this web site, but not much.

Position of Potential Energy

Potential energy is energy that is stored by virtue of position. There are several different types of storage, of which these four are examples.

Gravitational : This is the most familiar. A rock poised to roll down a hill has potential energy. A ball thrown into the air gains more and more potential energy as it rises. The higher in the gravity field you go, the more potential energy you gain. Generally speaking, chemistry does not concern itself with the potential energy from gravity.

Electrical : In certain materials, you can remove electrons from one area and send them to another. The area losing the electrons becomes more and more positive and the area gaining them becomes negative. The greater and greater the charge difference, the more energy is stored within the system. An example of this is a storm cloud about to "hurl" a lightning strike Earthwards.

Chemical : This is slightly more complex. Certain chemicals have bonds which require little energy to break. This energy must be put into the bond to break it. However, during the course of the chemical reaction, new bonds form which give off MORE energy than that which was put in. Commonly, these reactive compounds are said to "store" energy, but the truth is that the energy released came from a process of first putting in and then getting back more than you put in.

The positional aspect comes from first breaking bonds between atoms (which takes energy) and then rearranging the atoms in new positions to form new bonds (which gives off energy). If you get back more than you put it, this is called exothermic. The net potential energy converted in the reaction shows up as heat, that is the area around the reaction goes up in temperature. If you get back less than you put in, this is called endothermic. The increase in potential energy of the newly made compounds is reflected in a heat flow from the surroundings into the chemicals, resulting in a temperature drop in the surroundings.

Nuclear : The famous equation $E = mc^2$ governs this source of potential energy. We can consider the mass itself to be potential energy, since it can be converted from a form not being used (while it is the mass), to kinetic energy. This type of potential energy is released (in measurable amounts) during radioactive decay, fission and fusion.

ABSOLUTE TEMPERATURE

Generally speaking, the temperature discussed is absolute temperature, measured in Kelvins. Here's the definition:

temperature is a property which is directly proportional to the kinetic energy of the substance under examination.

By the way, it's OK to use temperature differences measured in degrees Celsius. That's because the "size" of one degree Celsius equals one Kelvin. Also, the term "degrees Kelvin" is NOT used.

Here's another definition I found: temperature is the property which determines the direction heat will flow when two objects are brought into contact.

It turns out that temperature is a rather sophisticated concept, but this short discussion will suffice until you get into the more sophisticated classes that chemistry majors take in college. We'll measure temperature with various devices and use it in calculations and pretty much leave it at that.

Two last points, just by the by:

- When two bodies are in thermal equilibrium with a third body, then they must be in thermal equilibrium with each other. This is called the Zeroth Law of Thermodynamics and is the basis for temperature measurements, since the thermometer must come to thermal equilibrium with the object being measured.
- An important issue in temperature measurement is the ability to accurately and reroducibly measure temperature. To that end, there are on-going efforts at the international level to set temperature standards and ensure that the scientific world gets good data. A recent issue of discussion concerns how to accurately measure temperatures below 0.1 Kelvin. After all, your ordinary laboratory thermometer just will not do at those very low temperatures.

SPECIFIC HEAT AND HEAT CAPACITY

The amount of energy needed to raise the temperature of a rock is proportional to the temperature increase and to the size of the rock; it also depends on what the rock is made of. We usually measure "the size of the rock" in terms of its mass (in kilograms).

A measurement shows that it takes about 800 Joules to increase the temperature of a particular 1 Kg rock by 1 C ° — we then say that the heat capacity of rock is 800 J/Kg-degree. We can use this result to calculate the amount of energy involved in increasing the temperature of a similar 0.4 kilogram rock by 38 C°: it is just 800 J/Kg-degree × 0.4 Kg × 38 C° = 12,160 J. (You will recall from the calculation you did earlier that this is not a great deal of energy). A smaller rock or a smaller temperature increase would require proportionally less energy, as you found out in the second activity.

For any material, we define the specific heat to be the amount of energy (in Joules) needed to increase the temperature of a 1 Kg sample by 1 C°. Defined this way, the specific heat of materials varies a lot — it is 4,186 Joules/Kg-degree for water and only 130 Joules/Kg-degree for lead. The reason would be obvious if you had the 1 kilogram samples in front of you: 1 Kg is a lot of water, but a rather small lump of lead. In fact, lead atoms are very heavy, and so you don't get very many in a kilogram; a kilogram of water contains 35 times as many atoms as a kilogram of lead.

The heat capacity of most materials would be rather similar if we were to measure "the size of a rock" in terms of the number of atoms it contains instead of the number of kilograms, and define the specific heat to be the amount of energy needed to raise the temperature of 1 atom (or 1,000,000,000,000,000,000,000,000 atoms, to get a practical kind of unit).

In the third activity involving pennies and tiles, you found that equal masses of copper and ceramic have different abilities to heat air. Assuming that the difference is due to having more atoms, which cup contained more atoms, the one with the pennies or the one with the tiles?

A related concept is heat capacity. This is the amount of energy needed to raise the temperature of an object by 1 C°. An object that contains a lot of atoms has a larger heat capacity than an object containing a small number — heat capacity is the property of an object, and depends on its size. In everyday experience, thin stuff like air doesn't have much heat capacity, because there are not many atoms there. This explains how you can run you hand through a candle flame without getting burned, while you definitely will get burned on the oven rack which is much cooler than the flame— the rack has lots of atoms in it, has a large heat capacity, and can give you lots of thermal energy!

FORCE AND POTENTIAL ENERGY

We will look at just two adjacent molecules in a solid and consider the force between them and their potential energies compared with each other. We will call the separation of the two molecules at the equilibrium position where the net force between the two molecules is zero r_0. This point is also the one of minimum potential energy for the system. Therefore ro would be the separation of the molecules when no external forces are acting in the solid – i.e. it is not being squashed or stretched. In a solid all the molecules exert a force on each other and these forces can give an explanation of some of the elastic and thermal properties of a material. The potential energy of two molecules and the force between them changes with their separation.

The force at any point is found from taking the gradient of he potential energy curve, in other words F = -dv/dr, where V is the potential energy. Two forces act between the molecules:

- The repulsive force which predominates at short distances
- The attractive force which predominates at long distances.

The molecules are close to each other the repulsive force predominates, while at greater distances the attractive force is larger. The resultant force is:

- Repulsive from 0 to M
- Attractive from M to B but increasing with distance, and
- Attractive from B to infinity but decreasing with distance.

The potential energy is a minimum at this point (as would be expected). Any disturbance from this position would produce a force tending to return the molecules to M. The force of attraction between the molecules increases as the molecules arc separated from M to B. The breaking point is at B, since beyond this point the force of attraction decreases with increasing separation.

THE KINETIC THEORY OF MATTER

The Kinetic Theory of Matter states that matter is composed of a large number of small particles-individual atoms or molecules—that are in constant motion. This theory is also called the Kinetic Molecular Theory of Matter. The ancients such as the philosophers Democritus and Lucretius held that matter was composed of minute particles. They also maintained that these particles were in a state of continuous random motion within solids, liquids and gases. The theory was therefore called the kinetic theory of matter, after the Greek work kinema-motion. Strong evidence for the existence of molecules is provided by the following observations:

- The diffusion of gases and liquids - diffusion in solids has actually also been observed: a slab of lead was clamped to a slab of gold for some years, and diffusion of each metal a few millimetres into the other was demonstrated by chemical analysis.
- The mixing of two liquids to give a final volume which is less than the sum of their original volumes;
- Dissolving a solid in a liquid.

Various phenomena dealt with elsewhere in detail may be explained in terms of the kinetic theory:

- *Evaporation* - molecules in the surface of a liquid gain sufficient energy to escape from it
- *Saturated vapour pressure* - there is a dynamic equilibrium between molecules entering and leaving a liquid surface in an enclosed space
- *Surface tension* - the intermolecular forces at a liquid surface explain capillary rise, liquid drop shapes, the wetting of surfaces and so on
- *Latent heat* - energy is required to overcome the intermolecular attraction to change the state of a substance

- *Viscosity* - the movement of molecules between adjacent layers of a moving fluid and their attraction gives the effect of viscous drag
- *The behaviour of gases,* both ideal and real, may be explained in terms of molecules.

ASSUMPTIONS OF THEORY

The Kinetic Theory of Matter is a prediction of how matter should behave, based on certain assumptions and approximations. The assumptions are made from observations and experiments, such as the fact that materials consist of small molecules or atoms. Approximations are made to keep the theory from being too complex. One assumption is that the size of the particles is so small that it can be considered a point.

Matter consists of Small Particles

The first assumption in this theory is that matter consists of a large number a very small particles—either individual atoms or molecules.

Large Separation between Particles

The next assumption concerns the separation of the particles.

- In a gas, the separation between particles is very large compared to their size, such that there are no attractive or repulsive forces between the molecules.
- In a liquid, the particles are still far apart, but now they are close enough that attractive forces confine the material to the shape of its container.
- In a solid, the particles are so close that the forces of attraction confine the material to a specific shape.

Particles in Constant Motion

Another assumption is that each particle is in constant motion. In gases, the movement of the particles is assumed to be random and free. In liquids, the movement is somewhat constrained by the volume of the liquid. In solids, the motion of the particles is severely constrained to a small area, in order for the solid to maintain its shape. The velocity of each particle determines its kinetic energy.

Transfer Energy of Collisions

The numerous particles often collide with each other. Also, if a gas or liquid is confined in a container, the particles collide with the particles that make up the walls of a container.

Approximations

When atoms or molecules collide, energy may be given off in the form of electromagnetic radiation. Taking this into account could make the theory highly complex, and since the amount of radiation is small in most situations, an approximation is made that this effect is negligible.

Also, atoms and molecules have a discrete size. But charting the collisions of such particles would again make the theory too complex. Thus an approximation is made to say the size of the particles is a simple point, especially compared to the distances involved.

No Energy Change

Thus, an assumption is that the particles transfer energy in a collision with no net energy change. That means the collisions between the particles are perfectly elastic and no energy is gained or lost during the collision. This follows the Law of the Conservation of Energy.

In reality, the collisions are not perfect, and some energy is lost. But for the sake of simplicity in drawing conclusions, this theory makes the collisions elastic.

HEAT FLOW OF THERMAL ENERGY

The motion of a particle determines its kinetic energy, according to the equation

$$KE = \tfrac{1}{2}mv^2$$

where;

- KE is the kinetic energy of the particle
- m is its mass
- v^2 is the square of its velocity

The total internal kinetic energy of all the particles is called its thermal energy.

The temperature of an object or collection of matter is the average kinetic energy of the particles. Faster particles means a higher temperature. A thermometer is used to measure the temperature and put it into temperature degrees instead of kinetic energy units.

The heat is the transfer of thermal energy from an object of higher temperature to one of lower temperature. For example, an object feels warm or hot if its temperature is higher than your skin temperature.

The Kinetic Theory of Matter explains heat transfer by conduction, where thermal energy seems to move through a material, warming up cooler areas. This is called heat transfer or heat flow

Processes not covered in this theory are heat transfer by convection and by radiation.

Collisions Transfer Energy

The Kinetic Theory of Matter states that the material's particles have greater kinetic energy and are moving faster at higher temperatures. When a fast moving particle collides with a slower moving particle, it transfers some of its energy to the slower moving particle, increasing the speed of that particle.

If that particle then collides with another particle that is moving faster, its speed will be increased even more. But if it hits a slow moving particle, then it will speed up the third particle.

With billions of moving particles colliding into each other, an area of high energy or high heat will slowly diffuse across the material, making other areas warm too. By the Conservation of Energy, the total energy or total heat of the object will remain the same, but the heat will be evenly distributed throughout the object.

Rate of Transfer Energy

The rate at which the kinetic or thermal energy is transferred from one particle to another depends on the separation of the particles and their freedom to move. In a gas, the particles are allowed to move freely, but their separation distance is great, so heat or energy transfer is slow. In a liquid, the heat transfer by conduction is faster because the particles are closer together.

In a solid, the molecules are constrained into a specific location within the material. Although the particles are closer together than in liquids, the constraints in some materials actually prevent the transfer of heat energy. A good example of that is in wood.

Temperature

One important result of the kinetic theory is that the average molecular kinetic energy is proportional to the absolute temperature of the material. Absolute temperature is measured in the Kelvin scale. But in general, you can say that temperature is the measurement of the average internal kinetic energy of the material or object.

PRESSURE, VOLUME AND TEMPERATURE

If a gas is enclosed in a container, it exerts pressure on the walls of the container. The Kinetic Theory of Matter explains gas pressure as the total force exerted by gas molecules colliding against the walls of a container. If the container can expand, like with a balloon or cylinder and piston, increasing the pressure can increase the volume. Like, the balloon will get bigger. Also, if you increase the temperature of the gas—and thus the kinetic energy of its molecules—you increase the pressure or the volume of the container. This leads to a relationship between pressure, volume and temperature in an ideal gas. (An ideal gas is a gas that follows the assumptions of the Kinetic Theory of Matter.) The relationship is;

$$PV = NkT$$

where:

- P is the pressure of the ideal gas
- V is the volume of the gas container
- N is the number of gas particles
- k is the Boltzman constant in joule per kelvin per particle
- T is the temperature in the absolute or kelvin scale

This equation has a number of implications, including:

- If you decrease the pressure and hold the volume constant, the temperature decreases (principle of a refrigerator)
- If you increase the temperature and hold the pressure constant, the volume increases (heating a balloon).

SUBSTANCE OF HEAT ENERGY

The heat energy of a substance is determined by how active its atoms and molecules are. A hot object is one whose atoms and molecules are excited and show rapid movement. A cooler object's molecules and atoms will be less excited and show less movement. When these guys are in the excited state, they take up a lot of space because they're moving around so fast. When the atoms and molecules settle down, or cool down, they take up less space.

SPECIFIC HEAT CAPACITY AND ENERGY

Why is it that you can put out a candle flame with moist fingers without hurting yourself although it is at 750 °C but it is very painful to put your fingers into a cup of hot water at 80 °C? The reason is because of the difference between heat energy and temperature. There is much more heat energy "locked away" in the hot water than in the candle flame, partly because of the low mass of the flame and partly because of a property of the gas in the flame and the water known as their specific heat capacity. The amount of heat energy transferred to your hand when you put it in water or the candle flame. For the candle flame this is about 1 J and for the hot water about 40 kJ!

The temperature of an object is a measure of the energy of each individual particle within it while the heat energy is a measure of the total energy of the object as a whole. In the candle flame the molecules are moving at very high speeds because of their high temperature but there are very few of them. In the cup of water although the speed of the molecules is much less there are very many more molecules and so the heat energy content is much greater. The amount of heat needed to change the temperature of a body depends on:

- The material of the body,
- The mass of the body, and
- The change in temperature (positive or negative).

For a given body we can define a quantity known as the thermal capacity as the heat energy needed to raise its temperature by 1 K. A rather more useful quantity is the specific heat capacity of a material defined as follows: The specific heat capacity of a material is the heat energy needed to raise the temperature of 1 kg of the material by 1 K. The units of thermal capacity are joules per kelvin ($J\ K^{-1}$) and those of specific heat capacity joules per kilogram kelvin ($Jkg^{-1}K^{-1}$). Therefore: Heat energy = mass × specific heat capacity × temperature change. The values of some specific heat capacities are given in the following table:

Material	*Specific heat capacity* $Jkg^{-1}K^{-1}$
Water	4200
Copper	385
Ethanol	2500
Lead	126
Paraffin oil	2130
Aluminium	913
Turpentine	1760
Sodium	1240
Hydrogen	14 300
Iron	106
Air	993
Steel	420
Helium	5240
Concrete	3350
Oxygen	913
Polypropylene	900
Granite	820
Marble	2100
Beryllium	1970
Glass	600

It is interesting to note the large specific heat capacity of water compared with other liquids, which makes it useful as a coolant.

Sodium too has a high specific beat capacity and is used in liquid form as a coolant in some nuclear reactors.

The specific heat capacity of air is also deceptive; it actually requires quite a large amount of energy to raise the temperature of a kilogram of air. Remember, however, that at normal atmospheric pressure this mass of air has a volume of about 1 m^3.

All specific heat capacities have been found to vary with temperature: the variation for three solids. The exact reasons for this variation are complex and outside the scope of this text.

MOLAR HEAT CAPACITIES

If the molar heat capacities (the heat required to raise the temperature of one mole of a substance by 1 K) of metals are considered, then it is found that they are all approximately the same and equal to about 25 J $mol^{-1}K^{-1}$, a fact first noticed by Dulong and Petit in 1819. It follows that the heat required to raise the temperature of a sample of metal depends on how many particles the sample contains, and not on the mass of an individual molecule. The specific heat capacity is therefore directly related to the molecular structure of the material.

Heat Capacity

Heat Capacity of a system is the amount of heat required to change the temperature of *the whole system* by *one degree.*

Specific Heat

Specific heat is the amount of heat required to change temperature of *one kilogram* of a substance by *one degree.* Specific heat may be measured in *kJ/kg K* or *Btu/lb°F.*

Since enthalpy of a fluid is a function of its temperature and pressure, the temperature dependence of the enthalpy can be estimated by measuring the rise in temperature caused by the flow of heat at constant pressure. The constant-pressure heat capacity - c_p - is a measure of the change in enthalpy at a particular temperature.

Similarly, the internal energy is a function of temperature and specific volume. The constant volume heat capacity - c_v -

is a measure of the change in internal energy at a particular temperature and constant volume. Unless the pressure is extremely high the work done by applied pressure on solids and liquids can be neglected, and enthalpy can be represented by the internal energy component alone. Constant-volume and constant-pressure heats can be said to be equal.

For solids and liquids;

$$c_p = = c_v$$

The specific heat represents the amount of energy required to raise *1 kg by 1°C,* and can be thought of as the ability of a substance to absorb heat. Therefore the SI units of specific heat capacity are *kJ/kg K (kJ/kg °C)*. Water has a very large specific heat capacity (*4.19 kJ/kg °C*) compared with many fluids.

MICROSCOPIC ORIGIN OF HEAT

Heat is a macroscopic characteristic of systems, but like other thermodynamic quantities it has a microscopic explanation given by statistical mechanics. Temperature in many systems is the kinetic energy of motion of microscopic particles, and heat is the exchange of such energy. An early and vague expression of this was by Francis Bacon. Precise and detailed versions of it were developed in the nineteenth century.

Entropy

In 1856, German physicist Rudolf Clausius defined the *second fundamental theorem* (the second law of thermodynamics) in the mechanical theory of heat (thermodynamics): "if two transformations which, without necessitating any other permanent change, can mutually replace one another, be called equivalent, then the generations of the quantity of heat Q from work at the temperature T, has the *equivalence-value:*"

$$\frac{Q}{T}.$$

In 1865, he came to define the entropy symbolized by S, such that, due to the supply of the amount of heat Q at temperature T the entropy of the system is increased by

$$\Delta S = \frac{Q}{T}$$

and thus, for small changes, quantities of heat δQ (an inexact differential) are defined as quantities of $T\mathrm{d}S$, with $\mathrm{d}S$ an exact differential:

$$\delta Q = T\mathrm{d}S.$$

This equality is only valid for a closed system and if no irreversible processes take place inside the system while the heat δQ is applied. If, in contrast, irreversible processes are involved, *e.g.* some sort of friction, then there is entropy production and, instead of the above equation, one has

$$\delta Q \leq T\mathrm{d}S \text{ (Second law)}$$

This is the second law of thermodynamics for closed systems.

HEAT TRANSFER IN ENGINEERING

The discipline of heat transfer, typically considered an aspect of mechanical engineering and chemical engineering, deals with specific applied methods by which thermal energy in a system is generated, or converted, or transferred to another system.

Although the definition of heat implicitly means the transfer of energy, the term *heat transfer* encompasses this traditional usage in many engineering disciplines and laymen language.

Heat transfer includes the mechanisms of heat conduction, thermal radiation, and mass transfer. In engineering, the term convective heat transfer is used to describe the combined effects of conduction and fluid flow and is often regarded as an additional mechanism of heat transfer.

Although distinct physical laws may describe the behaviour of each of these methods, real systems often exhibit a complicated combination which are often described by a variety of complex mathematical methods.

PRACTICAL APPLICATIONS

In accordance with the first law, heat may be converted to or from work. Heat engines operate by converting heat flow from a high temperature reservoir to a low temperature reservoir into work. One example are steam engines, where the high temperature reservoir is steam generated by boiling water. The flow of heat from the hot steam to water is converted into mechanical work via a turbine or piston. Heat engines achieve high efficiency when the difference between initial and final temperature is high. Heat pumps, by contrast, use work to cause thermal energy to flow from low to high temperature, the opposite direction heat would flow spontaneously. An example is a refrigerator or air conditioner, where electric power is used to cool a low temperature system (the interior of the refrigerator) while heating a higher temperature environment (the exterior). High efficiency is achieved when the temperature difference is small.

MOLE AND AVOGADRO

Molecules and atoms are extremely small objects-both in size and mass. Consequently, working with them in the laboratory requires a large collection of them. How large does this collection need to be? A standard needs to be introduced. This standard is the "mole". The mole is based upon the carbon-12 isotope. We ask the following question: How many carbon-12 atoms are needed to have a mass of exactly 12 g. That number is NA - Avogadro's number. Thus, NA is defined by

$$NA \times (\text{mass of carbon-12 atom}) = 12 \text{ g}$$

Careful measurements yield a value for NA = $6.0221367 \times 10^{+23}$. This is an incredibly large number-almost a trillion trillion. For example, if we stack NA pennies on top of one another how tall would the stack be? The answer is it would be so tall that the stack of pennies could reach the sun and back almost 500 million times!

A convenient name is given when there is an Avogadro's number of objects-it is called a "mole". Thus in the above example there was a mole of pennies.

$$1 \text{ mole} = NA \text{ objects}$$

The mole concept is no more complicated than the more familiar concept of a dozen : 1 dozen = 12 objects. From the penny example above one might suspect that the mass of a mole of objects is huge. Well, that is true if we're considering a mole of pennies, however a mole of atoms or molecules is a different story. Recall that the atomic mass unit (amu) is defined as 1/12 the mass of a carbon-12 atom. Consequently we have the relation

$$NA \times 12 \text{ amu} = 12 \text{ g}$$

Thus, a mole of carbon-12 atoms has a mass of just 12 g. What about other atoms? In the periodic table the atomic mass of the elements is given.

For example the atomic mass of magnesium is 24.305 amu. This is the average isotopic mass of naturally occurring magnesium. What is the molar mass of magnesium in grams? From the equation above we get 1 amu = 1g/NA or 1 amu = 1.66054×10^{-24} g. Thus, a mole of magnesium atoms has a mass of NA × 24.305 amu × (1.66054×10^{-24} g/amu) = 24.305 g. A mole of magnesium atoms has a mass of 24.305 g. This example demonstrates that the atomic mass of magnesium can be interpreted in one of two ways:

- The average mass of a single magnesium atom is 24.305 amu or
- The average mass of a mole of magnesium atoms is 24.305 g;

HISTORY OF THE MOLE

The number of objects in one mole, that is, 6.02×10^{23}, is commonly referred to as Avogadro's number. Amadeo Avogadro was an Italian physics professor who proposed in 1811 that equal volumes of different gases at the same temperature contain equal numbers of molecules.

About fifty years later, an Italian scientist named Stanislao Cannizzaro used Avogadro's hypothesis to develop a set of atomic weights for the known elements by comparing the masses of equal volumes of gas.

Building on this work, an Austrian high school teacher named Johann Josef Loschmidt calculated the size of a molecule of air in 1865, and thus developed an estimate for the number of molecules in a given volume of air. While these early estimates have since been refined, they led to the concept of the mole-that is, the theory that in a defined mass of an element (its atomic weight) there is a precise number of atoms: Avogadro's number.

MOLAR MASS

A sample of any element with a mass equal to that element's atomic weight (in grams) will contain precisely one mole of atoms (6.02×10^{23} atoms).

For example, helium has an atomic weight of 4.00. Therefore, 4.00 grams of helium will contain one mole of helium atoms. You can also work with fractions (or multiples) of moles:

Mole/Weight Relationship Examples Using Helium

Moles Helium	*# Helium Atoms*	*Grams Helium*
1/4	1.505×10^{23}	1 g
1/2	3.01×10^{23}	2 g
1	6.02×10^{23}	4 g
2	1.204×10^{24}	8 g
10	6.02×10^{24}	40 g

Other atomic weights are listed on the periodic table. For each element listed, measuring out a quantity of the element equal to its atomic weight in grams will yield 6.02×10^{23} atoms of that element.

The atomic weight of an element identifies both the mass of one mole of that element *and* the total number of protons and neutrons in an atom of that element. How can that be? Let's look at hydrogen. One mole of hydrogen atoms will weigh 1.01 grams.

Each hydrogen atom consists of one proton surrounded by one electron. But remember, the electron weighs so little that it does not contribute much to an atom's weight.

Ignoring the weight of hydrogen's electrons, we can say that one mole of protons (H nuclei) weighs approximately one gram.

Since protons and neutrons have about the same mass, a mole of either of these particles will weigh about one gram.

For example, in one mole of helium, there are two moles of protons and two moles of neutrons-four grams of particles.

MOLECULAR WEIGHT

If you stand on a scale with a friend, the scale will register the combined weight of both you and your friend. When atoms form molecules, the atoms bond together, and the molecule's weight is the combined weight of all of its parts.

For example, every water molecule (H_2O) has two atoms of hydrogen and one atom of oxygen. One mole of water molecules will contain two moles of hydrogen and one mole of oxygen.

Mole and Weight Relationships of Water and Its Parts;

2 moles H + 1 mole O = 1 mole water

2 * 1.01 g + 16.00 g = 18.02 g

A bottle filled with exactly 18.02 g water will contain 6.02×10^{23} water molecules. The concept of fractions and multiples applies to molecules: 9.01 g of water would contain 1/2 mole, or 3.01×10^{23} molecules. You can calculate the molecular weight of any compound simply by summing the weights of atoms that make up that compound.

THE MOLE AS A UNIT

Since its adoption into the International System of Units, there have been a number of criticisms of the concept of the mole as a unit like the meter or the second:

- the number of molecules, etc. in a given lump of material is a fixed dimensionless quantity that can be expressed simply as a number, so does not require its own base unit;
- the SI thermodynamic mole is irrelevant to analytical chemistry and is causing avoidable costs to advanced economies;
- the mole is not a true metric (*i.e.* measuring) unit, rather it is a parametric unit and amount of substance is a parametric base quantity;

- the concepts of the SI quantity 'amount of substance' and unit 'mole' are confusing and difficult to teach.
- the SI defines numbers of entities as quantities of dimension one, and thus ignores the ontological distinction between entities and units of continuous quantities.

In chemistry, it has been known since Proust's law of definite proportions (1794) that knowledge of the mass of each of the components in a chemical system is not sufficient to define the system. Amount of substance can be described as mass divided by Proust's "definite proportions", and contains information that is missing from the measurement of mass alone. As demonstrated by Dalton's law of partial pressures (1803), a measurement of mass is not even necessary to measure the amount of substance (although in practice it is usual). There are many physical relationships between amount of substance and other physical quantities, the most notable one being the ideal gas law (where the relationship was first demonstrated in 1857). The term "mole" was first used in a textbook describing these colligative properties.

Other Units called "Mole"

Chemical engineers use the concept extensively, but the unit is rather small for industrial use. For convenience in avoiding conversions, some American engineers adopted the pound-mole (noted lb-mol or lbmol), which is defined as the number of entities in 12 lb of ^{12}C. One lb-mol is equal to 453.59237 mol. In the metric system, chemical engineers once used the kilogram-mole (noted kg-mol), which is defined as the number of entities in 12 kg of ^{12}C, and often referred to the mole as the gram-mole (noted g-mol), when dealing with laboratory data. However modern chemical engineering practice is to use the kilomole (kmol), which is identical to the kilogram-mole, but whose name and symbol adopt the SI convention for standard multiples of metric units.

Proposed Future Definition

In 2011, the 24th meeting of the General Conference on Weights and Measures (CGPM) agreed a plan for a possible revision of the SI base unit definitions on an as yet undetermined date. This plan, set forward in the meeting's first resolution, included a proposal to redefine the mole in a way that will fix "the Avogadro constant to be equal to exactly 6.022 14X $\times 10^{23}$ when it is expressed in the SI unit mol^{-1}."

Related Units

The SI units for molar concentration are mol/m^3. However, most chemical literature traditionally uses mol/dm^3, or mol dm^{-3}, which is the same as mol/L. These traditional units are often denoted by a capital letter M (pronounced "molar"), sometimes preceded by an SI prefix, for example, millimoles per litre (mmol/L) or millimolar (mM), micromoles/litre (μmol/L) or micromolar (μM), or nanomoles/L (nmol/L) or nanomolar (nM).

AVOGADRO'S NUMBER AND THE MOLE

Avogadro's number and the mole are very important to the understanding of atomic structure. The Mole is like a dozen. You can have a dozen guitars, a dozen roosters, or a dozen rocks. If you have 12 of anything then you would have what we call a dozen. The concept of the mole is just like the concept of a dozen. You can have a mole of anything. The number associated with a mole is Avogadro's number. Avogadro's number is 602,000,000,000,000,000,000,000 (6.02×10^{23}). A mole of marbles would spread over the surface of the earth, and produce a layer about 50 miles thick. A mole of sand, spread over the United States, would produce a layer 3 inches deep. A mole of dollars could not be spent at the rate of a billion dollars a day over a trillion years. This shows you just how big a mole is. This number is so large that it is usually only represented in scientific notation:

$$6.02 \times 10^{23}$$

AVOGADRO'S NUMBER IN SCIENTIFIC NOTATION

Probably the only thing you will ever have a mole of is atoms or molecules. One mole of magnesium atoms (6.02×10^{23} magnesium atoms) weigh 24.3 grams. 6.02×10^{23}

carbon atoms weigh a total of 12.0 grams. 6.02×10^{23} molecules of CO_2 gas only weigh a total of 44.0 grams.

ATOMIC WEIGHT AND MASS

The decimal number on the periodic table is the atomic mass, the mass of one atom measured in atomic mass units (amu). Amu's are defined to be 1/12 the weight of the most common isotope of Carbon. This number in grams is the mass of 1 mole of that element. For example, 6.02×10^{23} iron atoms weigh only 55.847 grams. (This is equivalent to saying one mole of iron atoms weigh 55.847 grams.) One mole of sulfur weighs 32.066 grams. (This is the same as saying 6.02×10^{23} Sulfur atoms weigh 32.066 grams) As mentioned earlier, one proton weighs 1.0073 amu and 1 neutron weighs 1.0087 amu. So the atomic mass is the mass in amus of one atom of an element, but you rarely use the mass of one atom. Even if you have a tiny speck of a metal or a microgram of an element, you have billions and billions of atoms. Thus, the mass in grams of one mole of an element (the gram atomic weight) is more useful.

3

Scope of Thermal Physics

TEMPERATURE

A convenient operational definition of temperature is that it is a measure of the average translational kinetic energy associated with the disordered microscopic motion of atoms and molecules. The flow of heat is from a high temperature region towards a lower temperature region. The details of the relationship to molecular motion are described in kinetic theory. The temperature defined from kinetic theory is called the kinetic temperature. Temperature is not directly proportional to internal energy since temperature measures only the kinetic energy part of the internal energy, so two objects with the same temperature do not in general have the same internal energy. Temperatures are measured in one of the three standard temperature scales (Celsius, Kelvin, and Fahrenheit).

WHAT IS TEMPERATURE?

In a qualitative manner, we can describe the temperature of an object as that which determines the sensation of warmth or coldness felt from contact with it.

It is easy to demonstrate that when two objects of the same material are placed together (physicists say when they are put in thermal contact), the object with the higher temperature cools while the cooler object becomes warmer until a point is reached after which no more change occurs, and to our senses, they feel the same. When the thermal changes have stopped, we say that the two objects (physicists define them more rigorously as systems) are in *thermal equilibrium*. We can then define the temperature of the system by saying that the temperature is that quantity which is the same for both systems when they are in thermal equilibrium.

If we experiment further with more than two systems, we find that many systems can be brought into thermal equilibrium with each other; thermal equilibrium does not depend on the kind of object used. Put more precisely,

> if two systems are separately in thermal equilibrium with a third, then they must also be in thermal equilibrium with each other,

and they all have the same temperature regardless of the kind of systems they are. The statement in italics, called the zeroth law of thermodynamics may be restated as follows:

If three or more systems are in thermal contact with each other and all in equilibrium together, then any two taken separately are in equilibrium with one another.

Now one of the three systems could be an instrument calibrated to measure the temperature - *i.e.* a thermometer. When a calibrated thermometer is put in thermal contact with a system and reaches thermal equilibrium, we then have a quantitative measure of the temperature of the system. For example, a mercury-in-glass clinical thermometer is put under the tongue of a patient and allowed to reach thermal equilibrium in the patient's mouth - we then see by how much the silvery mercury has expanded in the stem and read the scale of the thermometer to find the patient's temperature.

WHAT IS A THERMOMETER?

A thermometer is an instrument that measures the temperature of a system in a quantitative way. The easiest way to do this is to find a substance having a property that changes in a regular way with its temperature. The most direct 'regular' way is a linear one:

$$t(x) = ax + b,$$

where t is the temperature of the substance and changes as the property × of the substance changes. The constants a and b depend on the substance used and may be evaluated by specifying two temperature points on the scale, such as 32° for the freezing point of water and 212° for its boiling point.

For example, the element mercury is liquid in the temperature range of -38.9° C to 356.7° C. As a liquid, mercury expands as it gets warmer, its expansion rate is linear and can be accurately calibrated.

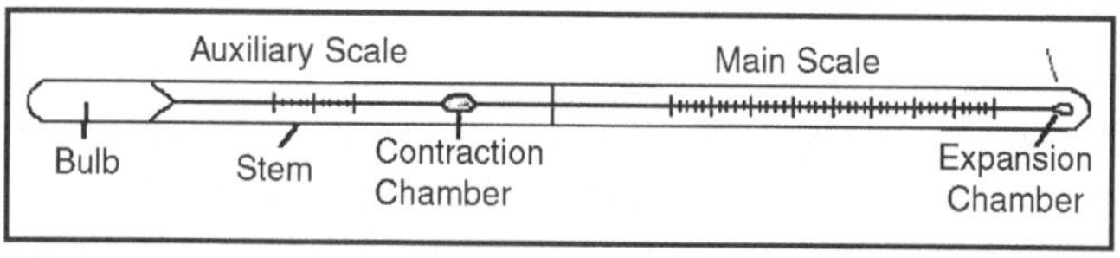

The mercury-in-glass thermometer contains a bulb filled with mercury that is allowed to expand into a capillary. Its rate of expansion is calibrated on the glass scale.

THE DEVELOPMENT OF THERMOMETERS AND TEMPERATURE SCALES

One of the first attempts to make a standard temperature scale occurred about AD 170, when Galen, in his medical writings, proposed a standard "neutral" temperature made up of equal quantities of boiling water and ice; on either side of this temperature were four degrees of heat and four degrees of cold, respectively.

The earliest devices used to measure the temperature were called thermoscopes.

They consisted of a glass bulb having a long tube extending downward into a container of coloured water, although Galileo in 1610 is supposed to have used wine. Some of the air in the bulb was expelled before placing it in the liquid, causing the liquid to rise into the tube. As the remaining air in the bulb was heated or cooled, the level of the liquid in the tube would vary reflecting the change in the air temperature. An engraved scale on the tube allowed for a quantitative measure of the fluctuations.

The air in the bulb is referred to as the thermometric medium, i.e. the medium whose property changes with temperature.

In 1641, the first sealed thermometer that used liquid rather than air as the thermometric medium was developed for Ferdinand II, Grand Duke of Tuscany. His thermometer used a sealed alcohol-in-glass device, with 50 "degree" marks on its stem but no "fixed point" was used to zero the scale. These were referred to as "spirit" thermometers.

Robert Hook, Curator of the Royal Society, in 1664 used a red dye in the alcohol. His scale, for which every degree represented an equal increment of volume equivalent to about 1/500 part of the volume of the thermometer liquid, needed only one fixed point. He selected the freezing point of water. By scaling it in this way, Hook showed that a standard scale could be established for thermometers of a variety of sizes. Hook's original thermometer became known as the standard of Gresham College and was used by the Royal Society until 1709. (The first intelligible meteorological records used this scale).

In 1702, the astronomer Ole Roemer of Copenhagen based his scale upon two fixed points: snow (or crushed ice) and the boiling point of water, and he recorded the daily temperatures at Copenhagen in 1708-1709 with this thermometer.

It was in 1724 that Gabriel Fahrenheit, an instrument maker of Däanzig and Amsterdam, used mercury as the thermometric liquid. Mercury's thermal expansion is large and fairly uniform, it does not adhere to the glass, and it remains a liquid over a wide range of temperatures. Its silvery appearance makes it easy to read.

Fahrenheit described how he calibrated the scale of his mercury thermometer: "placing the thermometer in a mixture of sal ammoniac or sea salt, ice, and water a point on the scale will be found which is denoted as zero. A second point is obtained if the same mixture is used without salt. Denote this position as 30. A third point, designated as 96, is obtained if the thermometer is placed in the mouth so as to acquire the heat of a healthy man."

On this scale, Fahrenheit measured the boiling point of water to be 212. Later he adjusted the freezing point of water to 32 so that the interval between the boiling and freezing points of water could be represented by the more rational number 180. Temperatures measured on this scale are designated as degrees Fahrenheit (° F).

In 1745, Carolus Linnaeus of Upsula, Sweden, described a scale in which the freezing point of water was zero, and the boiling point 100, making it a *centigrade* (one hundred steps) scale. Anders Celsius (1701-1744) used the reverse scale in which 100 represented the freezing point and zero the boiling point of water, still, of course, with 100 degrees between the two defining points.

In 1948 use of the Centigrade scale was dropped in favour of a new scale using degrees Celsius (° C). The Celsius scale is defined by the following two items:

- The triple point of water is defined to be 0.01° C.
- A degree Celsius equals the same temperature change as a degree on the ideal-gas scale.

On the Celsius scale the boiling point of water at standard atmospheric pressure is 99.975 C in contrast to the 100 degrees defined by the Centigrade scale.

To convert from Celsius to Fahrenheit: multiply by 1.8 and add 32.

$$^\circ F = 1.8^\circ C + 32$$

$$^\circ K = ^\circ C + 273.$$

In 1780, J. A. C. Charles, a French physician, showed that for the same increase in temperature, all gases exhibited the same increase in volume. Because the expansion coefficient of gases is so very nearly the same, it is possible to establish a temperature scale based on a single fixed point rather than the two fixed- point scales, such as the Fahrenheit and Celsius scales. This brings us back to a thermometer that uses a gas as the thermometric medium.

P. Chappuis in 1887 conducted extensive studies of gas thermometers with constant pressure or with constant volume using hydrogen, nitrogen, and carbon dioxide as the thermometric medium. Based on his results, the Comité International des Poids et Mesures adopted the constant-volume hydrogen scale based on fixed points at the ice point

(0° C) and the steam point (100° C) as the practical scale for international meteorology.

Experiments with gas thermometers have shown that there is very little difference in the temperature scale for different gases. Thus, it is possible to set up a temperature scale that is independent of the thermometric medium if it is a gas at low pressure. In this case, all gases behave like an "Ideal Gas" and have a very simple relation between their pressure, volume, and temperature:

$$pV = (\text{constant})T.$$

This temperature is called the thermodynamic temperature and is now accepted as the fundamental measure of temperature. Note that there is a naturally-defined zero on this scale - it is the point at which the pressure of an ideal gas is zero, making the temperature also zero. We will continue a discussion of "absolute zero". With this as one point on the scale, only one other fixed point need be defined. In 1933, the International Committee of Weights and Measures adopted this fixed point as the triple point of water, the temperature at which water, ice, and water vapour coexist in equilibrium); its value is set as 273.16. The unit of temperature on this scale is called the kelvin, after Lord Kelvin (William Thompson), 1824-1907, and its symbol is K (no degree symbol used).

To convert from Celsius to Kelvin, add 273.

$$K = {}^\circ C + 273.$$

Thermodynamic temperature is the fundamental temperature; its unit is the kelvin which is defined as the fraction 1/273.16 of the thermodynamic temperature of the triple point of water.

Sir William Siemens, in 1871, proposed a thermometer whose thermometric medium is a metallic conductor whose resistance changes with temperature. The element platinum does not oxidize at high temperatures and has a relatively uniform change in resistance with temperature over a large range. The *Platinum Resistance Thermometer* is now widely used as a thermoelectric thermometer and covers the temperature range from about -260° C to 1235° C.

Several temperatures were adopted as Primary reference points so as to define the International Practical Temperature Scale of 1968. The International Temperature Scale of 1990 was adopted by the International Committee of Weights and Measures at its meeting in 1989. Between 0.65K and 5.0K, the temperature is defined in terms of the vapour pressure-temperature relations of the isotopes of helium. Between 3.0K and the triple point of neon (24.5561K) the temperature is defined by means of a helium gas thermometer. Between the triple point of hydrogen (13.8033K) and the freezing point of silver (961.78°K) the temperature is defined by means of platinum resistance thermometers. Above the freezing point of silver the temperature is defined in terms of the Planck radiation law.

T. J. Seebeck, in 1826, discovered that when wires of different metals are fused at one end and heated, a current flows from one to the other. The electromotive force generated can be quantitatively related to the temperature and hence, the system can be used as a thermometer-known as a thermocouple. The thermocouple is used in industry and many different metals are used-platinum and platinum/rhodium, nickel-chromium and nickel-aluminum, for example. The National Institute of Standards and Technology (NIST) maintains databases for standardizing thermometers.

For the measurement of very low temperatures, the magnetic susceptibility of a paramagnetic substance is used as the thermometric physical quantity. For some substances, the magnetic susceptibility varies inversely as the temperature. Crystals such as cerrous magnesium nitrate and chromic potassium alum have been used to measure temperatures down to 0.05 K; these crystals are calibrated in the liquid helium range. This diagram and the last illustration in this text were taken from the Low Temperature Laboratory, Helsinki University of Technology's picture archive. For these very low, and even lower, temperatures, the thermometer is also the mechanism for cooling. Several low-temperature laboratories conduct interesting applied and theoretical research on how to reach the lowest possible temperatures and how work at these temperatures may find application.

HEAT AND THERMODYNAMICS

Prior to the 19th century, it was believed that the sense of how hot or cold an object felt was determined by how much "heat" it contained. Heat was envisioned as a liquid that flowed from a hotter to a colder object; this weightless fluid was called "caloric", and until the writings of Joseph Black (1728-1799), no distinction was made between heat and temperature. Black distinguished between the quantity (caloric) and the intensity (temperature) of heat.

Benjamin Thomson, Count Rumford, published a paper in 1798 entitled "an Inquiry Concerning the Source of Heat which is Excited by Friction". Rumford had noticed the large amount of heat generated when a cannon was drilled. He doubted that a material substance was flowing into the cannon and concluded "it appears to me to be extremely difficult if not impossible to form any distinct idea of anything capable of being excited and communicated in the manner the heat was excited and communicated in these experiments except motion."

But it was not until J. P. Joule published a definitive paper in 1847 that the caloric idea was abandoned. Joule conclusively showed that heat was a form of energy. As a result of the experiments of Rumford, Joule, and others, it was demonstrated (explicitly stated by Helmholtz in 1847), that the various forms of energy can be transformed one into another. When heat is transformed into any other form of energy, or when other forms of energy are transformed into heat, the total amount of energy (heat plus other forms) in the system is constant.

This is the first law of thermodynamics, the conservation of energy. To express it another way: it is in no way possible either by mechanical, thermal, chemical, or other means, to obtain a perpetual motion machine; *i.e.*, one that creates its own energy.

A second statement may also be made about how machines operate. A steam engine uses a source of heat to produce work. Is it possible to completely convert the heat energy into work, making it a 100% efficient machine? The answer is to be found in the second law of thermodynamics:

> No cyclic machine can convert heat energy wholly into other forms of energy. It is not possible to construct a cyclic machine that does nothing but withdraw heat energy and convert it into mechanical energy.

The second law of thermodynamics implies the irreversibility of certain processes-that of converting all heat into mechanical energy, although it is possible to have a cyclic machine that does nothing but convert mechanical energy into heat!

Sadi Carnot (1796-1832) conducted theoretical studies of the efficiencies of heat engines (a machine which converts some of its heat into useful work). He was trying to model the most efficient heat engine possible. His theoretical work provided the basis for practical improvements in the steam engine and also laid the foundations of thermodynamics. He described an ideal engine, called the Carnot engine, that is the most efficient way an engine can be constructed. He showed that the efficiency of such an engine is given by

$$\text{efficiency} = 1 - T''/T',$$

where the temperatures, T' and T'', are the hot and cold "reservoirs", respectively, between which the machine operates. On this temperature scale, a heat engine whose coldest reservoir is zero degrees would operate with 100% efficiency. This is one definition of *absolute zero,* and it can be shown to be identical to the absolute zero. The temperature scale is called the *absolute,* the *thermodynamic,* or the *kelvin* scale.

The way that the gas temperature scale and the thermodynamic temperature scale are shown to be identical is based on the *microscopic* interpretation of temperature, which postulates that the *macroscopic* measurable quantity called temperature is a result of the random motions of the microscopic particles that make up a system.

THE KINETIC THEORY

About the same time that thermodynamics was evolving, James Clerk Maxwell (1831-1879) and Ludwig Boltzmann (1844-

1906) developed a theory describing the way molecules moved-molecular dynamics. The molecules that make up a perfect gas move about, colliding with each other like billiard balls and bouncing off the surface of the container holding the gas. The energy associated with motion is called Kinetic Energy and this kinetic approach to the behaviour of ideal gases led to an interpretation of the concept of temperature on a microscopic scale.

The amount of kinetic energy each molecule has is a function of its velocity; for the large number of molecules in a gas (even at low pressure), there should be a range of velocities at any instant of time. The magnitude of the velocities of the various particles should vary greatly-no two particles should be expected to have the exact same velocity. Some may be moving very fast; others, quite slowly. Maxwell found that he could represent the distribution of velocities statistically by a function known as the Maxwellian distribution. The collisions of the molecules with their container gives rise to the pressure of the gas. By considering the average force exerted by the molecular collisions on the wall, Boltzmann was able to show that the average kinetic energy of the molecules was directly comparable to the measured pressure, and the greater the average kinetic energy, the greater the pressure. From Boyles' Law, we know that the pressure is directly proportional to the temperature, therefore, it was shown that the kinetic energy of the molecules related directly to the temperature of the gas. A simple relation holds for this:

average kinetic energy of molecules = $3kT/2$,

where k is the Boltzmann constant. Temperature is a measure of the energy of thermal motion and, at a temperature of zero, the energy reaches a minimum (quantum mechanically, the zero-point motion remains at 0 K).

In July, 1995, physicists in Boulder, Colo achieved a temperature far lower than has ever been produced before and created an entirely new state of matter predicted decades ago by Albert Einstein and Satyendra Nath Bose. The press release describes the nature of this experiment and a full description of this phenomenon is described by the University of Colorado's BEC Homepage.

Dealing with a system which contained huge numbers of molecules requires a statistical approach to the problem. About 1902, J. W. Gibbs (1839-1903) introduced *statistical mechanics* with which he demonstrated how average values of the properties of a system could be predicted from an analysis of the most probable values of these properties found from a large number of identical systems (called an ensemble). Again, in the statistical mechanical interpretation of thermodynamics, the key parameter is identified with a temperature which can be directly linked to the thermodynamic temperature, with the temperature of Maxwell's distribution, and with the perfect gas law:

> Temperature becomes a quantity definable either in terms of macroscopic thermodynamic quantities such as heat and work, or, with equal validity and identical results, in terms of a quantity which characterized the energy distribution among the particles in a system. (Quinn, "Temperature")

With this understanding of the concept of temperature, it is possible to explain how heat (thermal energy) flows from one body to another. Thermal energy is carried by the molecules in the form of their motions and some of it, through molecular collisions, is transferred to molecules of a second object when put in contact with it. This mechanism for transferring thermal energy by contact is called *conduction.*

A second mechanism of heat transport is illustrated by a pot of water set to boil on a stove-hotter water closest to the flame will rise to mix with cooler water near the top of the pot. Convection involves the bodily movement of the more energetic molecules in a liquid or gas.

The third way that heat energy can be transferred from one body to another is by radiation; this is the way that the sun warms the earth.

The radiation flows from the sun to the earth, where some of it is absorbed, heating the surface.

A major dilemma in physics since the time of Newton was how to explain the nature of this radiation.

THERMAL RADIATION

The nature of radiation has puzzled scientists for centuries. Maxwell proposed that this form of energy travels as a vibratory electric and magnetic disturbance through space in a direction perpendicular to those disturbances.

An electromagnetic wave can be defined in terms of the frequency of its oscillation, designated by the Greek letter nu (v). The wave moves in a straight line with a constant speed (designated as c if it is moving through a vacuum); the distance between successive 'peaks' of the wave is the wavelength, λ, of the wave and is equal to its speed divided by its frequency.

The electromagnetic spectrum covers an enormous range in wavelengths, from very short waves to very long ones.

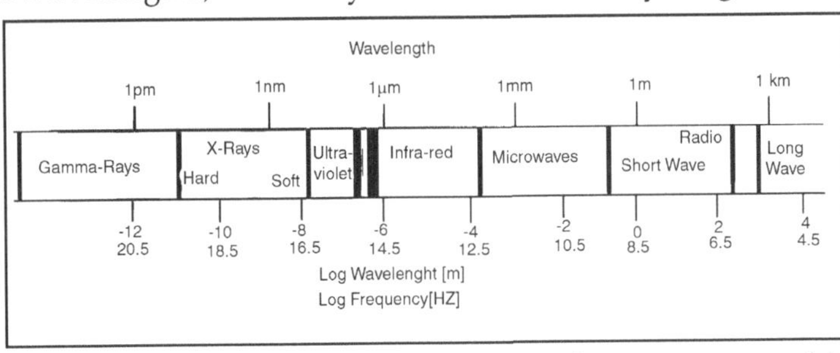

The only region of the electromagnetic spectrum to which our eye is sensitive is the "visible" range identified in the diagram by the rainbow colours.

The sun is not the only object that provides radiant energy; any object whose temperature is greater than 0 K will emit some radiant energy. The challenge to scientists was to show how this radiant energy is related to the temperature of the object.

If an object is placed in a container whose walls are at a uniform temperature, we expect the object to come into thermal equilibrium with the walls of the enclosure and the object should emit radiant energy just like the walls of the container. Such an object absorbs and radiates the same amount of energy. Now a blackened surface absorbs all radiation incident upon it and it must radiate in the same manner if it is in thermal equilibrium. Equilibrium thermal radiation is therefore called black body radiation.

The first relation between temperature and radiant energy was deduced by J. Stefan in 1884 and theoretically explained by Boltzmann about the same time. It states:

$$\textit{Total Energy} = \sigma T^4$$

where the total energy is per unit area per second emitted by the back body, T is its absolute (thermodynamic) temperature and σ is the Stefan-Boltzmann constant.

The great question at the turn of the century was to explain the way this total radiant energy emitted by a black body was spread out into the various frequencies or wavelengths of the radiation. Maxwell's "classical" theory of electromagnetic oscillators failed to explain the observed brightness distribution. It was left to Max Planck to solve the dilemma by showing that the energy of the oscillators must be *quantized*, *i.e.* the energies can not take any value but must change in steps, the size of each step, or quantum, is proportional to the frequency of the oscillator and equal to hv, where h is the Planck constant.

With this assumption, Planck derived the brightness distribution of a black body and showed that it is defined by its temperature. Once the temperature of a black body is specified, the Planck law can be used to calculate the intensity of the light emitted by the body as a function of wavelength. Conversely, if the brightness distribution of a radiating body is measured, then, by fitting a Planck curve to it, its temperature can be determined.

The hotter the body is, the brighter it is at shorter wavelengths. The surface temperature of the sun is 6000 K, and its Planck curve peaks in the visible wavelength range. For bodies cooler than the sun, the peak of the Planck curve shifts to longer wavelengths, until a temperature is reached such that very little radiant energy is emitted in the visible range.

The graphical representation of Wien's law, which states:

$$\lambda \text{ (max)} \sim 0.29/\text{T},$$

where λ(max) is the wavelength of maximum brightness in cm and T is the absolute temperature of the black body.

3 K - THE TEMPERATURE OF THE UNIVERSE

The sun and stars emit thermal radiation covering all wavelengths; other objects in the sky, like the great clouds of gas in the Milky Way, also emit thermal radiation but are much cooler. These objects are best detected by infrared and radio telescopes-telescopes whose detectors are sensitive to the longer wavelengths.

In 1965, Arno Penzias and Robert Wilson were conducting a careful calibration of their radio telescope at the Bell Laboratory at Whippany, New Jersey. The found that their receiver showed a "noise" pattern as if it were inside a container whose temperature was 3K - *i.e.* as if it were in equilibrium with a black body at 3 K. This "noise" seemed to be coming from every direction. Earlier theoretical predictions by George Gamow and other astrophysicists had predicted the existence of a cosmic 3 K background. Penzias' and Wilson's discovery was the observational confirmation of the isotropic radiation from the Universe, believed to be a relic of the "Big Bang". The enormous thermal energy released during the creation of the universe began to cool as the universe expanded. Some 12 billion years later, we are in a universe that radiates like a black body now cooled to 3 K. In 1978 Penzias and Wilson were awarded the Nobel prize in physics for this discovery.

A black body at 3K emits most of its energy in the microwave wavelength range. Molecules in the earth's atmosphere absorb this radiation so that from the ground, astronomers cannot make observations in this wavelength region. In 1989 the Cosmic Background Explorer (COBE) satellite, developed by NASA's Goddard Space Flight Center, was launched to measure the diffuse infrared and microwave radiation from the early universe. One of its instruments, the Far Infrared Absolute Spectrophotometer (FIRAS) compared the spectrum of the cosmic microwave background radiation with a precise blackbody. The cosmic microwave background spectrum was measured with a precision of 0.03% and it fit precisely with a black body of temperature 2.726 K. Even though there are billions of stars in the universe, these precise COBE measurements show that 99.97% of the radiant energy of the Universe was released within the first year after the Big Bang itself and now resides in this thermal 3 K radiation field.

TEMPERATURE EXPLAINED

Imagine a room full of air. The air is made of individual particles (molecules, to be precise). These particles don't stand still-they all have their own share of kinetic energy accumulated from the odd billiard table, as well as sources like the Sun. Remember, they can't lose their kinetic energy unless they transfer it elsewhere, and since this residual energy is already all around, that's kind of difficult to do. So, the gas particles are all doomed to travel at their own speed around the room, bouncing off the walls (and each other) like billiard balls. Now if you look at all the gas particles in the room together, and take the average energy of each particle; there's a name for that: it's called *temperature*. Well, not quite. You actually have to multiply the average kinetic energy by a conversion factor to convert it into units of kelvins, but that's all you have to do.

$$T = \frac{E}{k}$$

where

T = temperature,

E = average kinetic energy per particle, and

k is a conversion factor, known as the *Boltzmann Constant*

The Boltzmann constant, which is simply a conversion factor between temperature and energy units, has the following values, depending on whether you deal with energy in units of joules (J) or electron-volts (eV):

$$k = 1.3806505 \times 10^{-23} \text{ J/K}$$

$$= 8.617\ 339 \times 10^{-5} \text{ eV/K}$$

This also explains why it's impossible to get colder to a temperature colder than 0K (absolute zero). How, after all, can a particle have energy lower than zero? The very concept of temperatures lower than absolute zero simply doesn't make sense.

Heat Explained

Heating is the transfer of the kinetic energy of particles from one body to another. A hotter object placed next to a cooler object will always transfer heat from itself into the cooler object, until both objects are of equal temperature.

For example, if you place a cup of water, at room temperature; into a room, at the same temperature; then for every time an air particle rebounds off and transfers energy to a water particle, a water particle will transfer an equivalent amount of energy into the air-so that on average, the temperature of the water will remain unchanged.

If, on the other hand, the air and water are of different relative temperatures, then the amount of energy transferred between the two bodies will be unbalanced, hence the cooler body heats up and the hotter body cools down.

Incidently, remember that temperature is only the *average* kinetic energy per molecule. So, even though a cup of water may only be a few degrees above freezing (nowhere near boiling point), the interactions between molecules mean that some molecules will be moving much faster than others. In fact, some of the molecules in water move so fast that they fly right out of the cup and into the atmosphere.

TEMPERATURE SCALES AND MEASUREMENTS

Much of the world uses the Celsius scale (°C) for most temperature measurements. It has the same incremental scaling as the Kelvin scale used by scientists, but fixes its null point, at 0°C = 273.15K, approximately the freezing point of water (under one atmosphere of pressure). The United States uses the Fahrenheit scale for common purposes, a scale on which water freezes at 32 °F and boils at 212 °F (under one atmosphere of pressure). For practical purposes of scientific temperature measurement, the International System of Units (SI) defines a scale and unit for the thermodynamic temperature by using the easily reproducible temperature of the triple point of water as a second reference point.

The reason for this choice is that, unlike the freezing and boiling point temperatures, the temperature at the triple point is independent of pressure (since the triple point is a fixed point on a two-dimensional plot of pressure vs. temperature). For historical reasons, the triple point temperature of water is fixed at 273.16 units of the measurement increment, which has been named the kelvin in honour of the Scottish physicist who first defined the scale. The unit symbol of the kelvin is K.

Absolute zero is defined as a temperature of precisely 0 kelvins, which is equal to –273.15°C or –459.68 °F.

THERMODYNAMIC APPROACH TO TEMPERATURE

Temperature is one of the principal quantities studied in the field of thermodynamics. Thermodynamics investigates the relation between heat and work, using a special scale of temperature called the absolute temperature, and thus relates temperature to work, as considered below. In thermodynamic terms, temperature is a macroscopic intensive variable because it is independent of the bulk amount of elementary entities contained inside, be they atoms, molecules, or electrons. Real world systems are not homogeneous. For study, a body is usually spatially and temporally divided conceptually into imagined 'cells' of small size. If classical thermodynamic equilibrium conditions for matter are fulfilled to good approximation in each 'cell', then a temperature exists for each 'cell', and local thermodynamic equilibrium is said to prevail in the body.

Statistical Mechanics Approach to Temperature

Statistical mechanics provides a microscopic explanation of temperature, based on macroscopic systems' being composed of many particles, such as molecules and ions of various species, the particles of a species being all alike. It explains macroscopic phenomena in terms of the mechanics of the molecules and ions, and statistical assessments of their joint adventures. In the statistical thermodynamic approach, degrees of freedom are used instead of particles.

On the molecular level, temperature is the result of the motion of the particles that constitute the material. Moving particles carry kinetic energy. Temperature increases as this motion and the kinetic energy increase. The motion may be the translational motion of particles, or the energy of the particle due to molecular vibration or the excitation of an electron energy level. Although very specialized laboratory equipment is required to directly detect the translational thermal motions, thermal collisions by atoms or molecules with small particles suspended in a fluid produces Brownian motion that can be seen with an ordinary microscope. The thermal motions of atoms are very fast and temperatures close to absolute zero are required to directly observe them. For instance, when scientists at the NIST achieved a record-setting low temperature of 700 nK (1 nK = 10^{-9} K) in 1994, they used laser equipment to create an optical lattice to adiabatically cool caesium atoms. They then turned off the entrapment lasers and directly measured atom velocities of 7mm per second in order to calculate their temperature.

Molecules, such as oxygen (O_2), have more degrees of freedom than single spherical atoms: they undergo rotational and vibrational motions as well as translations. Heating results in an increase in temperature due to an increase in the average translational energy of the molecules. Heating will also cause, through equipartitioning, the energy associated with vibrational and rotational modes to increase. Thus a diatomic gas will require a higher energy input to increase its temperature by a certain amount, *i.e.* it will have a higher heat capacity than a monatomic gas.

The process of cooling involves removing thermal energy from a system. When no more energy can be removed, the system is at absolute zero, which cannot be achieved experimentally. Absolute zero is the null point of the thermodynamic temperature scale, also called absolute temperature. If it were possible to cool a system to absolute zero, all motion of the particles comprising matter would cease and they would be at complete rest in this *classical* sense. Microscopically in the description of quantum mechanics, however, matter still has zero-point energy even at absolute zero, because of the uncertainty principle.

TEMPERATURE MEASUREMENT

Temperature measurement using modern scientific thermometers and temperature scales goes back at least as far as the early 18th century, when Gabriel Fahrenheit adapted a thermometer (switching to mercury) and a scale both developed by Ole Christensen Rømer. Fahrenheit's scale is still in use in the United States for non-scientific applications.

Temperature is measured with thermometers that may be calibrated to a variety of temperature scales. In most of the world (except for Belize, Myanmar, Liberia and the United States), the Celsius scale is used for most temperature measuring purposes. Most scientist measures temperature using the Celsius scale and the thermodynamic temperature using the Kelvin scale, which is the Celsius scale offset so that its null point is 0K = –273.15°C, or absolute zero. Many engineering fields in the U.S., notably high-tech and US federal specifications (civil and military), also use the Kelvin and Celsius scales. Other engineering fields in the U.S. also rely upon the Rankine scale (a shifted Fahrenheit scale) when working in thermodynamic-related disciplines such as combustion.

Units

The basic unit of temperature in the International System of Units (SI) is the kelvin. It has the symbol K.

For everyday applications, it is often convenient to use the Celsius scale, in which 0°C corresponds very closely to the freezing point of water and 100°C is its boiling point at sea level. Because liquid droplets commonly exist in clouds at sub-zero temperatures, 0°C is better defined as the melting point of ice. In this scale a temperature difference of 1 degree Celsius is the same as a 1kelvin increment, but the scale is offset by the temperature at which ice melts (273.15 K).

By international agreement the Kelvin and Celsius scales are defined by two fixing points: absolute zero and the triple point of Vienna Standard Mean Ocean Water, which is water specially prepared with a specified blend of hydrogen and oxygen isotopes.

Absolute zero is defined as precisely 0K and –273.15°C. It is the temperature at which all classical translational motion of the particles comprising matter ceases and they are at complete rest in the classical model. Quantum-mechanically, however, zero-point motion remains and has an associated energy, the zero-point energy. Matter is in its ground state, and contains no thermal energy. The triple point of water is defined as 273.16K and 0.01°C. This definition serves the following purposes: it fixes the magnitude of the kelvin as being precisely 1 part in 273.16 parts of the difference between absolute zero and the triple point of water; it establishes that one kelvin has precisely the same magnitude as one degree on the Celsius scale; and it establishes the difference between the null points of these scales as being 273.15K (0K = –273.15°C and 273.16K = 0.01°C).

In the United States, the Fahrenheit scale is widely used. On this scale the freezing point of water corresponds to 32 °F and the boiling point to 212 °F. The Rankine scale, still used in fields of chemical engineering in the U.S., is an absolute scale based on the Fahrenheit increment.

Conversion

The following table shows the temperature conversion formulas for conversions to and from the Celsius scale:

	from Celsius	*to Celsius*
Fahrenheit	[°F] = [°C] × $^{9}D_{5}$ + 32	[°C] = ([°F] – 32) × $^{5}D_{9}$
Kelvin	[K] = [°C] + 273.15	[°C] = [K] – 273.15
Rankine	[°R] = ([°C] + 273.15) × $^{9}D_{5}$	[°C] = ([°R] – 491.67) × $^{5}D_{9}$
Delisle	[°De] = (100 – [°C]) × $^{3}D_{2}$	[°C] = 100 – [°De] × $^{2}D_{3}$
Newton	[°N] = [°C] × $^{33}D_{100}$	[°C] = [°N] × $^{100}D_{33}$
Réaumur	[°Ré] = [°C] × $^{4}D_{5}$	[°C] = [°Ré] × $^{5}D_{4}$
Rømer	[°Rø] = [°C] × $^{21}D_{40}$ + 7.5	[°C] = ([°Rø] – 7.5) × $^{40}D_{21}$

Plasma Physics

The field of plasma physics deals with phenomena of electromagnetic nature that involve very high temperatures.

It is customary to express temperature in electronvolts (eV) or kiloelectronvolts (keV), where 1 eV = 11605K. In the study of QCD matter one routinely encounters temperatures of the order of a few hundred MeV, equivalent to about 10^{12}K.

THEORETICAL FOUNDATION

Historically, there are several scientific approaches to the explanation of temperature: the classical thermodynamic description based on macroscopic empirical variables that can be measured in a laboratory; the kinetic theory of gases which relates the macroscopic description to the probability distribution of the energy of motion of gas particles; and a microscopic explanation based on statistical physics and quantum mechanics. In addition, rigorous and purely mathematical treatments have provided an axiomatic approach to classical thermodynamics and temperature. Statistical physics provides a deeper understanding by describing the atomic behaviour of matter, and derives macroscopic properties from statistical averages of microscopic states, including both classical and quantum states. In the fundamental physical description, using natural units, temperature may be measured directly in units of energy. However, in the practical systems of measurement for science, technology, and commerce, such as the modern metric system of units, the macroscopic and the microscopic descriptions are interrelated by the Boltzmann constant, a proportionality factor that scales temperature to the microscopic mean kinetic energy.

The microscopic description in statistical mechanics is based on a model that analyses a system into its fundamental particles of matter or into a set of classical or quantum-mechanical oscillators and considers the system as a statistical ensemble of microstates. As a collection of classical material particles, temperature is a measure of the mean energy of motion, called kinetic energy, of the particles, whether in solids, liquids, gases, or plasmas. Kinetic energy, a concept of classical mechanics, is one half the product of mass and the square of a particle's velocity. In this mechanical interpretation of thermal motion, the kinetic energies of material particles may reside in the velocity of the particles of their translational or vibrational motion or in the inertia of their rotational modes. In monoatomic perfect gases and, approximately, in most gases, temperature is a measure of the mean particle kinetic energy. It also determines the probability distribution function of the energy. In condensed matter, and particularly in solids, this purely mechanical description is often less useful and the oscillator model provides a better description to account for quantum mechanical phenomena. Temperature determines the statistical occupation of the microstates of the ensemble. The microscopic definition of temperature is only meaningful in the thermodynamic limit, meaning for large ensembles of states or particles, to fulfil the requirements of the statistical model.

In the context of thermodynamics, the kinetic energy is also referred to as thermal energy. The thermal energy may be partitioned into independent components attributed to the degrees of freedom of the particles or to the modes of oscillators in a thermodynamic system. In general, the number of these degrees of freedom that are available for the equipartitioning of energy depend on the temperature, *i.e.* the energy region of the interactions under consideration. For solids, the thermal energy is associated primarily with the vibrations of its atoms or molecules about their equilibrium position. In an ideal monatomic gas, the kinetic energy is found exclusively in the purely translational motions of the particles. In other systems, vibrational and rotational motions also contribute degrees of freedom.

KINETIC THEORY OF GASES

The kinetic theory of gases uses the model of the ideal gas to relate temperature to the average kinetic energy of the atoms in a container of gas. Classical mechanics defines the kinetic energy as follows:

$$E_k = \frac{1}{2}mv^2,$$

where m is the particle mass and v its velocity. The distribution of energies (and thus speeds) of the particles in any gas are given by the Maxwell-Boltzmann distribution. The temperature of a classical ideal gas is related to its average kinetic energy per degree of freedom E_k via the equation:

$$\overline{E}_k = \frac{1}{2}kT,$$

where the Boltzmann constant $k = R/n$ (n = Avogadro number, R = ideal gas constant). This relation is valid in the classical regime, *i.e.* when the particle density is much less than $1/\Lambda^3$, where Λ is the thermal de Broglie wavelength. A monoatomic gas has only the three translational degrees of freedom.

The second law of thermodynamics states that any two given systems when interacting with each other will later reach the same average energy per particle and hence the same temperature.

In a mixture of particles of various masses, the heaviest particles will move slower than lighter particles, but have the same average kinetic energy. A neon atom moves slower relative to a hydrogen molecule of the same kinetic energy; a pollen particle suspended in water moves in a slow Brownian motion among fast moving water molecules.

ZEROTH LAW OF THERMODYNAMICS

It has long been recognized that if two bodies of different temperatures are brought into thermal connection, conductive or radiative, they exchange heat accompanied by changes of other state variables. Left isolated from other bodies, the two connected bodies eventually reach a state of thermal equilibrium in which no further changes occur. This basic knowledge is relevant to thermodynamics. Some approaches to thermodynamics take this basic knowledge as axiomatic, other approaches select only one narrow aspect of this basic knowledge as axiomatic, and use other axioms to justify and express deductively the remaining aspects of it. The one aspect chosen by the latter approaches is often stated in textbooks as the zeroth law of thermodynamics, but other statements of this basic knowledge are made by various writers.

The usual textbook statement of the zeroth law of thermodynamics is that if two systems are each in thermal equilibrium with a third system, then they are also in thermal equilibrium with each other. This statement is taken to justify a statement that all three systems have the same temperature, but, by itself, it does not justify the idea of temperature as a numerical scale for a concept of hotness which exists on a one-dimensional manifold with a sense of greater hotness. Sometimes the zeroth law is stated to provide the latter justification. For suitable systems, an empirical temperature scale may be defined by the variation of one of the other state variables, such as pressure, when all other coordinates are fixed. The second law of thermodynamics is used to define an absolute thermodynamic temperature scale for systems in thermal equilibrium.

A temperature scale is based on the properties of some reference system to which other thermometers may be calibrated. One such reference system is a fixed quantity of gas. The ideal gas law indicates that the product of the pressure (p) and volume (V) of a gas is directly proportional to the thermodynamic temperature:

$$pV = nRT$$

where T is temperature, n is the number of moles of gas and R = 8.314472(15) $\text{Jmol}^{-1}\text{K}^{-1}$ is the gas constant. Reformulating the pressure-volume term as the sum of classical mechanical particle energies in terms of particle mass, m, and root-mean-square particle speed v, the ideal gas law directly provides the relationship between kinetic energy and temperature:

$$\frac{1}{2}mv_{rms}^2 = \frac{3}{2}kT$$

Thus, one can define a scale for temperature based on the corresponding pressure and volume of the gas: the temperature in kelvins is the pressure in pascals of one mole of gas in a container of one cubic metre, divided by the gas constant. In practice, such a gas thermometer is not very convenient, but other thermometers can be calibrated to this scale.

The pressure, volume, and the number of moles of a substance are all inherently greater than or equal to zero, suggesting that temperature must also be greater than or equal to zero. As a practical matter it is not possible to use a gas thermometer to measure absolute zero temperature since the gasses tend to condense into a liquid long before the temperature reaches zero. It is possible, however, to extrapolate to absolute zero by using the ideal gas law.

SECOND LAW OF THERMODYNAMICS

The certain properties of temperature were expressed by the zeroth law of thermodynamics. It is also possible to define temperature in terms of the second law of thermodynamics which deals with entropy. Entropy is often thought of as a measure of the disorder in a system. The second law states that any process will result in either no change or a net increase in the entropy of the universe. This can be understood in terms of probability.

For example, in a series of coin tosses, a perfectly ordered system would be one in which either every toss comes up heads or every toss comes up tails. This means that for a perfectly ordered set of coin tosses, there is only one set of toss outcomes possible: the set in which 100% of tosses come up the same. On the other hand, there are multiple combinations that can result in disordered or mixed systems, where some fraction are heads and the rest tails. A disordered system can be 90% heads and 10% tails, or it could be 98% heads and 2% tails, et cetera. As the number of coin tosses increases, the number of possible combinations corresponding to imperfectly ordered systems increases. For a very large number of coin tosses, the combinations to ~50% heads and ~50% tails dominates and obtaining an outcome significantly different from 50/50 becomes extremely unlikely. Thus the system naturally progresses to a state of maximum disorder or entropy.

It has been previously stated that temperature governs the flow of heat between two systems and it was just shown that the universe tends to progress so as to maximize entropy, which is expected of any natural system. Thus, it is expected that there is some relationship between temperature and entropy. To find this relationship, the relationship between heat, work and temperature is first considered. A heat engine is a device for converting thermal energy into mechanical energy, resulting in the performance of work, and analysis of the Carnot heat engine provides the necessary relationships. The work from a heat engine corresponds to the difference between the heat put into the system at the high temperature, q_H and the heat ejected at the low temperature, q_C. The efficiency is the work divided by the heat put into the system or:

$$\text{efficiency} = \frac{w_{cy}}{q_H} = \frac{q_H - q_C}{q_H} = 1 - \frac{q_C}{q_H}$$

where w_{cy} is the work done per cycle. The efficiency depends only on q_C/q_H. Because q_C and q_H correspond to heat transfer at the temperatures T_C and T_H, respectively, q_C/q_H should be some function of these temperatures:

$$\frac{q_C}{q_H} = f(T_H, T_C)$$

states that all reversible engines operating between the same heat reservoirs are equally efficient. Thus, a heat engine operating between T_1 and T_3 must have the same efficiency as one consisting of two cycles, one between T_1 and T_2, and the second between T_2 and T_3. This can only be the case if:

$$q_{13} = \frac{q_1 q_2}{q_2 q_3}$$

which implies:

$$q_{13} = f(T_1, T_3) = f(T_1, T_2) f(T_2, T_3)$$

Since the first function is independent of T_2, this temperature must cancel on the right side, meaning $f(T_1, T_3)$ is of the form $g(T_1)/g(T_3)$ (*i.e.* $f(T_1,T_3) = f(T_1,T_2)f(T_2,T_3) = g(T_1)/g(T_2)\cdot g(T_2)/g(T_3) = g(T_1)/g(T_3)$), where g is a function of a single temperature. A temperature scale can now be chosen with the property that:

$$\frac{q_C}{q_H} = \frac{T_C}{T_H}$$

A relationship for the efficiency in terms of temperature:

$$\text{efficiency} = 1 - \frac{q_C}{q_H} = 1 - \frac{T_C}{T_H}$$

Notice that for $T_C = 0$ K the efficiency is 100% and that efficiency becomes greater than 100% below 0 K. Since an efficiency greater than 100% violates the first law of thermodynamics, this implies that 0 K is the minimum possible temperature.

In fact the lowest temperature ever obtained in a macroscopic system was 20 nK, which was achieved in 1995 at NIST. Subtracting the right hand side of Equation 5 from the middle portion and rearranging gives:

$$\frac{q_H}{T_H} - \frac{q_C}{T_C} = 0$$

where the negative sign indicates heat ejected from the system. This relationship suggests the existence of a state function, S, defined by:

$$dS = \frac{dq_{\text{rev}}}{T}$$

where the subscript indicates a reversible process. The change of this state function around any cycle is zero, as is necessary for any state function. This function corresponds to the entropy of the system, which was described previously.

Rearranging Equation above gives a new definition for temperature in terms of entropy and heat:

$$T = \frac{dq_{\text{rev}}}{dS}$$

For a system, where entropy $S(E)$ is a function of its energy E, the temperature T is given by:

$$T^{-1} = \frac{d}{dE}S(E),$$

i.e. the reciprocal of the temperature is the rate of increase of entropy with respect to energy.

Definition from Statistical Mechanics

The historical derivation relating entropy and heat. A modern definition of temperature is given by statistical mechanics. It is defined in terms of the fundamental degrees of freedom of a system.

Generalized Temperature from Single Particle Statistics

It is possible to extend the definition of temperature even to systems of few particles, like in a quantum dot. The generalized temperature is obtained by considering time ensembles instead of configuration space ensembles given in statistical mechanics in the case of thermal and particle exchange between a small system of fermions (N even less than 10) with a single/double occupancy system. The finite quantum grand canonical ensemble, obtained under the hypothesis of ergodicity and orthodicity, allows to express the generalized temperature from the ratio of the average time of occupation τ_1 and $_2$ of the single/double occupancy system:

$$T = k^{-1}\ln 2\frac{\tau_2}{\tau_1}\left(E - E_F\left(1 + \frac{3}{2N}\right)\right),$$

where E_F is the Fermi energy which tends to the ordinary temperature when N goes to infinity.

Negative Temperature

On the empirical temperature scales, which are not referenced to absolute zero, a negative temperature is one below the zero-point of the scale used. For example, dry ice has a sublimation temperature of –78.5°C which is equivalent to –109.3°F. On the absolute Kelvin scale, however, this temperature is 194.6 K. On the absolute scale of thermodynamic temperature no material can exhibit a temperature smaller than or equal to 0 K, both of which are forbidden by the third law of thermodynamics.

In the quantum mechanical description of electron and nuclear spin systems that have a limited number of possible states, and therefore a discrete upper limit of energy they can attain, it is possible to obtain a negative temperature, which is numerically indeed less than absolute zero. However, this is not the macroscopic temperature of the material, but instead the temperature of only very specific degrees of freedom, that are isolated from others and do not exchange energy by virtue of the equipartition theorem.

A negative temperature is experimentally achieved with suitable radio frequency techniques that cause a population inversion of spin states from the ground state. As the energy in the system increases upon population of the upper states, the entropy increases as well, as the system becomes less ordered, but attains a maximum value when the spins are evenly distributed among ground and excited states, after which it begins to decrease, once again achieving a state of higher order as the upper states begin to fill exclusively. At the point of maximum entropy, the temperature function shows the behaviour of a singularity, because the slope of the entropy function decreases to zero at first and then turns negative.

Since temperature is the inverse of the derivative of the entropy, the temperature formally goes to infinity at this point, and switches to negative infinity as the slope turns negative. At energies higher than this point, the spin degree of freedom therefore exhibits formally a negative thermodynamic temperature. As the energy increases further by continued population of the excited state, the negative temperature approaches zero asymptotically. As the energy of the system increases in the population inversion, a system with a negative temperature is not colder than absolute zero, but rather it has a higher energy than at positive temperature, and may be said to be in fact hotter at negative temperatures. When brought into contact with a system at a positive temperature, energy will be transferred from the negative temperature regime to the positive temperature region.

MACROSCOPIC VS MICROSCOPIC

MICROSCOPIC AND MACROSCOPIC SYSTEMS

To make a distinction between the different sizes of the systems that we are going to examine. We shall call a system *microscopic* if it is roughly of atomic dimensions, or smaller. On the other hand, we shall call a system *macroscopic* when it is large enough to be visible in the ordinary sense. This is a rather inexact definition. The exact definition depends on the number of particles in the system, which we shall call N. A system is macroscopic if

$$\frac{1}{\sqrt{N}} \ll 1,$$

which means that statistical arguments can be applied to reasonable accuracy. For instance, if we wish to keep the statistical error below one per cent then a macroscopic system would have to contain more than about ten thousand particles. Any system containing less than this number of particles would be regarded as essentially microscopic, and, hence, statistical arguments could not be applied to such a system without unacceptable error.

MACROSCOPIC SCALE

The macroscopic scale is the length scale on which objects or processes are of a size that is measurable and observable by the naked eye.

When applied to phenomena and abstract objects, the macroscopic scale describes existence in the world as we perceive it, often in contrast to experiences (microscopy) or theories (microphysics, statistical physics) considering objects of geometric lengths smaller than one millimetre.

A macroscopic view of a ball is just that: a ball. A microscopic view could reveal a thick round skin seemingly composed entirely of puckered cracks and fissures (as viewed through a microscope) or, further down in scale, a collection of molecules in a roughly spherical shape.

In classical mechanics, describing the movements of the above mentioned ball, can be considered a mainly macroscopic theory; on the much smaller scale of atoms and molecules, classical mechanics no longer applies and the movement of particles is described by quantum mechanics. As another example, near the absolute minimum of temperature, the Bose–Einstein condensate exhibits elementary quantum effects on macroscopic scale.

The term may also refer to a "larger view", namely a view available only from a large perspective. A macroscopic position could be considered the "big picture".

The opposite to the macroscopic scale is the microscopic scale: objects smaller than those that can easily be seen by the naked eye and that require a lens or microscope to see them clearly.

USE OF MICROSCOPIC SCALE

The microscopic scale is the scale of size or length used to describe objects smaller than those that can easily be seen by the naked eye and which require a lens or microscope to see them clearly.

History

By convention it is also used to describe classes of objects which are most commonly too small to see but of which some members are large enough to be observed with the eye. Such groups include the *Cladocera,* planktonic green algae of which *Volvox* is readily observable, and the protozoa of which *Stentor* can be easily seen without aid. The term submicroscopic is a similar term used to describe objects that are too small to see with any optical microscope.

Microscopic is also by association used to classify and describe the units and measurements relevant to very small objects. The antonym to microscopic is macroscopic. The units used to describe objects on a microscopic length scale are most commonly the Micrometer (μm)-one millionth of 1 metre, and smaller units.

Microscopic is also commonly used as a hyperbole in the English language to describe small objects of a class that would be expected to be bigger-as in *"Her feet are microscopic!"*

EXTENSIVE VS INTENSIVE STATE VARIABLES

Thus far we have discussed a number of "process variables" (variables that may be measured and used to characterize the operation of a process). It is helpful, prior to discussing state variables to group these variables into two categories:

Definition: An extensive variable is one which depends on system size (like mass or volume). While extensive variables are useful for characterizing the specific system being analysed, they are not general and do not help us to determine the "state" of the system.

An intensive variable is one which does not depend on system size (like temperature, pressure, or density).

While it may not be immediately obvious, intensive variables tell us much more about the system than extensive variables. In particular, the temperature and pressure are two of the most critical intensive variables.

INTENSIVE AND EXTENSIVE PROPERTIES

In the physical sciences, an intensive property (also called a bulk property, intensive quantity, or intensive variable), is a physical property of a system that does not depend on the system size or the amount of material in the system: it is scale invariant.

By contrast, an extensive property (also extensive quantity, extensive variable, or extensive parameter) is one that is additive for independent, noninteracting subsystems. It is directly proportional to the amount of material in the system.

For example, density is an intensive property of a substance because it does not depend on the amount of that substance; mass and volume, which are measures of the amount of the substance, are extensive properties. In general the ratio of two extensive properties (such as mass and volume) that scale in the same way is scale-invariant, and hence an intensive property (such as density).

Intensive Properties

An intensive property is a physical quantity whose value does not depend on the amount of the substance for which it is measured. For example, the temperature of a system in thermal equilibrium is the same as the temperature of any part of it. If the system is divided the temperature of each subsystem is identical. The same applies to the density of a homogeneous system: if the system is divided in half, the mass and the volume change in the identical ratio and the density remains unchanged. According to the state postulate, for a sufficiently simple system, only two independent intensive variables are needed to fully specify the entire state of a system. Other intensive properties can be derived from the two known values. Some intensive properties, such as viscosity, are empirical macroscopic quantities and are not relevant to extremely small systems.

Combined Intensive Properties

There are four properties in any thermodynamic system, two intensive ones and two extensive ones.

If a set of parameters, $\{a_i\}$, are intensive properties and another set, $\{A_j\}$, are extensive properties, then the function $F(\{a_i\},\{A_j\})$ is an intensive property if for all α,

$$F(\{a_i\}, \{\alpha A_j\}) = F(\{a_i\}, \{A_j\})$$

It follows, for example, that the ratio of two extensive properties is an intensive property-density (intensive) is equal to mass (extensive) divided by volume (extensive).

Joining Systems

Let there be a system or piece of substance a of amount m_a and another piece of substance b of amount m_b which can be combined without interaction. [For example, lead and tin combine without interaction, but common salt dissolves in water and the properties of the resulting solution are not a simple combination of the properties of its constituents.] Let V be an intensive variable. The value of variable V corresponding to the first substance is V_a, and the value of V corresponding to the second substance is V_b. If the two pieces a and b are put together, forming a piece of substance "a+b" of amount $m_{a+b} = m_a + m_b$, then the value of their intensive variable V is:

$$V = \frac{m_a V_a + m_b V_b}{m_a + m_b},$$

which is a weighted mean. Further, if $V_a = V_b$ then $V_{a+b} = V_a = V_b$, *i.e.* the intensive variable is independent of the amount. Note that this property holds only as long as other variables on which the intensive variable depends stay constant.

In a thermodynamic system composed of two monatomic ideal gases, a and b, if the two gases are mixed, the final temperature T is

$$T = \frac{N_a T_a + N_b T_b}{N_a + N_b},$$

a weighted mean where N_i is the number of particles in gas i, and T_i is the corresponding temperature.

Note that you have to measure the amounts in the same unit that was used to calculate the intensive property from the extensive property. So when you interpolate density, you have to measure the properties in volume, as density is mass per volume. The formula makes no sense when you measure the properties in mass (kg).

INTENSIVE AND EXTENSIVE VARIABLES

Consider two bodies each with the same volume N_i and the same pressure. Bring the bodies together, what is the result?

$$V^{total} = V_1 + V_2 P^{total} = P_1 = P_2$$

Variables that are additive like V are called *extensive variables*, they depend on the size or the extent of the system. Variables that do no add, but combine like P are called *intensive variables,* they are intrinsic to the system and can vary from point to point. Fields and potentials are intensive variables.

ENERGY IN MECHANICS

MECHANICAL ENERGY

In physics, mechanical energy is the sum of potential energy and kinetic energy present in the components of a mechanical system. It is the energy associated with the motion and position of an object. The law of conservation of energy states that in an isolated system that is only subject to conservative forces, like the gravitational force, the mechanical energy is constant. If an object is moved in the opposite direction of a conservative net force, the potential energy will increase and if the speed (not the velocity) of the object is changed, the kinetic energy of the object is changed as well. In all real systems, however, non-conservative forces, like frictional forces, will be present, but often they are of negligible values and the mechanical energy's being constant can therefore be a useful approximation. In elastic collisions, the mechanical energy is conserved but in inelastic collisions, some mechanical energy is converted into heat. The equivalence between lost mechanical energy and an increase in temperature was discovered by James Prescott Joule.

Many modern devices, such as the electric motor or the steam engine, are used today to convert mechanical energy into other forms of energy, *e.g.* electrical energy, or to convert other forms of energy, like heat, into mechanical energy.

General

Energy is a scalar quantity and the mechanical energy of a system is the sum of the potential energy which is measured by the position of the parts of the system, and the kinetic energy which is also called the energy of motion:

$$E_{mechanical} = U + K$$

The law of conservation of mechanical energy states that if a body or system is subjected only to conservative forces, the total mechanical energy of that body or system remains constant. The difference between a conservative and a non-conservative force is that when a conservative force moves an object from one point to another, the work done by the conservative force is independent of the path. On the contrary, when a non-conservative force acts upon an object, the work done by the non-conservative force is dependent of the path.

The potential energy, U, depends on the position of an object subjected to a conservative force. It is defined as the object's ability to do work and is increased as the object is moved in the opposite direction of the direction of the force. If F represents the conservative force and × the position, the potential energy of the force between the two positions x_1 and x_2 is defined as the negative integral of F from x_1 to x_2:

$$U = -\int_{x_1}^{x_2} \vec{F} \cdot d\vec{x}$$

The kinetic energy, K, depends on the speed of an object and is the ability of a moving object to do work on other objects when it collides with them. It is defined as one half the product of the object's mass with the square of its speed, and the total kinetic energy of a system of objects is the sum of the kinetic energies of the respective objects:

$$K = \frac{1}{2} m v^2 .$$

CONSERVATION AND INTERCONVERSION OF ENERGY

Of the three great conservation laws of classical mechanics, the conservation of energy is regarded as the most important. According to this law, the mechanical energy of an isolated system remains constant in time, as long as the system is free of all frictional forces, including eventual internal friction from collisions of the objects of the system.

In any real situation, frictional forces and other non-conservative forces are always present, but in many cases their effects on the system are so small that the principle of conservation of mechanical energy can be used as a fair approximation.

Though energy cannot be created nor destroyed in an isolated system, it can be internally converted to any other form of energy.

Thus, in a mechanical system like a swinging pendulum subjected to the conservative gravitational force where frictional forces like air drag and friction at the pivot are negligible, energy passes back and forth between kinetic and potential energy but never leaves the system.

The pendulum reaches greatest kinetic energy and least potential energy when in the vertical position, because it will have the greatest speed and be nearest the Earth at this point. On the other hand, it will have its least kinetic energy and greatest potential energy at the extreme positions of its swing, because it has zero speed and is farthest from Earth at these points. However, when taking the frictional forces into account, the system loses mechanical energy with each swing because of the work done by the pendulum to oppose these non-conservative forces.

That the loss of mechanical energy in a system always resulted in an increase of the system's temperature has been known for a long time, but it was the amateur physicist James Prescott Joule who first experimentally demonstrated how a certain amount of work done against friction resulted in a definite quantity of heat which should be conceived as the random motions of the particles that matter is composed of. This equivalence between mechanical energy and heat is especially important when considering colliding objects. In an elastic collision, mechanical energy is conserved; *i.e.* the sum of the kinetic energies of the colliding objects is the same before and after the collision.

After an inelastic collision, however, the total mechanical energy of the system will have changed. Usually, the total mechanical energy after the collision is smaller than the initial total mechanical energy and the lost mechanical energy is converted into heat. However, the total mechanical energy can be greater after an inelastic collision if for example the collision causes an explosion which converts chemical energy into mechanical energy. In inelastic collisions, the smaller particles of which the colliding objects consist are shaken up and rattle around. These small-scale motions are perceived as an increase in heat and need kinetic energy which must be taken from the large-scale motion of the objects that are observed directly. Thus, the total energy of the system remains unchanged though the mechanical energy has been changed.

ELEMENTARY KINETIC THEORY OF GASES

However, when dealing with kinetic theory, granular flow-and population balance modelling in chemical reactor engineering, basic knowledge of the principles of mechanics is required. Hence, a very brief but essential overview of the disciplines of mechanics and the necessary prescience on the historical development of kinetic theory are given before the more detailed and mathematical principles of kinetic theory are presented.

Mechanics is a branch of physics concerned with the motions of physical bodies and the interacting forces. The science of mechanics is commonly divided into two major disciplines of study called classical mechanics and quantum mechanics. Classical mechanics, which can be seen as the prime discipline of mechanics, describes the behaviour of bodies with forces acting upon them. Quantum mechanics is a relatively modern field of science invented at about 1900. The term classical mechanics normally refers to the motion of relatively large objects, whereas the study of motion at the level of the atom or smaller is the domain of quantum mechanics. Classical mechanics is commonly divided into *statics* and *dynamics*. Statics deals with bodies at rest, while dynamics deals with bodies in motion. The study of dynamics is sometimes further divided into *kinematics* and *kinetics*. Kinematics denotes the description of motion without regard to its cause, while in kinetics one intends to explain the change in motion as a result of forces. A third and very recent branch of dynamics is *non-linear dynamics and chaos,* which denotes the study of systems in which small changes in a variable may have large effects.

The behaviour of large populations of interacting molecules in solids, gases and liquids, particulate systems, dense suspensions and dispersions. The science of classical mechanics may thus be grouped according to the state of matter being studied, into solid mechanics and fluid mechanics, both disciplines are often considered sub-disciplines of *continuum mechanics* dealing with continuous matter. Hence, fluid mechanics or *fluid dynamics* denotes the study of the macroscopic physical properties and behaviour of fluids. The continuity assumption, however, considers fluids to be continuous. That is, properties such as density, pressure, temperature, and velocity are taken to be well-defined at infinitely small points, and are assumed to vary continuously from one point to another. The discrete, molecular nature of a fluid is ignored. Hence, in many physical sciences this mathematical representation of the system is considered a simplifying engineering approach often useful in engineering practice, but of limited accuracy especially when the system considered doesn't allow sufficient inherent separation of scales. For those problems for which the continuity assumption does not give answers of desired accuracy we may (not always!) obtain better results using more fundamental concepts.

Statistical mechanics is the application of statistics, which includes mathematical tools for dealing with large populations, to the field of dynamics. Although the nature of each individual element of a system and the interactions between any pair of elements may both be well understood, the large number of elements and possible interactions present an infeasible problem to the investigators who seek to understand the behaviour of the system. Statistical mechanics provides a mathematical framework upon which such an understanding may be built.

The statistical mechanics theory, which are typified by the work of Boltzmann and Gibbs. The main difference between the two approaches lies in the choice of statistical unit. In the method of Boltzmann the statistical unit is the molecule and the statistical ensemble is a large number of molecules constituting a system, thus the system properties are said to be calculated as average over a phase space trajectory resembling time average properties. In the method of Gibbs the entire system is taken as a single statistical unit and the statistics are those of an ensemble of such systems, hence the system properties are calculated as averages over a large collection of imaginary systems each of which is an independent replica of the system of interest. The collection of independent systems supposedly spans the assembly of all possible micro-states consistent with the constraints with which the system is characterized macroscopically. The very first steps developing the theory dealing with irreversible processes was principally in accordance with the method of Boltzmann as outlined shortly. In the more modern research in statistical mechanics the method of Gibbs has achieved considerable attention as it can be extended in a relatively simple and general way to the description of irreversible processes.

The implications of choosing either of these methods usually goes along the following lines. If the positions and velocities of all the particles in a given system were known at any time, the behaviour of the system could be determined by applying the laws of classical and quantum mechanics. This procedure is, of course, not feasible firstly because the actual positions and velocities of the individual particles are not known and secondly because the computational efforts needed calculating the macroscopic properties from the states of the individual particles are prohibitively great taking into consideration the large number of particles commonly present in the systems of interest. Instead, statistical methods are introduced with the object of predicting the most probable behaviour of a large collection of particles without actually being concerned with the precise states of the individual particles. For this purpose the most probable particle states or a hypothetical ensemble of systems are considered calculating the macroscopic properties. Therefore, we may loosely say that the main reason for introducing the idea of an ensemble was to make it easier to accomplish averaging in statistical mechanics.

The experimental characteristics are usually given as time average properties, the equivalence of the calculation and measurement data may be questionable. The ultimate question is whether the average over the ensemble of systems is the same as the average over an infinite time for a single system. Time averages and micro-canonical ensemble averages are commonly assumed to be identical by the *ergodic hypothesis*. Statistical mechanics is normally further divided into two branches, one dealing with equilibrium systems, the other with non-equilibrium systems. Equilibrium statistical mechanics is sometimes called statistical thermodynamics. Kinetic theory of gases is a particular field of non-equilibrium statistical mechanics that focuses on dilute gases which are only slightly removed from equilibrium.

Performing kinetic theory analyses is to explain physical phenomena that are measurable at the macroscopic level in a gas at-or near equilibrium in terms of the properties of the individual molecules and the intermolecular forces. For instance, one of the original aims of kinetic theory was to explain the experimental form of the ideal gas law from basic principles. The kinetic theory of transport processes determines the transport coefficients (*i.e.*, conductivity, diffusivity, and viscosity) and the mathematical form of the heat, mass and momentum fluxes. Nowadays the kinetic theory of gases originating in statistical mechanics is thus strongly linked with irreversible-or non-equilibrium thermodynamics which is a modern field in thermodynamics describing transport processes in systems that are not in global equilibrium.

Maxwell provided most of the fundamental concepts constituting the statistical theory recognizing that the molecular motion has a random character. When the molecular motion is random, the absolute molecular velocity cannot be described deterministically in accordance with a physical law so a probabilistic (stochastic) model is required.

The conceptual ideas of kinetic theory rely on the assumption that the mean flow, transport and thermodynamic properties of a collection of gas molecules can be obtained from the knowledge of their masses, number density, and a probabilistic velocity distribution function. The gas is thus described in terms of the *distribution function* which contains information of the spatial distributions of molecules, as well as about the molecular velocity distribution, in the system under consideration. Maxwellian velocity distribution function heuristically derived for a gas at equilibrium.

It is emphasized that a gas at thermodynamic equilibrium contains no macroscopic gradients, so that the fluid properties like velocity, temperature and density are uniform in space and time. When the gas is out of equilibrium non-uniform spatial distributions of the macroscopic quantities occur, thus additional phenomena arise as a result of the molecular motion. The random movement of molecules from one region to another tend to transport with them the macroscopic properties of the region from which they depart. Therefore, at their destination the molecules find themselves out of equilibrium with the properties of the region in which they arrive. At the continuous macroscopic level the net effect of these molecular transport processes is expressed through the non-equilibrium phenomena of viscosity, heat conduction and diffusion. Nowadays the phrase *transport processes* thus refers to the transport of mass, momentum and energy within a fluid smoothing out the macroscopic gradients in the physical variable fields enabling non-equilibrium systems to approach equilibrium states.

The transport coefficients have been deduced in several ways, mostly based on the mean free path concept, the Maxwellian moment equations, and the Boltzmann equation. A preliminary theory of transport processes was suggested by Maxwell in which the transport coefficients were determined on the basis of Clausius' empirical mean free path hypothesis. In a subsequent study by Maxwell the equation of transfer for non-equilibrium gases was derived, describing the total rate of change of any mean property of a gas consisting of molecules having certain predefined properties, neatly simplifying the analytical solution. The so-called *Maxwellian molecules* are point centres of force repelling each other with forces which are inversely proportional to the fifth power of their mutual distance. Almost needless to say, the resulting equations of change for the mean variables (or moments of the distribution function), also called *moment equations* or *equations of transfer*, play an important role in kinetic theory. Based on these equations Maxwell deduced more accurate analytical relationships for the transport coefficients. A few years later Boltzmann presented the derivation of a more general integro-differential equation which describes the evolution of the distribution function in space and time. Two approximate methods for solving the Boltzmann equation were given independently by Chapman and Enskog, leading to the same novel relations for the transport coefficients. In this way the Boltzmann equation provides a more rigorous derivation of Maxwell's formulas quantifying the transport coefficients for a gas of Maxwellian molecules. Another important contribution was the H-theorem showing that the molecular collisions tend to increase entropy in an irreversible manner providing a firm theoretical justification of the second law of thermodynamics which was already accepted at that time.

A spin-off result of the foregoing analysis determining the transport coefficients, a rigorous procedure deriving the governing equations of fluid dynamics from first principles was established. It is stressed that in classical fluid dynamics the continuum hypothesis is used so that the governing equations of change are derived directly on the macroscopic scales applying the balance principle over a suitable control volume. Thereafter, closure laws are required relating the internal stresses and diffusive transport fluxes of mass and energy (heat) to the gradients of the macroscopic quantities (*e.g.*, Newtons law of viscosity, Fick's law of mass diffusion, and Fourier's law of conduction are commonly adopted). By using these constitutive relationships we also introduce several unknown parameters, the so-called transport coefficients of viscosity, mass diffusivities and thermal conductivity into the governing equations. Unfortunately, fluid dynamics does neither provide any guidelines on how to determine the mathematical form of the constitutive relations nor the values of transport coefficients.

A unique application of kinetic theory emerges provided that an approximate solution of the Boltzmann equation is available. In this case particular moments of the distribution function can be obtained multiplying the Boltzmann equation by an invariant function (*i.e.*, successively representing molecular mass, momentum and energy), and thereafter integrating the resulting equation over the whole velocity space. The moments of the distribution function (also called the probability-weighted average functions) represent macroscopic (ensemble) mean quantities like gas velocity, pressure, mass density, temperature and energy. In this way it is possible to derive rigorous equations of change for the evolution of the mean quantities starting out from the Boltzmann equation. The resulting transport equations are recognized as being analogue to the conservation equations of continuum mechanics. In addition, in contrast to the continuum mechanic formulation the ensemble averaged equations obtained from kinetic theory do not contain any unknown coefficients. That is, a particular set of closure laws is established. Alternatively, by comparing the kinetic theory results with the classical fluid dynamic equations, we may verify both the form of the constitutive laws and the values of the transport coefficients.

The kinetic theory of multi-component non-reactive mixtures was first described by Maxwell and Stefan and later thoroughly described by Hirschfelder et al.. Hirschfelder et al. also considers reactive systems. The latest contributions are reviewed by Curtiss and Bird. Basically, the Boltzmann equation is considered valid as long as the density of the gas is sufficiently low and the gas properties are sufficiently uniform in space. Although an exact solution is only achieved for a gas at equilibrium for which the Maxwell velocity distribution is supposed to be valid, one can still obtain approximate solutions for gases near equilibrium states. However, it is evident that the range of densities for which a formal mathematical theory of transport processes can be deduced from Boltzmann's equation is limited to *dilute* gases, since this relation is reflecting an asymptotic formulation valid in the limit of no collisional transfer fluxes and restricted to binary collisions only. Hence, this theory cannot without ad hoc modifications be applied to dense gases and liquids.

Enskog made the first heuristic attempt to extend the kinetic theory of dilute mono-atomic gases to higher density gas systems. Enskog introduced corrections to the Boltzmann equation accounting for the finite size of the colliding molecules (a free volume correction), and that the centres of the two colliding particles are no longer at the same point. These model extensions resulted in a novel flux accounting for the mechanisms of instantaneous momentum and energy transfer over the distance separating the centres of the two colliding molecules. It is later stated that even at moderate densities the collisional transfer fluxes may become significant compared to the kinetic contribution, and they may dominate at slightly higher densities.

PRESSURE OF AN IDEAL GAS

GAS PRESSURE

Gas molecules inside a volume (*e.g.* a balloon) are constantly moving around freely. During this molecular motion they frequently collide with each other and with the surface of any enclosure there may be (in a small balloon that would be many thousands of billions of collisions each second).

The force of impact of a single one such collision is too small to be sensed. However, taken all together, this large number of impacts of gas molecules exerts a considerable force onto the surface of the enclosure: the gas pressure.

The larger the number of collisions per area of enclosure, the larger the pressure:

$$\text{Pressure} = \frac{\text{Force}}{\text{Area}} \text{ or } P = \frac{F}{A}\left[\frac{N}{m^2} = Pa\right]_{SI}$$

The SI-unit of pressure is Pascal [Pa], but in Meteorology it is accepted to use millibars [mb], where 100 kPa = 1000 mb.

The *direction* of this gas pressure force is *always perpendicular to the surface* of the enclosure at every point.

ATMOSPHERIC PRESSURE – PRESSURE PROFILE

In the example of the balloon (above), there is not only gas inside the balloon (exerting pressure from the inside), but there is also gas (air) on the outside, exerting pressure onto the outside surface of the balloon.

The rate, at which the skin of the balloon is bombarded by air molecules, is dependent on how tightly the gas molecules are packed, or on the gas density:

$$(\text{Gas})\ \text{Density} = \frac{\text{Mass(of gas)}}{\text{Volume}} \quad or \quad \rho = \frac{m}{V}\left[\frac{kg}{m^3}\right]_{SI}$$

Since gas is compressible, its density depends on the force that is used to compress it. In the atmosphere, the force that compresses the air at the surface is just the weight of all the air in the atmospheric column above it.

$$\text{Atmospheric Pressure} = \frac{\text{Weight to } f \text{ Overlying Air}}{\text{Unit Area}}$$

At the surface the atmospheric pressure is on average $P_0 = 101.3$ kPa = 1013 mb

The higher we go in the atmosphere, the less air remains in the column above us. Thus, the atmospheric pressure always decreases with height. Similarly, air density decreases with height, because the overload to compress the air gets less and less, as we go higher.

Clearly, at the surface, the air is densest. Thus, as we rise from the surface through the first kilometer of the atmosphere, we leave a lot of dense air below us: the overload (and thus the density and pressure) decreases quickly. As a result, the air in the next km is already much less dense than below, and the overload (density and pressure) decrease more slowly. This ever slower decrease of the overload, of density and pressure, is continued for every consecutive vertical stretch of atmosphere.

In fact, at 6 km height, we already have approximately half of the mass of air below us. Thus, the atmospheric pressure at 6 km height is only half that at the surface (*i.e.*, P_{6km} » 500 mb). Between 6 and 12 km the overload (and the pressure) is halved again: only ¼ of the surface pressure is left. This consecutive halving gives rise to the following (approximate) pressure profile, starting at a surface pressure of P_0 = 1000 mb:

Height (km)	*Pressure (mb)*	*Fraction of P_0*
0	1000 (= P_0)	1
6	500	1/2
12	250	1/4
18	125	1/8
24	63	1/16
...	...	...

The shape of this profile-curve is called a negative exponential decrease. The density profile behaves in a similar way.

$$\frac{P(z)}{P_0} = \exp\left(-\alpha(z - z_0)\right)$$

where a is a temperature dependent parameter.

HYDROSTATIC PRESSURE – MERCURY BAROMETER

The principle that the pressure at a given level is equivalent to the weight of the overlying column is not only true for air, but for fluids (gases and liquids) in general. The pressure generated by an overlying column of fluid is thus termed the hydrostatic pressure.

The upper boundary of the air column that gives rise to atmospheric pressure is the vacuum of space. Being rather light, the mass of a column of air with a 1 cm^2 cross section is almost exactly 1 kg. If a much heavier liquid substance is used to balance this air column, only a relatively small length would be needed. In addition, because the density of liquids does not change with height (most liquids are incompressible), such an equivalent liquid column has a well defined upper boundary (below a vacuum),

One of the heaviest liquids at room temperature is mercury (Hg) and the height of the Hg-column that is equivalent to normal pressure (1013 mb) is only 760 mm long (29.92"). For this reason, columns of mercury, "hanging" in an inverted vacuum tube, can be used as practical instruments to measure atmospheric pressure.

If water were used instead of mercury, the height of the column equivalent to normal pressure would be 10.33 m-not a very practical length of tube to work with.

IDEAL GAS LAW

An ideal gas is defined as one in which all collisions between atoms or molecules are perfectly eleastic and in which there are no intermolecular attractive forces. One can visualize it as a collection of perfectly hard spheres which collide but which otherwise do not interact with each other. In such a gas, all the internal energy is in the form of kinetic energy and any change in internal energy is accompanied by a change in temperature.

An ideal gas can be characterized by three state variables: absolute pressure (P), volume (V), and absolute temperature (T). The relationship between them may be deduced from kinetic theory and is called the

$$\text{Ideal gas law}: PV = nRT = NkT$$

- n = number of moles
- R = universal gas constant = 8.3145 J/mol K
- N = number of molecules
- k = Boltzmann constant = 1.38066×10^{-23} J/K = 8.617385×10^{-5} eV/K
- $k = R/N_A$
- N_A = Avogadro's number = 6.0221×10^{23}/mol

The ideal gas law can be viewed as arising from the kinetic pressure of gas molecules colliding with the walls of a container in accordance with Newton's laws. But there is also a statistical element in the determination of the average kinetic energy of those molecules. The temperature is taken to be proportional to this average kinetic energy; this invokes the idea of kinetic temperature. One mole of an ideal gas at STP occupies 22.4 litres.

IDEAL GAS LAW WITH CONSTRAINTS

For the purpose of calculations, it is convenient to place the ideal gas law in the form:

$$\frac{P_i V_i}{T_i} = \frac{P_f V_f}{T_f}$$

where the subscripts i and f refer to the initial and final states of some process. If the temperature is constrained to be constant, this becomes:

$$P_i V_i = P_f V_f$$

which is referred to as Boyle's Law.

If the pressure is constant, then the ideal gas law takes the form

$$\frac{V_i}{T_i} = \frac{V_f}{T_f} \quad or \quad V_f = V_i \frac{T_f}{T_i}$$

which has been historically called Charles' Law. It is appropriate for experiments performed in the presence of a constant atmospheric pressure.

All the possible states of an ideal gas can be represented by a PvT surface. The behaviour when any one of the three state variables is held constant is also shown.

DEVIATIONS FROM IDEAL GAS LAW BEHAVIOUR

VAN DER WAALS EQUATION

The behaviour of real gases usually agrees with the predictions of the ideal gas equation to within ±5% at normal temperatures and pressures. At low temperatures or high pressures, real gases deviate significantly from ideal gas behaviour. In 1873, while searching for a way to link the behaviour of liquids and gases, the Dutch physicist Johannes van der Waals developed an explanation for these deviations and an equation that was able to fit the behaviour of real gases over a much wider range of pressures.

Van der Waals realised that two of the assumptions of the kinetic molecular theory were questionable. The kinetic theory assumes that gas particles occupy a negligible fraction of the total volume of the gas. It also assumes that the force of attraction between gas molecules is zero.

The first assumption works at pressures close to 1 atm. But something happens to the validity of this assumption as the gas is compressed. Imagine for the moment that the atoms or molecules in a gas were all clustered in one corner of a cylinder. At normal pressures, the volume occupied by these particles is a negligibly small fraction of the total volume of the gas. But at high pressures, this is no longer true. As a result, real gases are not as compressible at high pressures as an ideal gas. The volume of a real gas is therefore larger than expected from the ideal gas equation at high pressures.

Van der Waals proposed that we correct for the fact that the volume of a real gas is too large at high pressures by *subtracting* a term from the volume of the real gas before we substitute it into the ideal gas equation. He therefore introduced a constant (b) into the ideal gas equation that was equal to the volume actually occupied by a mole of gas particles. Because the volume of the gas particles depends on the number of moles of gas in the container, the term that is subtracted from the real volume of the gas is equal to the number of moles of gas times b.

$$P(V - nb) = nRT$$

When the pressure is relatively small, and the volume is reasonably large, the nb term is too small to make any difference in the calculation. But at high pressures, when the volume of the gas is small, the nb term corrects for the fact that the volume of a real gas is larger than expected from the ideal gas equation.

The assumption that there is no force of attraction between gas particles cannot be true. If it was, gases would never condense to form liquids. In reality, there is a small force of attraction between gas molecules that tends to hold the molecules together. This force of attraction has two consequences:

- Gases condense to form liquids at low temperatures and
- The pressure of a real gas is sometimes smaller than expected for an ideal gas.

To correct for the fact that the pressure of a real gas is smaller than expected from the ideal gas equation, van der Waals *added* a term to the pressure in this equation. This term contained a second constant (a) and has the form: an^2/V^2. The complete van der Waals equation is therefore written as follows.

$$\left[P + \frac{an^2}{V^2}\right](V - nb) = nRT$$

This equation is something of a mixed blessing. It provides a much better fit with the behaviour of a real gas than the ideal gas equation. But it does this at the cost of a loss in generality. The ideal gas equation is equally valid for any gas, whereas the van der Waals equation contains a pair of constants (a and b) that change from gas to gas.

The ideal gas equation predicts that a plot of PV versus P for a gas would be a horizontal line because PV should be a constant. Experimental data for PV versus P for H_2 and N_2 gas at 0ºC and CO_2 at 40C. Values of the van der Waals constants for these and other gases are given in the table below:

van der Waals Constants for Various Gases

Compound	*a (L^2-atm/mol^2)*	*b (L/mol)*
He	0.03412	0.02370
Ne	0.2107	0.01709
H_2	0.2444	0.02661
Ar	1.345	0.03219
O_2	1.360	0.03803
N_2	1.390	0.03913
CO	1.485	0.03985
CH_4	2.253	0.04278
CO_2	3.592	0.04267
NH_3	4.170	0.03707

The magnitude of the deviations from ideal gas behaviour can be illustrated by comparing the results of calculations using the ideal gas equation and the van der Waals equation for 1.00 mole of CO_2 at 0°C in containers of different volumes. Let's start with a 22.4 L container.

4

Thermal Properties of Heat Capacity

SPECIFIC HEAT CAPACITY

Temperature and heat are not the same thing:

- Temperature is a measure of how hot something is
- Heat is a measure of the thermal energy contained in an object.

Temperature is measured in °C, and heat is measured in J. When heat energy is transferred to an object, its temperature increase depends upon the:

- The mass of the object
- The substance the object is made from
- The amount energy transferred to the object.

For a particular object, the more heat energy transferred to it, the greater its temperature increase. The specific heat capacity of a substance is the amount of energy needed to change the temperature of 1 kg of the substance by 1°C. Different substances have different specific heat capacities. The table shows some examples.

Heat Capacities of Different Substances

Substance	*Specific heat capacity in J/kg °C*
Water	4181
Oxygen	918
Lead	128

Notice that water has a particularly high specific heat capacity. This makes water useful for storing heat energy, and for transporting it around the home using central heating pipes.

Calculating Specific Heat Capacity

Here is the equation relating energy to specific heat capacity:

$$E = m \times c \times \theta$$

- E is the energy transferred in joules, J
- m is the mass of the substances in kg
- c is the specific heat capacity in J/kg °C
- θ (theta) is the temperature change in degrees Celsius, °C.

For example, how much energy must be transferred to raise the temperature of 2 kg of water from 20°C to 30°C?

$$E = m \times c \times \theta \ (\theta = 30 - 20 = 10°C)$$

$$E = 2 \times 4181 \times 10 = 83{,}620 \text{ J or } 83.62 \text{ kJ}$$

MEASUREMENT OF HEAT CAPACITY

The heat capacity of most systems is not a constant. Rather, it depends on the state variables of the thermodynamic system under study. In particular it is dependent on temperature itself, as well as on the pressure and the volume of the system, and the ways in which pressures and volumes have been allowed to change while the system has passed from one temperature to another. The reason for this is that pressure-volume work done to the system raises its temperature by a mechanism other than heating, while pressure-volume work done *by* the system absorbs heat without raising the system's temperature.

Different measurements of heat capacity can therefore be performed, most commonly at constant pressure and constant volume. The values thus measured are usually subscripted (by p and V, respectively) to indicate the definition. Gases and liquids are typically also measured at constant volume. Measurements under constant pressure produce larger values than those at constant volume because the constant pressure values also include heat energy that is used to do work to expand the substance against the constant pressure as its temperature increases. This difference is particularly notable in gases where values under constant pressure are typically 30% to 66.7% greater than those at constant volume.

The specific heat capacities of substances comprising molecules are not fixed constants and vary somewhat depending on temperature. Accordingly, the temperature at which the measurement is made is usually also specified. Examples of two common ways to cite the specific heat of a substance are as follows:

- Water (liquid): $c_p = 4.1855$ [J/(g·K)] (15 °C, 101.325 kPa)
- Water (liquid): $C_vH = 74.539$ J/(mol·K) (25 °C)

For liquids and gases, it is important to know the pressure to which given heat-capacity data refer. Most published data are given for standard pressure. However, quite different standard conditions for temperature and pressure have been defined by different organizations. The International Union of Pure and Applied Chemistry changed its recommendation from one atmosphere to the round value 100 kPa (≈750.062 Torr).

CALCULATION FROM FIRST PRINCIPLES

The path integral Monte Carlo method is a numerical approach for determining the values of heat capacity, based on quantum dynamical principles. However, good approximations can be made for gases in many states using simpler methods outlined below. For many solids composed of relatively heavy atoms (atomic number > iron), at non-cryogenic temperatures, the heat capacity at room temperature approaches 3R = 24.94 joules per kelvin per mole of atoms. Low temperature approximations for both gases and solids at temperatures less than their characteristic Einstein temperatures or Debye temperatures can be made by the methods of Einstein and Debye.

Thermodynamic Relations and Definition of Heat Capacity

The internal energy of a closed system changes either by adding heat to the system or by the system performing work. Written mathematically we have

$$dU = \delta Q - \delta W.$$

For work as a result of an increase of the system volume we may write,

$$dU = \delta Q - PdV.$$

If the heat is added at constant volume, then the second term of this relation vanishes and one readily obtains

$$\left(\frac{\partial U}{\partial T}\right)_V = \left(\frac{\partial Q}{\partial T}\right)_V = C_V.$$

This defines the *heat capacity at constant volume*, C_V. Another useful quantity is the *heat capacity at constant pressure*, C_P. With the *enthalpy* of the system given by

$$H = U + PV$$

our equation for dU changes to;

$$dH = \delta Q + VdP,$$

and therefore, at constant pressure, we have;

$$\left(\frac{\partial H}{\partial T}\right)_P = \left(\frac{\partial Q}{\partial T}\right)_P = C_P.$$

RELATION BETWEEN HEAT CAPACITIES

Measuring the heat capacity, sometimes referred to as specific heat, at constant volume can be prohibitively difficult for liquids and solids. That is, small temperature changes typically require large pressures to maintain a liquid or solid at constant volume implying the containing vessel must be nearly rigid or at least very strong. Instead it is easier to measure the heat capacity at constant pressure (allowing the material to expand or contract freely) and solve for the heat capacity at constant volume using mathematical relationships derived from the basic thermodynamic laws. Starting from the fundamental Thermodynamic Relation one can show

$$C_p - C_V = T\left(\frac{\partial p}{\partial T}\right)_{V,N}\left(\frac{\partial V}{\partial T}\right)_{p,N}$$

where the partial derivatives are taken at constant volume and constant number of particles, and constant pressure and constant number of particles, respectively.

This can also be rewritten;

$$C_p - C_V = VT\frac{\alpha^2}{\beta_T}$$

where α

is the coefficient of thermal expansion,

β_T is the isothermal compressibility.

The heat capacity ratio or adiabatic index is the ratio of the heat capacity at constant pressure to heat capacity at constant volume.

It is sometimes also known as the isentropic expansion factor.

Ideal Gas

For an ideal gas, evaluating the partial derivatives above according to the equation of state;

$$pV = nRT$$

the relation can be found to reduce to;

$$C_p - C_V = nR$$

where n is number of moles of gas in the thermodynamic system under consideration, and R is the universal gas constant. Dividing through by n, this equation reduces simply to Mayer's relation,

$$C_{p,m} - C_{v,m} = R$$

where $C_{p,m}$ and $C_{v,m}$ are intensive property heat capacities expressed on a per mole basis at constant pressure and constant volume, respectively.

Specific Heat Capacity

The specific heat capacity of a material on a per mass basis is;

$$c = \frac{\partial C}{\partial m},$$

which in the absence of phase transitions is equivalent to;

$$c = E_m = \frac{C}{m} = \frac{C}{\rho V},$$

where

C is the heat capacity of a body made of the material in question,

m is the mass of the body,

V is the volume of the body, and

$\rho = \frac{m}{V}$ is the density of the material.

For gases, and also for other materials under high pressures, there is need to distinguish between different boundary conditions for the processes under consideration (since values differ significantly between different conditions). Typical processes for which a heat capacity may be defined include isobaric (constant pressure, $dp = 0$) or isochoric (constant volume, $dV = 0$) processes. The corresponding specific heat capacities are expressed as;

$$c_p = \left(\frac{\partial C}{\partial m}\right)_p,$$

$$c_V = \left(\frac{\partial C}{\partial m}\right)_V.$$

From the results, dividing through by the mass gives the relation;

$$c_p - c_V = \frac{\alpha^2 T}{\rho \beta_T}.$$

A related parameter to c is CV^{-1}, the volumetric heat capacity.

In engineering practice, c_V for solids or liquids often signifies a volumetric heat capacity, rather than a constant-volume one. In such cases, the mass-specific heat capacity (specific heat) is often explicitly written with the subscript m, as c_m.

Of course, from the above relationships, for solids one writes;

$$c_m = \frac{C}{m} = \frac{c_{volumetric}}{\rho}.$$

For pure homogeneous chemical compounds with established molecular or molar mass or a molar quantity is established, heat capacity as an intensive property can be expressed on a per mole basis instead of a per mass basis by the following equations analogous to the per mass equations:

$$C_{p,m} = \left(\frac{\partial C}{\partial n}\right)_p = \text{molar heat capacity at constant pressure}$$

$$C_{V,m} = \left(\frac{\partial C}{\partial n}\right)_V = \text{molar heat capacity at constant volume}$$

where n = number of moles in the body or thermodynamic system. One may refer to such a *per mole* quantity as molar heat capacity to distinguish it from specific heat capacity on a per mass basis.

Heat Capacity of Polytropic

The polytropic heat capacity is calculated at processes if all the thermodynamic properties (pressure, volume, temperature) change;

$$C_{i,m} = \left(\frac{\partial C}{\partial n}\right) = \text{molar heat capacity at polytropic process.}$$

The most important polytropic processes run between the adiabatic and the isotherm functions, the polytropic index is between 1 and the adiabatic exponent (γ or κ)

Heat Capacity of Dimensionless

The dimensionless heat capacity of a material is;

$$C^* = \frac{C}{nR} = \frac{C}{Nk}$$

where

C is the heat capacity of a body made of the material in question (J/K)

n is the amount of substance in the body (mol)

R is the gas constant (J/(K·mol))

N is the number of molecules in the body. (dimensionless)

k is Boltzmann's constant (J/(K·molecule)).

In the ideal gas article, dimensionless heat capacity C^* v is expressed as $\hat{c}$, and is related there directly to half the number of degrees of freedom per particle. This holds true for quadratic degrees of freedom, a consequence of the equipartition theorem. More generally, the dimensionless heat capacity relates the logarithmic increase in temperature to the increase in the dimensionless entropy per particle $S^* = S / Nk$, measured in nats.

$$C^* = \frac{dS^*}{d\ln T}$$

Alternatively, using base 2 logarithms, C^* relates the base-2 logarithmic increase in temperature to the increase in the dimensionless entropy measured in bits.

HEAT CAPACITY AT ABSOLUTE ZERO

From the definition of entropy;

$$T dS = \delta Q$$

the absolute entropy can be calculated by integrating from zero kelvins temperature to the final temperature T_f;

$$S(T_f) = \int_{T=0}^{T_f} \frac{\delta Q}{T} = \int_0^{T_f} \frac{\delta Q}{dT}\frac{dT}{T} = \int_0^{T_f} C(T)\frac{dT}{T}.$$

The heat capacity must be zero at zero temperature in order for the above integral not to yield an infinite absolute entropy, which would violate the third law of thermodynamics. One of the strengths of the Debye model is that (unlike the preceding Einstein model) it predicts the proper mathematical form of the approach of heat capacity towards zero, as absolute zero temperature is approached.

Negative Heat Capacity of Stars

Most physical systems exhibit a positive heat capacity. However, even though it can seem paradoxical at first, there are some systems for which the heat capacity is *negative*. These include gravitating objects such as stars; and also sometimes some nano-scale clusters of a few tens of atoms, close to a phase transition. A negative heat capacity can result in a negative temperature.

According to the virial theorem, for a self-gravitating body like a star or an interstellar gas cloud, the average potential energy U_{Pot} and the average kinetic energy U_{Kin} are locked together in the relation;

$$U_{Pot} = -2U_{Kin},$$

The total energy U ($= U_{Pot} + U_{Kin}$) therefore obeys;

$$U = -U_{Kin},$$

If the system loses energy, for example by radiating energy away into space, the average kinetic energy and with it the average temperature actually *increases*. The system therefore can be said to have a negative heat capacity.

A more extreme version of this occurs with black holes. According to black hole thermodynamics, the more mass and energy a black hole absorbs, the colder it becomes. In contrast, if it is a net emitter of energy, through Hawking radiation, it will become hotter and hotter until it boils away.

THEORY OF HEAT CAPACITY

Factors that Affect Specific of Heat Capacity

For any given substance, the heat capacity of a body is directly proportional to the amount of substance it contains (measured in terms of mass or moles or volume). Doubling the amount of substance in a body doubles its heat capacity, etc.

However, when this effect has been corrected for, by dividing the heat capacity by the quantity of substance in a body, the resulting specific heat capacity is a function of the structure of the substance itself. In particular, it depends on the number of degrees of freedom that are available to the particles in the substance, each of which type of freedom allows substance particles to store thermal energy. The kinetic energy of substance particles is the only one of the many possible degrees of freedom which manifests as temperature change, and thus the larger the number of degrees of freedom available to the particles of a substance other than kinetic energy, the larger will be the specific heat capacity for the substance.

In addition, quantum effects require that whenever energy be stored in any mechanism associated with a bound system which confers a degree of freedom, it must be stored in certain minimal-sized deposits (quanta) of energy, or else not stored at all. Such effects limit the full ability of some degrees of freedom to store energy when their lowest energy storage quantum amount is not easily supplied at the average energy of particles at a given temperature. In general, for this reason, specific heat capacities tend to fall at lower temperatures where the average thermal energy available to each particle degree of freedom is smaller, and thermal energy storage begins to be limited by these quantum effects. Due to this process, as temperature falls towards absolute zero, so also does heat capacity.

DEGREES OF FREEDOM

Molecules are quite different from the monatomic gases like helium and argon. With monatomic gases, thermal energy comprises only translational motions. Translational motions are ordinary, whole-body movements in 3D space whereby particles move about and exchange energy in collisions—like rubber balls in a vigorously shaken container. These simple movements in the three dimensions of space mean individual atoms have three translational degrees of freedom. A degree of freedom is any form of energy in which heat transferred into an object can be stored. This can be in translational kinetic energy, rotational kinetic energy, or other forms such as potential energy in vibrational modes. Only three translational degrees of freedom (corresponding to the three independent directions in space) are available for any individual atom, whether it is free, as a monatomic molecule, or bound into a polyatomic molecule.

As to turning round about an atom's axis (again, whether the atom is bound or free), its energy of rotation is proportional to the moment of inertia for the atom, which is extremely small compared to moments of inertia of collections of atoms. This is because almost all of the mass of a single atom is concentrated in its nucleus, which has a radius too small to give a significant moment of inertia. In contrast, the *spacing* of quantum energy levels for a rotating object is inversely proportional to its moment of inertia, and so this spacing becomes very large for objects with very small moments of inertia. For these reasons, the contribution from rotation of atoms on their axes is essentially zero in monatomic gases, because the energy spacing of the associated quantum levels is too large for significant thermal energy to be stored in rotation of systems with such small moments of inertia. For similar reasons, axial rotation around bonds joining atoms in diatomic gases (or along the linear axis in a linear molecule of any length) can also be neglected as a possible "degree of freedom" as well, since such rotation is similar to rotation of monatomic atoms, and so occurs about an axis with a moment of inertia too small to be able to store significant heat energy.

Other rotational modes may become active, due to the much higher moments of inertia about certain axes which do not coincide with the linear axis of a linear molecule. These modes take the place of some translational degrees of freedom for individual atoms, since the atoms are moving in 3-D space, as the molecule rotates. The narrowing of quantum mechanically determined energy spacing between rotational states results from situations where atoms are rotating around an axis that does not connect them, and thus form an assembly that has a large moment of inertia. This small difference between energy states allows the kinetic energy of this type of rotational motion to store heat energy at ambient temperatures. Furthermore (although usually at higher temperatures than are able to store heat in rotational motion) internal vibrational degrees of freedom also may become active (these are also a type of translation, as seen from the view of each atom). In summary, molecules are complex objects with a population of atoms that may move about within the molecule in a number of different ways, and each of these ways of moving is capable of storing energy if the temperature is sufficient.

The heat capacity of molecules (on a per-atom, or atom-molar, basis) does not exceed the heat capacity of monatomic gases, unless vibrational modes are brought into play. The reason for this is that vibrational modes allow energy to be stored as potential energy in intra-atomic bonds in a molecule, which are not available to atoms in monatomic gases. Up to about twice as much energy (on a per-atom basis) per unit of temperature increase can be stored in a solid as in a monatomic gas, by this mechanism of storing energy in the potentials of interatomic bonds. This gives many solids about twice the atom-molar heat capacity of monatomic gases, at the highest temperatures their structure can withstand.

Quantum effects heavily affect the actual ratio at lower temperatures, especially in solids with light and tightly bound atoms (*e.g.*, beryllium metal).

Smaller polyatomic gases store intermediate amounts of energy, giving them a per-atom heat capacity that is between that of monatomic gases (${}^3D_2$ *R* per mole, where *R* is the ideal gas constant), and the maximum of fully excited warmer solids (3 *R* per mole). For gases, heat capacity never falls below the minimum of ${}^3D_2$ *R* per mole of atoms, since the kinetic energy of gas molecules is always available to store at least this much thermal energy. However, at cryogenic temperatures in solids, heat capacity falls towards zero, as temperature approaches absolute zero.

Temperature-dependent Specific Heat Capacity

The role of various degrees of freedom in storing heat, we may consider nitrogen, a diatomic molecule that has five active degrees of freedom at room temperature: the three comprising translational motion plus two rotational degrees of freedom internally. Although the constant-volume molar heat capacity of nitrogen at this temperature is five-thirds that of monatomic gases, on a per-mole of atoms basis, it is five-sixths that of a monatomic gas.

The reason for this is the loss of a degree of freedom due to the bond when it does not allow storage of thermal energy. Two separate nitrogen atoms would have a total of six degrees of freedom—the three translational degrees of freedom of each atom. When the atoms are bonded the molecule will still only have three translational degrees of freedom, as the two atoms in the molecule move as one.

However, the molecule cannot be treated as a point object, and the moment of inertia has increased sufficiently about two axes to allow two rotational degrees of freedom to be active at room temperature to give five degrees of freedom. The moment of inertia about the third axis remains small, as this is the axis passing through the centres of the two atoms, and so is similar to the small moment of inertia for atoms of a monatomic gas. Thus, this degree of freedom does not act to store heat, and does not contribute to the heat capacity of nitrogen. The heat capacity *per atom* for nitrogen (5/2 per mole molecules = 5/4 per mole atoms) is therefore less than for a monatomic gas (3/2 per mole molecules or atoms), so long as the temperature remains low enough that no vibrational degrees of freedom are activated.

At higher temperatures, however, nitrogen gas gains two more degrees of internal freedom, as the molecule is excited into higher vibrational modes that store thermal energy. Now the bond is contributing heat capacity, and is contributing more than if the atoms were not bonded. With full thermal excitation of bond vibration, the heat capacity per volume, or per mole of gas *molecules* approaches seven-thirds that of monatomic gases.

Significantly, this is seven-sixths of the monatomic gas value on a mole-of-atoms basis, so this is now a *higher* heat capacity *per atom* than the monatomic figure, because the vibrational mode enables for diatomic gases allows an extra degree of *potential energy* freedom per pair of atoms, which monatomic gases cannot possess.

Though, even at these large temperatures where gaseous nitrogen is able to store $7/6^{\text{ths}}$ of the energy *per atom* of a monatomic gas (making it more efficient at storing energy on an atomic basis), it still only stores 7/12^{ths} of the maximal per-atom heat capacity of a *solid,* meaning it is not nearly as efficient at storing thermal energy on an atomic basis, as solid substances can be. This is typical of gases, and results because many of the potential bonds which might be storing potential energy in gaseous nitrogen (as opposed to solid nitrogen) are lacking, because only one of the spatial dimensions for each nitrogen atom offers a bond into which potential energy can be stored without increasing the kinetic energy of the atom. In general, solids are most efficient, on an atomic basis, at storing thermal energy (that is, they have the highest per-atom or per-mole-of-atoms heat capacity).

HEAT CAPACITY OF THE CALORIMETER

In calorimetry it is often desirable to know the heat capacity of the calorimeter itself rather than the heat capacity of the entire calorimeter system (calorimeter and water). The heat (q) released by a reaction or process is absorbed by the calorimeter and any substances in the calorimeter. If the only other substance in the calorimeter is water, the following energy balance exists:

$$q = q_{cal} + q_w$$

where q_{cal} is the heat flow for the calorimeter and q_w is the heat flow for the water. Both of these individual heat flows can be related to the heat capacity and temperature change for the substance.

$$q_{cal} = C_{cal}\,\Delta T$$

$$q_w = C_w\,\Delta T$$

where C_{cal} is the heat capacity of the calorimeter and C_w is the heat capacity of the water. Because the water and calorimeter are in thermal equilibrium, they both have the same temperature and thus ΔT is the same for both. The consequence is that the heat capacity of the entire system (C) is the sum of the heat capacities for the individual components.

$$C = C_{cal} + C_w$$

The heat capacity is an extensive property; that is, the heat capacity depends upon the amount of substance present. The calorimeter exists as a fixed unit, thus its heat capacity is a fixed value. The amount of water in the calorimeter, however, can vary, and thus the heat capacity of the water can vary. When dealing with variable amounts of material, one often prefers to use an intensive measure of the heat capacity. One common intensive version of the heat capacity is the specific heat capacity (s), which is the heat capacity of one gram of a substance.

$$S_w = \frac{C_w}{m_w}$$

Because the mass of water (m_w) and the specific heat capacity of water are both known, one can readily calculate the heat capacity of the water. The joule (J) is defined based upon the specific heat capacity of water:

$$s_w = 4.184 \text{ J } ^{o}\text{C}^{-1} \text{ g}^{-1}$$

Overall one can write

$$C = C_{cal} + s_w m_w$$

Quantity	*Symbol*	*Unit*	*Meaning*
heat	q	J	Energy transfer that produces or results from a difference in temperature
temperature	T	^{o}C or K	Measure of the kinetic energy of molecular motion
temperature change	ΔT	^{o}C or K	Difference between the final and initial temperatures for a process
mass	m	g	Amount of material present
heat capacity	C	J $^{o}C^{-1}$ or J K^{-1}	Heat required to change the temperature of a substance one degree
specific heat capacity	s	J $^{o}C^{-1}$ g^{-1} or J K^{-1} g^{-1}	Heat required to change the temperature of one gram of a substance one degree

HEAT CAPACITY

Concepts of Heat

When heat is transferred to an object, the temperature of the object increases. When heat is removed from an object, the temperature of the object decreases. The relationship between the heat (q) that is transferred and the change in temperature (ΔT) is

$$q = C\,\Delta T = C\,(T_f - T_i)$$

The proportionality constant in this equation is called the heat capacity (C). The heat capacity is the amount of heat required to raise the temperature of an object or substance one degree. The temperature change is the difference between the final temperature (T_f) and the initial temperature (T_i).

A calorimeter is an experimental device in which a chemical reaction or physical process takes place. The calorimeter is well-insulated so that, ideally, no heat enters or leaves the calorimeter from the surroundings. For this reason, any heat liberated by the reaction or process being studied must be picked up by the calorimeter and other substances in the calorimeter.

A thermometer is typically inserted in the calorimeter to measure the change in temperature that results from the reaction or physical process. A stirrer is employed to keep the contents of the calorimeter well-mixed and to ensure uniform heating.

Some water and is equipped with a thermometer, a stirrer, and a heating element.

When activated, an electric current is passed through the heating element to generate heat, which is transferred to the calorimeter. In this simulation, you can set the heating rate (units of J sec^{-1}) and the heating time (units of sec).

ADIABATIC CALORIMETERS

An adiabatic calorimeter is a calorimeter used to examine a runaway reaction. Since the calorimeter runs in an adiabatic environment, any heat generated by the material sample under test causes the sample to increase in temperature, thus fuelling the reaction.

No adiabatic calorimeter is truly adiabatic-some heat will be lost by the sample to the sample holder.

A mathematical correction factor, known as the phi-factor, can be used to adjust the calorimetric result to account for these heat losses. The phi-factor is the ratio of the thermal mass of the sample and sample holder to the thermal mass of the sample alone.

Examples of adiabatic calorimeters are:-

- THT EV-Accelerating Rate Calorimeter
- HEL Phi-Tec.

A Simple Dewar Flask

Systag FlexyTSC a successor of their SIKAREX unit-the electronics of which could be used to apply a feedback system to heat the sample holder to give a result closer to true adiabaticy, however as the sample holder is an open ended glass tube, one soon loses the sample as a great deal of smoke.

REACTION CALORIMETERS

A reaction calorimeter is a calorimeter in which a chemical reaction is initiated within a closed insulated container. Reaction heats are measured and the total heat is obtained by integrating heatflow versus time. This is the standard used in industry to measure heats since industrial processes are engineered to run at constant temperatures. Reaction calorimetry can also be used to determine maximum heat release rate for chemical process engineering and for tracking the global kinetics of reactions. There are four main methods for measuring the heat in reaction calorimeter:

Heat Flow of Calorimetry

The cooling/heating jacket controls either the temperature of the process or the temperature of the jacket. Heat is measured by monitoring the temperature difference between heat transfer fluid and the process fluid. In addition fill volumes (*i.e.* wetted area), specific heat, heat transfer coefficient have to be determined to arrive at a correct value. It is possible with this type of calorimeter to do reactions at reflux, although the accuracy is not as good.

Heat Balance of Calorimeter

The cooling/heating jacket controls the temperature of the process. Heat is measured by monitoring the heat gained or lost by the heat transfer fluid.

Power Compensation

Power compensation uses a heater placed within the vessel to maintain a constant temperature. The energy supplied to this heater can be varied as reactions require and the calorimetry signal is purely derived from this electrical power.

Constant Flux of Calorimetry

Constant flux calorimetry (or COFLUX as it is often termed) is derived from heat balance calorimetry and uses specialized control mechanisms to maintain a constant heat flow (or flux) across the vessel wall.

BOMB CALORIMETERS

A bomb calorimeter is a type of constant-volume calorimeter used in measuring the heat of combustion of a particular reaction. Bomb calorimeters have to withstand the large pressure within the calorimeter as the reaction is being measured. Electrical energy is used to ignite the fuel; as the fuel is burning, it will heat up the surrounding air, which expands and escapes through a tube that leads the air out of the calorimeter. When the air is escaping through the copper tube it will also heat up the water outside the tube. The temperature of the water allows for calculating calorie content of the fuel.

The whole bomb, pressurized with excess pure oxygen (typically at 30atm) and containing a weighed mass of a sample (typically 1-1.5 g) and a small fixed amount of water (to saturate the internal atmosphere, thus ensuring that all water produced is liquid, and removing the need to include enthalpy of vapourization in calculations), is submerged under a known volume of water (ca. 2000 ml) before the charge is electrically ignited. The bomb, with the known mass of the sample and oxygen, form a closed system-no air escapes during the reaction.

The weighted reactant put inside the steel container is then ignited. Energy is released by the combustion and heat flow from this crosses the stainless steel wall, thus raising the temperature of the steel bomb, its contents, and the surrounding water jacket.

The temperature change in the water is then accurately measured with a thermometer. This reading, along with a bomb factor (which is dependent on the heat capacity of the metal bomb parts), is used to calculate the energy given out by the sample burn. A small correction is made to account for the electrical energy input, the burning fuse, and acid production (by titration of the residual liquid). After the temperature rise has been measured, the excess pressure in the bomb is released.

Basically, a bomb calorimeter consists of a small cup to contain the sample, oxygen, a stainless steel bomb, water, a stirrer, a thermometer, the dewar or insulating container (to prevent heat flow from the calorimeter to the surroundings) and ignition circuit connected to the bomb. By using stainless steel for the bomb, the reaction will occur with no volume change observed. Since there is no heat exchange between the calorimeter and surroundings $\rightarrow Q = 0$ (adiabatic); no work performed $\rightarrow W = 0$. Thus, the total internal energy change $\Delta U(\text{total}) = Q + W = 0$

Also, total internal energy change $\Delta U(\text{total}) = \Delta U(\text{system}) + \Delta U(\text{surroundings}) = 0 \rightarrow \Delta U(\text{system}) = - \Delta U(\text{surroundings}) = -C_V\, \Delta T$ (constant volume $\rightarrow dV = 0$)
where C_V = heat capacity of the bomb.

Before the bomb can be used to determine heat of combustion of any compound, it must be calibrated. The value of C_V can be estimated by C_V (calorimeter) = m (water). C_V (water) + m (steel). C_V (steel)

m (water) and m (steel) can be measured;

C_V(water) = 1 cal/g.K

C_V(steel) = 0.1 cal/g.K

In laboratory, C_V is determined by running a compound with known heat of combustion value:

$$C_V = H_c/\Delta T$$

Common compounds are benzoic acid (H_c = 6318 cal/g) or p-methyl benzoic acid (H_c = 6957 cal/g).

Temperature (T) is recorded every minute and

$$\Delta T = T(\text{final}) - T(\text{initial})$$

A small factor contributes to the correction of the total heat of combustion is the fuse wire. Nickel fuse wire is often used and has heat of combustion = 981.3 cal/g In order to calibrate the bomb, a small amount (~ 1 g) of benzoic acid, or p-methyl benzoic acid is weighed. A length of Nickel fuse wire (~10 cm) is weighed both before and after the combustion process. Mass of fuse wire burned Δm = m(before) - m(after)

The combustion of sample (benzoic acid) inside the bomb $\Delta H_c = \Delta H_c$ (benzoic acid) × m (benzoic acid) + ΔH_c (Ni fuse wire) × Δm (Ni fuse wire)

$$\Delta H_c = C_V.\Delta T \rightarrow C_V = \Delta H_c/\Delta T$$

Once C_V value of the bomb is determined, the bomb is ready to use to calculate heat of combustion of any compounds by $\Delta H_c = C_V.\ \Delta T$.

CALVET-TYPE CALORIMETERS

The detection is based on a three-dimensional fluxmeter sensor. The fluxmeter element consists of a ring of several thermocouples in series. The corresponding thermopile of high thermal conductivity surrounds the experimental space within the calorimetric block. The radial arrangement of the thermopiles guarantees an almost complete integration of the heat. This is verified by the calculation of the efficiency ratio that indicates that an average value of 94 % ± 1 % of heat is transmitted through the sensor on the full range of temperature of the Calvet-type calorimeter. In this setup, the sensitivity of the calorimeter is not affected by the crucible, the type of purgegas, or the flow rate. The main advantage of the setup is the increase of the experimental vessel's size and consequently the size of the sample, without affecting the accuracy of the calorimetric measurement.

The calibration of the calorimetric detectors is a key parameter and has to be performed very carefully. For Calvet-type calorimeters, a specific calibration, so called Joule effect or electrical calibration, has been developed to overcome all the problems encountered by a calibration done with standard materials. The main advantages of this type of calibration are as follows:

It is an absolute calibration. The use of standard materials for calibration is not necessary. The calibration can be performed at a constant temperature, in the heating mode and in the cooling mode. It can be applied to any experimental vessel volume. It is a very accurate calibration. An example of Calvet-type calorimeter is the C80 Calorimeter (reaction, isothermal and scanning calorimeter).

CONSTANT-PRESSURE CALORIMETER

A constant-pressure calorimeter measures the change in enthalpy of a reaction occurring in solution during which the atmospheric pressure remains constant. An example is a coffee-cup calorimeter, which is constructed from two nested Styrofoam cups and a lid with two holes, allowing insertion of a thermometer and a stirring rod. The inner cup holds a known amount of a solute, usually water, that absorbs the heat from the reaction. When the reaction occurs, the outer cup provides insulation. Then;

$$Cp = \frac{W\Delta H}{M\Delta T}$$

where

Cp = Specific heat at constant pressure

ΔH = Enthalpy of solution

ΔT = Change in temperature

W = mass of solute

M = molecular mass of solute.

The measurement of heat using a simple calorimeter, like the coffee cup calorimeter, is an example of constant-pressure calorimetry, since the pressure (atmospheric pressure) remains constant during the process. Constant-pressure calorimetry is used in determining the changes in enthalpy occurring in solution. Under these conditions the change in enthalpy equals the heat.

DIFFERENTIAL SCANNING CALORIMETER

In a differential scanning calorimeter (DSC), heat flow into a sample—usually contained in a small aluminium capsule or 'pan'—is measured differentially, *i.e.*, by comparing it to the flow into an empty reference pan.

In a heat flux DSC, both pans sit on a small slab of material with a known (calibrated) heat resistance K. The temperature of the calorimeter is raised linearly with time (scanned), *i.e.*, the heating rate $dT/dt = \beta$ is kept constant. This time linearity requires good design and good (computerized) temperature control. Of course, controlled cooling and isothermal experiments are also possible.

Heat flows into the two pans by conduction. The flow of heat into the sample is larger because of its heat capacity C_p. The difference in flow dq/dt induces a small temperature difference ΔT across the slab. This temperature difference is measured using a thermocouple. The heat capacity can in principle be determined from this signal:

$$\Delta T = K\frac{dq}{dt} = KC_p\beta$$

Note that this formula (equivalent to Newton's law of heat flow) is analogous to, and much older than, Ohm's law of electric flow:

$$\Delta V = R\, dQ/dt = R\, I.$$

When suddenly heat is absorbed by the sample (*e.g.*, when the sample melts), the signal will respond and exhibit a peak.

$$\frac{dq}{dt} = C_p\beta + f(t,T)$$

From the integral of this peak the enthalpy of melting can be determined, and from its onset the melting temperature. Differential scanning calorimetry is a workhorse technique in many fields, particularly in polymer characterization. A modulated temperature differential scanning calorimeter (MTDSC) is a type of DSC in which a small oscillation is imposed upon the otherwise linear heating rate.

This has a number of advantages. It facilitates the direct measurement of the heat capacity in one measurement, even in (quasi-)isothermal conditions. It permits the simultaneous measurement of heat effects that are reversible and not reversible at the timescale of the oscillation (reversing and non-reversing heat flow, respectively). It increases the sensitivity of the heat capacity measurement, allowing for scans at a slow underlying heating rate.

Safety Screening

DSC may also be used as an initial safety screening tool. In this mode the sample will be housed in a non-reactive crucible (often Gold, or Gold plated steel), and which will be able to withstand pressure (typically up to 100 bar). The presence of an exothermic event can then be used to assess the stability of a substance to heat. However, due to a combination of relatively poor sensitivity, slower than normal scan rates (typically 2-3°/min - due to much heavier crucible) and unknonwn activation energy, it is necessary to deduct about 75-100°C from the initial start of the observed exotherm to suggest a maximum temperature for the material. A much more accurate data set can be obtained from an adiabatic calorimeter, but such a test may take 2–3 days from ambient at a rate of 3°C increment per half hour.

ISOTHERMAL TITRATION CALORIMETER

In an isothermal titration calorimeter, the heat of reaction is used to follow a titration experiment. This permits determination of the mid point (stoichiometry) (N) of a reaction as well as its enthalpy (delta H), entropy (delta S) and of primary concern the binding affinity (Ka) The technique is gaining in importance particularly in the field of biochemistry, because it facilitates determination of substrate binding to enzymes. The technique is commonly used in the pharmaceutical industry to characterize potential drug candidates.

SPECIFIC HEAT AND CALORIMETRY

The amount of heat, Q, required to raise the temperature of a solid body at constant pressure depends on the change in temperature, ΔT, of the body, its mass, m, and a characteristic of the material forming the body called its specific heat, C. This relationship is expressed by the equation $Q = mC\Delta T$ and the dimensions of C are thus heat per unit mass per unit temperature change. The values of C do depend on temperature with those of common metals such as aluminum and brass increasing a few per cent as the temperature increases from 20°C to 100°C, for example, while that for iron or steel increases about 10% over the same range. Since these are not large changes, average specific heats are often quoted in handbooks for such fairly broad temperature ranges.

Historically the amount of heat, Q, was originally expressed in terms of calories. The calorie was defined most accurately as the amount of heat required to raise the temperature of 1 *gram* of water from 14.5°C to 15.5°C at 1 atmosphere pressure. With this definition the specific heat of water between 0°C and 100°C is 1.00 *cal/gm.* °C to within better than 1%. The use of the calorie began before it was established that heat was a form of energy and that 1 calorie is the equivalent of about 4.18 *Joules*. Thus in the SI system of units specific heats, that is the values of C for particular materials, are expressed as *J/kg.* °C and there is no need for the *calorie.* However, since so much work involving heat has used the *calorie* and since the specific heat of water is unity when it is employed, it remains a common unit and will be used in this work. The food *Calorie,* with a capital C is 1000 of these *calories* or 1 *kilo-calorie.*

The process of measuring quantities of heat exchanged is called calorimetry. In this experiment your objective will be to determine the average specific heat of several metals over a certain temperature range by the calorimeter method of mixtures.

Theory

We know that when two bodies, initially at different temperatures, are placed in intimate contact, in time they will come to equilibrium at some intermediate temperature. Provided no heat is lost to or gained from the surroundings, the quantity of heat lost by the hotter body is equal to that gained by the colder body. This is the process which occurs in the method of mixtures that you will use. The metal sample whose specific heat is to be measured is heated in boiling water to about 100°C. It is then quickly transferred to an aluminum calorimeter cup which contains cold water of known temperature. When the metal sample and calorimeter cup come to equilibrium, the common temperature is measured with a thermometer. It is assumed that the transfer of heat between the thermometer and the system is small enough to be neglected. If the net heat exchange with the surroundings can be kept small, then the heat lost by the metal sample equals the heat gained by the water and the calorimeter cup.

Let M_s be the mass of the sample whose specific heat is C_s. Let T_s be its temperature before it is placed in the calorimeter. Let M_w and C_w be the mass and specific heat of the water and let M_c and C_c the mass and specific heat of the calorimeter cup. Denote the temperature of the water and calorimeter cup before the sample is added by T_w and the final temperature of the mixture by T_f. Now use these symbols to express mathematically the situation when a hot object (the sample) is placed in contact with a cooler one (the water and the calorimeter cup) and the two are allowed to exchange heat until they reach a common temperature. From this equation derive an expression for the specific heat of the sample in terms of the other quantities.

Procedure

Fill a beaker with enough water so that the sample when placed in it will be covered with some to spare. Bring the water to a boil using a bunsen burner. Weigh the aluminum sample and the dry inner calorimeter cup. Note that the plastic top on the calorimeter is a thermal insulator whose temperature like that of the outer cup is assumed to be unaffected by changes in the temperature of the inner calorimeter cup during the course of experiment. Suspend the sample in the boiling water with string and a glass rod making sure not to touch the sides or bottom.

While the aluminum sample is reaching equilibrium, fill the calorimeter cup about $^2/_3$ full of cool water (about 5°C below room temperature). Cool water can be had from a water cooler. Ice is also available. Weigh the cup plus water. Care should be taken that the water is not so cold as to cause condensation on the outside of the calorimeter. If condensation does occur, dry the outside of the inner cup before proceeding.

Place the thermometer in the boiling water near the sample, not touching the bottom. When equilibrium is reached, record the sample temperature. Remove the thermometer, cool it with tap water, wipe it dry and then place it in the calorimeter cup. Record the temperature as soon as it is reasonably steady and then quickly transfer the sample from the boiling water to the calorimeter. Care must be taken not to carry any hot water over with the sample nor to splash any cold water out of the calorimeter. Stir the water in the calorimeter gently with the glass rod and observe the temperature. When equilibrium is reached, record the temperature. Always read the thermometer as accurately as you can, interpolating between the marks.

Calculate the average specific heat of your aluminum sample as determined by your experiment and specify the temperature range over which your value applies. Since the specific heat of the aluminum calorimeter cup is also an unknown, approximate its value by assuming it to be the same as the sample even though the cup and the sample are subject to different temperature ranges. (Later when you check the effect of this approximation you will see that it introduces little error.)

If the value you obtain for the specific heat of your sample is not between 0.19 and 0.25 *cal/g.* °C, repeat the experiment to improve your technique. You may, for example, want to use a different temperature for the cool water. The objective is to have the cool water as far below room temperature initially as the final temperature of the mixture is above room temperature.

Perform the experiment for the other samples and determine their specific heats. Compare your results with the accepted values (which your instructor will furnish) and calculate the percentage error and estimate the uncertainty in your experimental technique.

LATENT HEAT SUPPLIES WEATHER ENERGY

Anyone can tell the differences between water in its three phases, but what makes the phases different isn't quite as obvious. Water when it's the gas known as water vapour, but if enough of it is in the air we feel it as humidity. The liquid form of water is so familiar that we just call it "water"- the stuff we drink and dive into when we go swimming. The solid form of water, which we usually just call "ice" is common today even in places were nature never turns it cold enough to freeze water.

No matter what phase it's in, a water molecule is the same- an atom of oxygen with two atoms of hydrogen attached. Their energy, as exhibited by their speed of movement, is the only thing that makes millions of water molecules act differently when they get together in water's different phases.

The conversation of energy is one of the very basic laws of nature. It says that energy cannot be created or destroyed, but it can change form. This means that when water molecules slow down enough to change from vapour to liquid or ice, the kinetic energy of their movement changes into another form of energy, heat. When water evaporates from a pond to become water vapour, heat energy becomes the kinetic energy of the added motion.

Some Technical Stuff

Scientists talk about different kinds of latent heat, depending on what's going on when it's taken up or released. These kinds are listed below with the amounts of energy involved in each.

Note: You will sometimes see different figures for some of these. The amount of latent heat involved in a process depends to some extent on the temperature at which the process is occurring. The normally found in meteorology texts and are for temperatures found in the atmosphere, such as 0 Celsius (32 F).

Latent heat of condensation (Lc): Refers to the heat gained by the air when water vapour changes into a liquid. Lc = 2500 Joules per gram (J/g) of water or 600 calories per gram (cal/g) of water.

Latent heat of fusion (Lf): Refers to the heat lost or gained by the air when liquid water changes to ice or *vice versa.*

Lf = 333 Joules per gram (J/g) of water or 80 calories per gram (cal/g) of water.

Latent heat of sublimation (Ls): Refers to the heat lost or gained by the air when ice changes to vapour or *vice versa.* Ls = 2833 Joules per gram (J/g) of water or 680 calories per gram (cal/g) of water.

Latent heat of vaporization (Lv): Refers to the heat lost by the air when liquid water changes into vapour. This is also commonly known as the latent heat of evaporation.

Lv = -2500 Joules per gram (J/g) of water or -600 calories per gram (cal/g) of water.

LATENT HEAT AND SENSIBLE HEAT

Heat is a form of energy associated with the motion of atoms, molecules and other particles which comprise matter. Heat can be created by chemical reactions (such as burning), nuclear reactions (such as fusion taking place inside the Sun), electromagnetic dissipation (as in electric stoves), or mechanical dissipation (such as friction). Heat can be transferred between objects by radiation, conduction and convection.

When an object is heated, its temperature rises as heat is added. The increase in heat is called sensible heat. Similarly, when heat is removed from an object and its temperature falls, the heat removed is also called sensible heat. Heat that causes a change in temperature in an object is called sensible heat.

Latent Heat

All pure substances in nature are able to change their state. Solids can become liquids (ice to water) and liquids can become gases (water to vapour) but changes such as these require the addition or removal of heat. The heat that causes these changes is called latent heat.

Latent heat however, does not affect the temperature of a substance- for example, water remains at 100°C while boiling. The heat added to keep the water boiling is latent heat. Heat that causes a change of state with no change in temperature is called latent heat.

A = Sensible heat of ice
B = Latent heat of fusion of ice
C = Sensible heat of water
D = Latent heat of vaporization of water
E = Sensible heat of steam.

Latent Heat of Fusion

To raise the temperature of 1 pound of ice from 0°F to 32°F, you must add 16 BTU. To change the pound of ice at 32°F to a pound of water at 32°F, you add 144 BTU (latent heat of fusion). There is no change in temperature while the ice is melting.

Example

Five pounds of ice at 32°F is inserted into 25 pounds of water at 68°F. The ice melts and the final temperature of water is 38°F. Find the latent heat of fusion of ice.

Solution

H1 = latent heat of fusion of ice
= heat gained by 5 pounds of ice changing state from solid at 32°F to liquid at 32°F
H2 = heat lost by 25 pounds of water cooling from 68°F to 38°F
H3 = heat gained by 5 pounds of water (produced by ice after melting) warming from 32°F to 38°F
H1 + H3 = H2
H2 = 25 lbs. × 1 × (68°F - 38°F) = 750 BTU's
H3 = 5 lbs. × 1 × (38°F - 32°F) = 30 BTU's
H1 = H2 - H3
H1 = 750 BTU's - 30 BTU's = 720 BTU's
720 BTU's is the amount of heat required to melt 5 pounds of ice.
The latent heat of fusion for 1 pound of ice = 720 BTU's/5
Therefore, Latent Heat of Fusion of Ice = 144 BTU's per

pound. Amount of heat gained in fusion of ice = amount of heat lost in crystallization of water

BTU's = (mass) × (specific heat) × (difference in temperature)

BTU: unit of heat. One BTU is the energy required to raise 1 pound of water by 1 degree Fahrenheit. Specific heat: the ratio of the amount of heat required to increase the temperature of one pound of any substance by one degree to the amount necessary to increase one pound of water. The specific heat of water is 1, by adoption as a standard, and specific heat of another substance (solid, liquid, or gas) is determined experimentally by comparing it to water.

$$S_h = \frac{H_q}{M(t_1 - t_2)}$$

Sh = Specific heat

Hq = Heat quantity (BTU)

M = Mass (weight in lbs.)

t1 - t2 = Temperature change (°F)

Large quantities of BTU's are stated as MBTU's:

1,000 BTU = 1 MBTU

Material	*Specific Heat (BTU/Lb./°F)*
Water	1
Ice	0.53
Steam	0.48

Latent Heat of Vapourization

After the ice is melted, however, the temperature of the water is raised when more heat is applied. When 180 BTU are added, the water boils. To change a pound of water at 212°F to a pound of steam at 212°F, you must add 970 BTU (latent heat of vaporization). After the water is converted to steam at 212°F, the application of additional heat causes a rise in the temperature of the steam.

Example

One pound of steam is added to 19 pounds of water. The initial temperature of the water is 40°F, the temperature of the steam is 212°F, and the temperature of the resulting mixture is 97.1°F. Find the latent heat of vaporization of water.

USAGE OF LATENT HEAT

Two of the more common forms of latent heat (or enthalpies or energies) encountered are latent heat of fusion (melting or freezing) and latent heat of vaporization (boiling or condensing). These names describe the direction of energy flow when changing from one phase to the next: from solid to liquid, and to gas. In both cases, the change is endothermic, meaning that the system absorbs energy on going from solid to liquid to gas. The change is exothermic (the process releases energy) for the opposite direction. For example, in the atmosphere, when a molecule of water evaporates from the surface of any body of water, energy is transported by the water molecule into a lower temperature air parcel that contains less water vapour than its surroundings. Because energy is needed to overcome the molecular forces of attraction between water particles, the process of transition from a parcel of water to a parcel of vapour requires the input of energy causing a drop in temperature in its surroundings. If the water vapour condenses back to a liquid or solid phase onto a surface, the latent energy absorbed during evaporation is released as sensible heat onto the surface. The large value of the enthalpy of condensation of water vapour is the reason that steam is a far more effective heating medium than boiling water, and is more hazardous.

The terms sensible heat and latent heat are not special forms of energy; instead they characterize the same form of energy, heat, in terms of their effect on a material or a thermodynamic system. Heat is thermal energy in the process of transfer between a system and its surroundings or between two systems with a different temperature. Both sensible and latent heats are observed in many processes while transporting energy in nature. Latent heat is associated with the phase changes of atmospheric water vapour, mostly vaporization and condensation, whereas sensible heat is energy transferred that affects the temperature of the atmosphere.

The original usage of the term, as introduced by Black, was applied to systems that were intentionally held at constant temperature. Such usage referred to latent heat of expansion and several other related latent heats. These latent heats are defined independently of the conceptual framework of thermo-dynamics. When a body is heated at constant temperature by thermal radiation in a microwave field for example, it may expand by an amount described by its latent heat with respect to volume or latent heat of expansion, or increase its pressure by an amount described by its latent heat with respect to pressure.

Meteorology

In meteorology, latent heat flux is the flux of heat from the Earth's surface to the atmosphere that is associated with evaporation or transpiration of water at the surface and subsequent condensation of water vapour in the troposphere. It is an important component of Earth's surface energy budget. Latent heat flux has been commonly measured with the Bowen ratio technique, or more recently since the mid-1900s by the eddy covariance method.

History

The English word *latent* comes from Latin *latçns,* meaning lying hid. The term latent heat was introduced into calorimetry around 1750 by Joseph Black when studying system changes, such as of volume and pressure, when the thermodynamic system was held at constant temperature in a thermal bath. James Prescott Joule characterized latent energy as the energy of interaction in a given configuration of particles, *i.e.* a form of potential energy, and the sensible heat as an energy that was indicated by the thermometer, relating the latter to thermal energy.

SPECIFIC LATENT HEAT

A specific latent heat (*L*) expresses the amount of energy in form of heat (*Q*) required to completely affect a phase change of a unit of mass (*m*), usually 1kg, of a substance as an intensive property:

$$L = \frac{Q}{m}$$

Intensive properties are material characteristics and are not dependent on the size or extent of the sample. Commonly quoted and tabulated in the literature are the specific latent heat of fusion and the specific latent heat of vaporization for many substances. From this definition, the latent heat for a given mass of a substance is calculated by

$$Q = mL$$

where:

Q is the amount of energy released or absorbed during the change of phase of the substance (in kJ or in BTU),

m is the mass of the substance (in kg or in lb), and

L is the specific latent heat for a particular substance (kJ-kg_m^{-1} or in BTU-lb_m^{-1}), either L_f for fusion, or L_v for vaporization.

Table of Latent Heats

The following table shows the latent heats and change of phase temperatures of some common fluids and gases.

Substance	Latent Heat Fusion kJ/kg	Melting Point °C	Latent Heat Vaporization kJ/kg	Boiling Point °C
Alcohol, ethyl	108	-114	855	78.3
Ammonia	339	-75	1369	-33.34
Carbon dioxide	184	-78	574	-57
Helium			21	-268.93
Hydrogen	58	-259	455	-253
Lead	24.5	327.5	871	1750
Nitrogen	25.7	-210	200	-196
Oxygen	13.9	-219	213	-183
R134a		-101	215.9	-26.6
Toluene		-93	351	110.6
Turpentine			293	
Water	334	0	2260	100

Latent Heat for Condensation of Water

The latent heat of condensation of water in the temperature range from –40 °C to 40 °C is approximated by the following empirical cubic function:

$$L_{\text{water}}(T) = (2500.8 - 2.36T + 0.0016T^2 - 0.00006T^3)\,\text{J/g},$$

where the temperature T is taken to be the numerical value in °C. For sublimation and deposition from and into ice, the latent heat is almost constant in the temperature range from –40 °C to 0 °C and can be approximated by the following empirical quadratic function:

$$L_{\text{water}}(T) = (2500.8 - 2.36T + 0.0016T^2 - 0.00006T^3)\,\text{J/g},$$

CHANGES OF PHASE OR STATE

When a substance changes from one state, or phase, of matter to another we say that it has undergone a change of state, or we say that it has undergone a change of phase. These changes of phase always occur with a change of heat. Heat, which is energy, either comes into the material during a change of phase or heat comes out of the material during this change. However, although the heat content of the material changes, the temperature does not.

So, how could there be a change in heat during a state change without a change in temperature? During a change in state the heat energy is used to change the bonding between the molecules. In the case of melting, added energy is used to break the bonds between the molecules. In the case of freezing, energy is subtracted as the molecules bond to one another. These energy exchanges are *not* changes in kinetic energy. They are changes in bonding energy between the molecules.

If heat is coming into a substance during a phase change, then this energy is used to break the bonds between the molecules of the substance. The example we will use here is ice melting into water. Immediately after the molecular bonds in the ice are broken the molecules are moving at the same average speed as before, so their average kinetic energy remains the same, and, thus, their Kelvin temperature remains the same. The molecule of ice and the molecule of water are moving with the same rate of vibration in this diagram. This is meant to show that they have the same average speed and thus the same average kinetic energy (since they have the same mass) and thus the same Kelvin temperature. The motions are, though, greatly exagerated. Actually, the motions of the molecules should be considered tiny vibrations.

Here are the five changes of phase. They are diagrammed in the above animation and listed below:

Description of Phase Change	**Term for Phase Change**	**Heat Movement During Phase Change**	**Temperature Change During Phase Change**
Solid to liquid	Melting	Heat goes into the solid as it melts.	None
Liquid to solid	Freezing	Heat leaves the liquid as it freezes.	None
Liquid to gas	Vaporization, which includes boiling and evaporation	Heat goes into the liquid as it vaporizes.	None
Gas to liquid	Condensation	Heat leaves the gas as it condenses.	None
Solid to gas	Sublimation	Heat goes into the solid as it sublimates.	None

In the ice the molecules are strongly bonded to one another, thus forming a rigid solid. When heat is added to the ice it melts, and these bonds are broken, The molecules afterward bond to one another with less strength, and water is formed. The molecules were actually moving when in the solid state. They were vibrating back and forth. They had an average kinetic energy. So they had a Kelvin temperature proportional to this average kinetic energy.

After the melting the water molecules are moving, also. And they have the same average kinetic energy as they had before the melting. So, the water is at the same temperature the moment after the melting that the ice was at the moment before the melting. Heat came into the situation, but it was not used to change the kinetic energy of the molecules. It was used to change the bonding between the molecules. Breaking the bonds between the molecules of the ice requires energy, and this energy is the added heat.

In a similar way heat enters a liquid to change the molecular bonding when the liquid boils or evaporates into a gas, and heat enters a solid to change the molecular bonding when it sublimates into a gas. In an inverse way heat leaves a gas to change the molecular bonding when the gas condenses into a liquid, and heat leaves a liquid to change the molecular bonding when it freezes into a solid.

In none of these changes of state is the heat (energy) that is input or output used to change the speed of the molecules. The average speed of the molecules is the same before and after a phase change, and so is the average kinetic energy. And so, again, note that the temperature does not change during a change in phase, since it is proportional, in Kelvin degrees, to the average kinetic energy, which does not change.

HYDROGEN AS A FUEL FOR HEAT OR ELECTRICITY

Water is perhaps the most important substance to life on Earth. It is a simple compound made from the two elements hydrogen (H) and oxygen (O), and each molecule of water consists of two hydrogen atoms and one oxygen atom. Thus we write the chemical formula for water as "H_2O".

Hydrogen itself is also a very important element in the universe. For example, it is the fuel for the Sun, which generates power by fusing (combining) hydrogen atoms into a helium in a process call nuclear fusion. Because it can be obtained from water, as this project demonstrates, the German's call hydrogen "wasserstoff", which literally means "water stuff". Suppose that you just happen to have some pure hydrogen gas on hand, stored in a container. The hydrogen gas consists of H_2 molecules zipping around in a container (hydrogen atoms like to bond together into H_2 molecules). If there also happens to be oxygen gas around (O_2), and there is always plenty oxygen in the air (air consists of about 20% oxygen), then the oxygen can react violently with the hydrogen gas, such that the hydrogen *burns,* or *combusts,* with the oxygen to form water and heat, according to the chemical reaction

$$2H_2 + O_2 \rightarrow 2\, H_2O + \text{energy (heat)}.$$

Therefore, if you have some hydrogen, you can burn it for fuel to generate heat!

Generating heat, however, is not always the best thing to do, because *entropy,* which may be thought of as molecular *disorder,* is created when heat is generated, and that can limit the efficiency of devices that use that heat energy to do useful work (For more info on entropy, see the section on entropy in our Energy Physics Primer). Fortunately, there exists a device called a *fuel cell,* which can chemically combine hydrogen with oxygen to make electricity. After you complete this project, you may want to also want to cover our project on exploring fuel cells.

Fuel cells can also accomplish what this project demonstrates - electrolysis - which generates hydrogen from water.

Carbon-based Fuels

Notice from the equation above that, unlike burning a fossil (carbon-based) fuel such as coal, burning hydrogen doesn't produce any byproducts except water, which is environmentally benign. Hydrogen burns clean!

Burning fossil fuels on the other hand, always results in carbon monoxide (CO) and/or carbon dioxide (CO_2), which is produced when the carbon atoms combine with oxygen. These compounds are now considered pollutants because they are greenhouse gases - that is, they help trap heat near the Earth's surface, causing the Earth's surface temperature to rise, i.e. global warming. Burning fossil fuels such as coal also usually releases other pollutants, including sulfur dioxide, mercury, and uranium to the atmosphere, because these substances are usually present to varying extent in fossil fuels. But if we can obtain hydrogen without producing greenhouse gases or these other pollutants, then hydrogen is a better fuel to use than fossil fuels. Many people are now hopeful that a "hydrogen-economy" will soon replace our fossil fuel economy.

Obstacles to a Hydrogen-economy

There are two obstacles to a hydrogen-economy.

- It takes alot of volume (or energy) to store hydrogen - usually five times or so the volume, at reasonable pressures, needed to store an equivalent amount of energy with gasoline. One company that has made headway on solving this problem, however, is Dynetek.
- There is no hydrogen infrastructure: Making the transition to a hydrogen economy might mean having to scrap the fossil fuel infrastructure that we have already developed. One company that has made progress on refueling equipment is Stuart Energy.

Both of these problems might be surmounted by using synthetic fuels. For example, it is possible, using a catalyst, to combine water, carbon dioxide (extracted from the air), and renewable electricity to make fuels such as methanol, a carbon-based fuel. When this fuel is burned, water and carbon dioxide are produced. But because the carbon dioxide used initially to make the fuel was extracted from the air, the cycle is closed with respect to both water and carbon dioxide, and so won't contribute excess carbon dioxide to the atmosphere. Fuel cells can already use such fuels (either by extracting the hydrogen from the fuel prior to the fuel cell, or even directly in certain types of fuel cells).

Is Hydrogen Dangerous? Some people are worried that hydrogen might be too dangerous. It is true that hydrogen is a very explosive fuel, but so is natural gas and gasoline. For example, movies commonly depict automobiles burning up after crashing, and explosions involving natural gas are reported in the press from time to time. Two famous disasters involving hydrogen are the explosion of a zeppelin (an airship) called the Hindenburg (in 1937), and the explosion of the Space Shuttle Challenger (in 1986). You may want to study these disasters as a class project. The Hindenburg explosion, although often cited as an example of the danger of hydrogen, is thought by many to have been caused by flammable paint that caught fire from an electrical spark, and so might have caught fire even if the zeppelin had been filled with helium (an inert, nonflammable gas). Moreover, most of the people that died may have done so from coming into contact with burning diesel fuel (which powered the Hindenburg's airplane-type prop-engines) or from jumping of the Zeppelin before it landed.

5

Applications and Techniques of Heat Transfer

HEAT TRANSFER

Heat transfer has broad application to the functioning of numerous devices and systems. Heat-transfer principles may be used to preserve, increase, or decrease temperature in a wide variety of circumstances.

Insulation and Radiant Barriers

Thermal insulators are materials specifically designed to reduce the flow of heat by limiting conduction, convection, or both. Radiant barriers are materials that reflect radiation, and therefore reduce the flow of heat from radiation sources. Good insulators are not necessarily good radiant barriers, and *vice versa*. Metal, for instance, is an excellent reflector and a poor insulator.

The effectiveness of an insulator is indicated by its R-value, or resistance value. The R-value of a material is the inverse of the conduction coefficient (k) multiplied by the thickness (d) of the insulator. In most of the world, R-values are measured in SI units: square-meter kelvins per watt ($m^2 \cdot K/W$). In the United States, R-values are customarily given in units of British thermal units per hour per square-foot degrees Fahrenheit ($Btu/h \cdot ft^2 \cdot °F$).

$$R = \frac{d}{k}$$

$$C = \frac{Q}{m\Delta T}$$

Rigid fibreglass, a common insulation material, has an R-value of four per inch, while poured concrete, a poor insulator, has an R-value of 0.08 per inch.

The tog is a measure of thermal resistance, commonly used in the textile industry, and often seen quoted on, for example, duvets and carpet underlay.

The effectiveness of a radiant barrier is indicated by its reflectivity, which is the fraction of radiation reflected. A material with a high reflectivity (at a given wavelength) has a low emissivity (at that same wavelength), and *vice versa*. At any specific wavelength, reflectivity = 1 - emissivity. An ideal radiant barrier would have a reflectivity of 1, and would therefore reflect 100 per cent of incoming radiation. Vacuum flasks, or Dewars, are silvered to approach this ideal. In the vacuum of space, satellites use multi-layer insulation, which consists of many layers of aluminized (shiny) Mylar to greatly reduce radiation heat transfer and control satellite temperature.

Critical Insulation Thickness

Low thermal conductivity (k) materials reduce heat fluxes. The smaller the k value, the larger the corresponding thermal resistance (R) value. Thermal conductivity is measured in watts-per-meter per kelvin ($W \cdot m^{-1} \cdot K^{-1}$), represented as k. As the thickness of insulating material increases, the thermal resistance—or R-value—also increases.

However, adding layers of insulation has the potential of increasing the surface area, and hence the thermal convection area.

For example, as thicker insulation is added to a cylindrical pipe, the outer radius of the pipe-and-insulation system increases, and therefore surface area increases. The point where the added resistance of increasing insulation thickness becomes overshadowed by the effect of increased surface area is called the critical insulation thickness. In simple cylindrical pipes, this is calculated as a radius:

$$R_{critical} = \frac{k}{h}.$$

HEAT EXCHANGERS

A heat exchanger is a tool built for efficient heat transfer from one fluid to another, whether the fluids are separated by a solid wall so that they never mix, or the fluids are in direct contact. Heat exchangers are widely used in refrigeration, air conditioning, space heating, power generation, and chemical processing. One common example of a heat exchanger is a car's radiator, in which the hot coolant fluid is cooled by the flow of air over the radiator's surface.

Common types of heat exchanger flows include parallel flow, counter flow, and cross flow. In parallel flow, both fluids move in the same direction while transferring heat; in counter flow, the fluids move in opposite directions; and in cross flow, the fluids move at right angles to each other. Common constructions for heat exchanger include shell and tube, double pipe, extruded finned pipe, spiral fin pipe, u-tube, and stacked plate.

When engineers calculate the theoretical heat transfer in a heat exchanger, they must contend with the fact that the driving temperature difference between the two fluids varies with position. To account for this in simple systems, the log mean temperature difference (LMTD) is often used as an "average" temperature. In more complex systems, direct knowledge of the LMTD is not available, and the number of transfer units (NTU) method can be used instead.

Heat Sink and Dissipation

A heat sink is a component that transfers heat generated within a solid material to a fluid medium, such as air or a liquid. Examples of heat sinks are the heat exchangers used in refrigeration and air conditioning systems, and the radiator in a car (which is also a heat exchanger). Heat sinks also help to cool electronic and optoelectronic devices such as CPUs, higher-power lasers, and light-emitting diodes (LEDs). A heat sink uses its extended surfaces to increase the surface area in contact with the cooling fluid.

Buildings and Cold Climates

In cold climates, houses with their heating systems form dissipative systems, often resulting in a loss of energy (known colloquially as "Heat Bleed") that makes home interiors uncomfortably cool or cold.

For the comfort of the inhabitants, the interiors must be maintained out of thermal equilibrium with the external surroundings. In effect, these domestic residences are islands of warmth in a sea of cold, and the thermal gradient between the inside and outside is often quite steep. This can lead to problems such as condensation and uncomfortable air currents, which—if left unaddressed—can cause cosmetic or structural damage to the property.

Such issues can be prevented through the execution of an energy audit, and the implementation of recommended corrective procedures (such as the installation of adequate insulation, the air sealing of structural leaks, and the addition of energy-efficient windows and doors.

Thermal transmittance is the rate of transfer of heat through a structure divided by the difference in temperature across the structure. It is expressed in watts per square meter per kelvin, or W/m^2K. Well-insulated parts of a building have a low thermal transmittance, whereas poorly-insulated parts of a building have a high thermal transmittance.

A thermostat is a device capable of starting the heating system when the house's interior falls below a set temperature, and of stopping that same system when another (higher) set temperature has been achieved. Thus, the thermostat controls the flow of energy into the house, that energy eventually being dissipated to the exterior.

Thermal Energy Storage and Thermal Reservoir

Thermal energy storage refers to technologies that store energy in a thermal reservoir for later use. They can be employed to balance energy demand between daytime and nighttime. The thermal reservoir may be maintained at a temperature above (hotter) or below (colder) than that of the ambient environment. Applications include later use in space heating, domestic or process hot water, or to generate electricity. Most practical active solar heating systems have storage for a few hours to a day's worth of heat collected.

Evaporative Cooling and Physical Phenomenon

Evaporative cooling is a physical phenomenon in which evaporation of a liquid, typically into surrounding air, cools an object or a liquid in contact with it. Latent heat describes the amount of heat that is needed to evaporate the liquid; this heat comes from the liquid itself and the surrounding gas and surfaces. The greater the difference between the two temperatures, the greater the evaporative cooling effect. When the temperatures are the same, no net evaporation of water in air occurs; thus, there is no cooling effect. A simple example of natural evaporative cooling is perspiration, or sweat, which the body secretes in order to cool itself. An evaporative cooler is a device that cools air through the simple evaporation of water.

Process of Radiative Cooling

Radiative cooling is the process by which a body loses heat by radiation. It is an important effect in the Earth's atmosphere. In the case of the Earth-atmosphere system, it refers to the process by which long-wave (infrared) radiation is emitted to balance the absorption of short-wave (visible) energy from the Sun. Convective transport of heat and evaporative transport of latent heat both remove heat from the surface and redistribute it in the atmosphere, making it available for radiative transport at higher altitudes.

Techniques of Laser Cooling

Laser cooling refers to techniques in which atomic and molecular samples are cooled through the interaction with one or more laser light fields. The most common method of laser cooling is Doppler cooling. In Doppler cooling, the frequency of the laser light is tuned slightly below an electronic transition in the atom. Thus, the atoms would absorb more photons if they moved towards the light source, due to the Doppler effect. If an excited atom then emits a photon spontaneously, it will be accelerated. The result of the absorption and emission process is to reduce the speed of the atom. Eventually the mean velocity, and therefore the kinetic energy of the atoms, will be reduced. Since the temperature of an ensemble of atoms is a measure of the random internal kinetic energy, this is equivalent to cooling the atoms. Sympathetic cooling is a process in which particles of one type cool particles of another type. Typically, atomic ions that can be directly laser-cooled are used to cool nearby ions or atoms. This technique allows cooling of ions and atoms that cannot be laser cooled directly.

Evaporatie of Magnetic Cooling

Magnetic evaporative cooling is a technique for lowering the temperature of a group of atoms. The process confines atoms using a magnetic field. Over time, individual atoms will become much more energetic than the others due to random collisions, and will escape—removing energy from the system and reducing the temperature of the remaining group. This process is similar to the familiar process by which standing water becomes water vapour.

HEAT TRANSFER IN THE HUMAN BODY

The principles of heat transfer in engineering systems can be applied to the human body in order to determine how the body transfers heat. Heat is produced in the body by the continuous metabolism of nutrients which provides energy for the systems of the body. The human body must maintain a consistent internal temperature in order to maintain healthy bodily functions. Therefore, excess heat must be dissipated from the body to keep it from overheating. When a person engages in elevated levels of physical activity, the body requires additional fuel which increases the metabolic rate and the rate of heat production. The body must then use additional methods to remove the additional heat produced in order to keep the internal temperature at a healthy level.

Heat transfer by convection is driven by the movement of fluids over the surface of the body. This convective fluid can be either a liquid or a gas. For heat transfer from the outer surface of the body, the convection mechanism is dependent on the surface area of the body, the velocity of the air, and the temperature gradient between the surface of the skin and the ambient air.

The normal temperature of the body is approximately 37°C. Heat transfer occurs more readily when the temperature of the surroundings is significantly less than the normal body temperature. This concept explains why a person feels "cold" when not enough covering is worn when exposed to a cold environment. Clothing can be considered an insulator which provides thermal resistance to heat flow over the covered portion of the body. This thermal resistance causes the temperature on the surface of the clothing to be less than the temperature on the surface of the skin. This smaller temperature gradient between the surface temperature and the ambient temperature will cause a lower rate of heat transfer than if the skin were not covered.

In order to ensure that one portion of the body is not significantly hotter than another portion, heat must be distributed evenly through the bodily tissues. Blood flowing through blood vessels acts as a convective fluid and helps to prevent any buildup of excess heat inside the tissues of the body.

This flow of blood through the vessels can be modelled as pipe flow in an engineering system. The heat carried by the blood is determined by the temperature of the surrounding tissue, the diameter of the blood vessel, the thickness of the fluid, velocity of the flow, and the heat transfer coefficient of the blood. The velocity, blood vessel diameter, and the fluid thickness can all be related with the Reynolds Number, a dimensionless number used in fluid mechanics to characterize the flow of fluids.

Latent heat loss, also known as evaporative heat loss, accounts for a large fraction of heat loss from the body. When the core temperature of the body increases, the body triggers sweat glands in the skin to bring additional moisture to the surface of the skin. The liquid is then transformed into vapour which removes heat from the surface of the body. The rate of evaporation heat loss is directly related to the vapour pressure at the skin surface and the amount of moisture present on the skin. Therefore, the maximum of heat transfer will occur when the skin is completely wet. The body continuously loses water by evaporation but the most significant amount of heat loss occurs during periods of increased physical activity.

BASICS OF HEAT TRANSFER

In the simplest of terms, the discipline of heat transfer is concerned with only two things: temperature, and the flow of heat. Temperature represents the amount of thermal energy available, whereas heat flow represents the movement of thermal energy from place to place. On a microscopic scale, thermal energy is related to the kinetic energy of molecules. The greater a material's temperature, the greater the thermal agitation of its constituent molecules (manifested both in linear motion and vibrational modes). It is natural for regions containing greater molecular kinetic energy to pass this energy to regions with less kinetic energy.

Several material properties serve to modulate the heat tranfered between two regions at differing temperatures. Examples include thermal conductivities, specific heats, material densities, fluid velocities, fluid viscosities, surface emissivities, and more. Taken together, these properties serve to make the solution of many heat transfer problems an involved process.

HEAT TRANSFER MECHANISMS

Heat transfer mechanisms can be grouped into 3 broad categories:

Conduction: Regions with greater molecular kinetic energy will pass their thermal energy to regions with less molecular energy through direct molecular collisions, a process known as conduction. In metals, a significant portion of the transported thermal energy is also carried by conduction-band electrons.

Convection: When heat conducts into a static fluid it leads to a local volumetric expansion. As a result of gravity-induced pressure gradients, the expanded fluid parcel becomes buoyant and displaces, thereby transporting heat by fluid motion (*i.e.* convection) in addition to conduction. Such heat-induced fluid motion in initially static fluids is known as free convection.

Radiation: All materials radiate thermal energy in amounts determined by their temperature, where the energy is carried by photons of light in the infrared and visible portions of the electromagnetic spectrum.

When temperatures are uniform, the radiative flux between objects is in equilibrium and no net thermal energy is exchanged. The balance is upset when temperatures are not uniform, and thermal energy is transported from surfaces of higher to surfaces of lower temperature.

CONVECTIVE HEAT TRANSFER

Convective heat transfer, often referred to simply as convection, is the transfer of heat from one place to another by the movement of fluids. Convection is usually the dominant form of heat transfer in liquids and gases. Although often discussed as a distinct method of heat transfer, convective heat transfer involves the combined processes of conduction (heat diffusion) and heat transfer by bulk fluid flow, a process technically called *heat advection*.

The term convection can refer to transfer of heat with any fluid movement, but advection is the more precise term for the transfer due only to bulk fluid flow. The process of transfer of heat from a solid to a fluid, or the reverse, requires not only transfer of heat by bulk motion of the fluid, but also diffusion/ conduction of heat through the still boundary layer next to the solid. Thus, this process with a moving fluid requires both diffusion and advection of heat, a summed process that is generally called convection.

Convection can be "forced" by movement of a fluid by means other than buoyancy forces (for example, a water pump in an automobile engine). In some cases, natural buoyancy forces alone are entirely responsible for fluid motion when the fluid is heated, and this process is called "natural convection." An example is the draft in a chimney or around any fire. In natural convection, an increase in temperature produces a reduction in density, which causes fluid motion due to pressures and forces when fluids of different densities are affected by gravity (or any g-force). For example, when water is heated on a stove, hot water from the bottom of the pan rises, displacing the colder denser liquid which falls. After heating has stopped, mixing and conduction from this natural convection eventually result in a nearly homogeneous density, and even temperature.

The convection heat transfer mode is comprised to two mechanisms. In addition to energy transfer due to random molecular motion (diffusion), energy is also transferred by bulk, or macroscopic, motion of the fluid. This motion is associated with the fact that, at any instant, large numbers of molecules are moving collectively or as aggregates. Such motion, in the presence of a temperature gradient, contributes to heat transfer. Because the molecules in aggregate retain their random motion, the total heat transfer is then due to the superposition of energy transport by random motion of the molecules and by the bulk motion of the fluid. It is customary to use the term convection when referring to this cumulative transport and the term advection when referring to the transport due to bulk fluid motion.

Overview of Transfer of Thermal Energy

Convection is the transfer of thermal energy from one place to another by the movement of fluids or gases. Convection is usually the dominant form of heat transfer in liquids and gases. Although often discussed as a distinct method of heat transfer, convection describes the combined effects of conduction and fluid flow or mass exchange.

Two types of convective heat transfer may be distinguished: Free or natural convection: when fluid motion is caused by buoyancy forces that result from the density variations due to variations of temperature in the fluid. In the absence of an external source, when the fluid is in contact with a hot surface, its molecules separate and scatter, causing the fluid to be less dense. As a consequence, the fluid is displaced while the cooler fluid gets denser and the fluid sinks. Thus, the hotter volume transfers heat towards the cooler volume of that fluid. Familiar examples are the upward flow of air due to a fire or hot object and the circulation of water in a pot that is heated from below.

Forced convection: when a fluid is forced to flow over the surface by an external source such as fans, by stirring, and pumps, creating an artificially induced convection current.

Internal and external flow can also classify convection. Internal flow occurs when a fluid is enclosed by a solid boundary such when flowing through a pipe. An external flow occurs when a fluid extends indefinitely without encountering a solid surface. Both of these types of convection, either natural or forced, can be internal or external because they are independent of each other. The bulk temperature, or the average fluid temperature, is a convenient reference point for evaluating properties related to convective heat transfer, particularly in applications related to flow in pipes and ducts.

For a visual experience of natural convection, a glass filled with hot water and some red food dye may be placed inside a fish tank with cold, clear water. The convection currents of the red liquid may be seen to rise and fall in different regions, then eventually settle, illustrating the process as heat gradients are dissipated.

NEWTON'S LAW OF COOLING

Convection-cooling can sometimes be described by Newton's law of cooling in cases where the heat transfer coefficient is independent or relatively independent of the temperature difference between object and environment. This is sometimes true, but is not guaranteed to be the case. Newton's law, which requires a constant heat transfer coefficient, states that *the rate of heat loss of a body is proportional to the difference in temperatures between the body and its surroundings*. The rate of heat transfer in such circumstances is derived below:

Newton's cooling law is a solution of the differential equation given by Fourier's law:

$$\frac{dQ}{dt} = \dot{Q} = h \cdot A(T_{env} - T(t)) = -h \cdot A \Delta T(t)$$

where

Q is the thermal energy in joules

h is the heat transfer coefficient (assumed independent of T here) (W/m^2 K)

A is the surface area of the heat being transferred (m^2)

T is the temperature of the object's surface and interior (since these are the same in this approximation)

is the temperature of the environment; *i.e.* the temperature suitably far from the surface

$\Delta T(t) = T(t) - T_{env}$ is the time-dependent thermal gradient between environment and object

The heat transfer coefficient h depends upon physical properties of the fluid and the physical situation in which convection occurs. Therefore, a single usable heat transfer coefficient (one that does not vary significantly across the temperature-difference ranges covered during cooling and heating) must be derived or found experimentally for every system analysed. Formulas and correlations are available in many references to calculate heat transfer coefficients for typical configurations and fluids. For laminar flows, the heat transfer coefficient is rather low compared to the turbulent flows; this is due to turbulent flows having a thinner stagnant fluid film layer on heat transfer surface. However, note that Newton's law breaks down if the flows should transition between laminar or turbulent flow, since this will change the heat transfer coefficient h which is assumed constant in solving the equation.

Newton's law requires that internal heat conduction within the object be large in comparison to the loss/gain of heat by convection (lumped capacitance model), and this may not be true. Also, an accurate formulation for temperatures may require analysis based on changing heat transfer coefficients at different temperatures, a situation frequently found in free-convection situations, and which precludes accurate use of Newton's law. Assuming these are not problems, then the solution can be given if heat transfer within the object is considered to be far more rapid than heat transfer at the boundary (so that there are small thermal gradients within the object). This condition, in turn, allows the heat in the object to be expressed as a simple product of the object's mass, its heat capacity, and its temperature.

Terms of Object Heat Capacity

If the entire body is treated as lumped capacitance thermal energy reservoir, with a total thermal energy content which is proportional to simple total heat capacity *C*, and *T*, the temperature of the body, or $Q = CT$, it is expected that the system will experience exponential decay with time in the temperature of a body.

From the definition of heat capacity *C* comes the relation $C = dQ / dT$. Differentiating this equation with regard to time gives the identity (valid so long as temperatures in the object are uniform at any given time): $dQ / dt = C(dT / dt)$. This expression may be used to replace dQ / dt in the first equation which begins. Then, if $T(t)$ is the temperature of such a body at time *t*, and T_{env} is the temperature of the environment around the body:

$$\frac{dT(t)}{dt} = -r(T(t) - T_{\text{env}}) = -r\Delta T(t)$$

where

$r = hA / C$ is a positive constant characteristic of the system, which must be in units of s^{-1}, and is therefore sometimes expressed in terms of a characteristic time constant t_0 given by: $r = 1 / t_0 = -(dT(t) / dt) / \Delta T$. Thus, in thermal systems, $t_0 = C / hA$. The solution of this differential equation, by standard methods of integration and substitution of boundary conditions, gives:

$$T(t) = T_{\text{env}} + (T(0) - T_{\text{env}})\, e^{-rt}.$$

If $\Delta T(t)$ is defined as : $T(t) - T_{\text{env}}$, where $\Delta T(0)$ is the initial temperature difference at time 0,

then the Newtonian solution is written as:

$$\Delta T(t) = \Delta T(0)\, e^{-rt} = \Delta T(0)\, e^{-t/t_0}.$$

This same solution is more immediately apparent if the initial differential equation is written in terms of $\Delta T(t)$, as a single function of time to be found, or "solved for." '

$$\frac{dT(t)}{dt} = \frac{d\Delta T(t)}{dt} = -\frac{1}{t_0}\Delta T(t)$$

FOURIER LAW OF HEAT CONDUCTION

When there exists a temperature gradient within a body, heat energy will flow from the region of high temperature to the region of low temperature. This phenomenon is known as conduction heat transfer, and is described by Fourier's Law (named after the French physicist Joseph Fourier),

$$q = -k\vec{\nabla} T$$

This equation determines the heat flux vector q for a given temperature profile T and thermal conductivity k. The minus sign ensures that heat flows down the temperature gradient.

CONVECTION OF HEAT ENERGY

Heat energy transfers between a solid and a fluid when there is a temperature difference between the fluid and the solid. This is known as "convection heat transfer". Generally, convection heat transfer can not be ignored when there is a significant fluid motion around the solid.

The temperature of the solid due to an external field such as fluid buoyancy can induce a fluid motion. This is known as "natural convection" and it is a strong function of the temperature difference between the solid and the fluid. Blowing air over the solid by using external devices such as fans and pumps can also generate a fluid motion. This is known as "forced convection".

Fluid mechanics plays a major role in determining convection heat transfer.

For each kind of convection heat transfer, the fluid flow can be either laminar or turbulent.

Laminar flow generally occurs in relatively low velocities in a smooth laminar boundary layer over smooth small objects, while turbulent flow forms when the boundary layer is shedding or breaking due to higher velocities or rough geometries.

TERMINOLOGY

The term *convection* may have slightly different but related usages in different scientific or engineering contexts or applications. The broader sense is in fluid mechanics, where *convection* refers to the motion of fluid regardless of cause. However in thermodynamics "convection" often refers specifically to heat transfer by convection.

Additionally, convection includes fluid movement both by bulk motion (advection) and by the motion of individual particles (diffusion).

However in some cases, convection is taken to mean only advective phenomena.

For instance, in the transport equation, which describes a number of different transport phenomena, terms are separated into "convective" and "diffusive" effects, with "convective" meaning purely advective in context.

A similar differentiation is made in the Navier–Stokes equations. In such cases the precise meaning of the term may be clear only from context.

EXAMPLES AND APPLICATIONS OF CONVECTION

Convection occurs on a large scale in atmospheres, oceans, planetary mantles, and it provides the mechanism of heat transfer for a large fraction of the outermost interiors of our sun and all stars. Fluid movement during convection may be invisibly slow, or it may be obvious and rapid, as in a hurricane. On astronomical scales, convection of gas and dust is thought to occur in the accretion disks of black holes, at speeds which may closely approach that of light.

HEAT TRANSFER

Convective heat transfer is a mechanism of heat transfer occurring because of bulk motion (observable movement) of fluids. Heat is the entity of interest being advected (carried), and diffused (dispersed). This can be contrasted with conductive heat transfer, which is the transfer of energy by vibrations at a molecular level through a solid or fluid, and radiative heat transfer, the transfer of energy through electromagnetic waves.

Heat is transferred by convection in numerous examples of naturally occurring fluid flow, such as: wind, oceanic currents, and movements within the Earth's mantle. Convection is also used in engineering practices to provide desired temperature changes, as in heating of homes, industrial processes, cooling of equipment, etc. The rate of convective heat transfer may be improved by the use of a heat sink, often in conjunction with a fan. For instance, a typical computer CPU will have a purpose-made fan to ensure its operating temperature is kept within tolerable limits.

Convection Cells

A convection cell, also known as a Bénard cell is a characteristic fluid flow pattern in many convection systems. A rising body of fluid typically loses heat because it encounters a cold surface. In liquid this occurs because it exchanges heat with colder liquid through direct exchange. In the example of the Earth's atmosphere, this occurs because it radiates heat. Because of this heat loss the fluid becomes denser than the fluid underneath it, which is still rising. Since it cannot descend through the rising fluid, it moves to one side. At some distance, its downward force overcomes the rising force beneath it, and the fluid begins to descend. As it descends, it warms again and the cycle repeats itself.

ATMOSPHERIC CIRCULATION

Atmospheric circulation is the large-scale movement of air, and the means by which thermal energy is distributed on the surface of the Earth, together with the much slower (lagged) ocean circulation system. The large-scale structure of the atmospheric circulation varies from year to year, but the basic climatological structure remains fairly constant.

Latitudinal circulation is the consequence of the fact that incident solar radiation per unit area is highest at the heat equator, and decreases as the latitude increases, reaching its minimum at the poles. It consists of two primary convection cells, the Hadley cell and the polar vortex, with the Hadley cell experiencing stronger convection as a consequence of the release of latent heat energy upon condensation at higher altitudes.

Longitudinal circulation, on the other hand, comes about because water has a higher specific heat capacity than land and thereby absorbs and releases more heat, but the temperature changes less than land. This effect is noticeable; it is what brings the sea breeze, air cooled by the water, ashore in the day, and carries the land breeze, air cooled by contact with the ground, out to sea during the night. Longitudinal circulation consists of two cells, the Walker circulation and El Niño/Southern Oscillation.

Weather

More localized phenomena than global atmospheric movement are also due to convection, including wind and some of the hydrologic cycle. For example, a foehn wind is a type of down-slope wind which occurs in the downwind side of a mountain range. It results from the adiabatic warming of air which has dropped most of its moisture on windward slopes. As a consequence of the different adiabatic lapse rates of moist and dry air, the air on the leeward slopes becomes warmer than equivalent elevations on the windward slopes.

A thermal column (or thermal) is a vertical section of rising air in the lower altitudes of the Earth's atmosphere. Thermals are created by the uneven heating of the Earth's surface from solar radiation. The Sun warms the ground, which in turn warms the air directly above it. The warmer air expands, becoming less dense than the surrounding air mass, and creating a thermal low. The mass of lighter air rises, and as it does, it cools due to its expansion at lower high-altitude pressures. It stops rising when it has cooled to the same temperature as the surrounding air. Associated with a thermal is a downward flow surrounding the thermal column. The downward moving exterior is caused by colder air being displaced at the top of the thermal. Another convection-driven weather effect is the sea breeze.

Warm air has a lower density than cool air, so warm air rises within cooler air, similar to hot air balloons. Clouds form as relatively warmer air carrying moisture rises within cooler air. As the moist air rises, it cools causing some of the water vapour in the rising packet of air to condense. When the moisture condenses, it releases energy known as latent heat of fusion which allows the rising packet of air to cool less than its surrounding air, continuing the cloud's ascension. If enough instability is present in the atmosphere, this process will continue long enough for cumulonimbus clouds to form, which support lightning and thunder. Generally, thunderstorms require three conditions to form: moisture, an unstable airmass, and a lifting force (heat).

All thunderstorms, regardless of type, go through three stages: the developing stage, the mature stage, and the dissipation stage. The average thunderstorm has a 24 km (15 mi) diameter. Depending on the conditions present in the atmosphere, these three stages take an average of 30 minutes to go through.

OCEANIC CIRCULATION

Solar radiation affects the oceans: warm water from the Equator tends to circulate towards the poles, while cold polar water heads towards the Equator. The surface currents are initially dictated by surface wind conditions. The trade winds blow westward in the tropics, and the westerlies blow eastward at mid-latitudes. This wind pattern applies a stress to the subtropical ocean surface with negative curl across the Northern Hemisphere, and the reverse across the Southern Hemisphere. The resulting Sverdrup transport is equatorward.

Because of conservation of potential vorticity caused by the poleward-moving winds on the subtropical ridge's western periphery and the increased relative vorticity of poleward moving water, transport is balanced by a narrow, accelerating poleward current, which flows along the western boundary of the ocean basin, outweighing the effects of friction with the cold western boundary current which originates from high latitudes.

The overall process, known as western intensification, causes currents on the western boundary of an ocean basin to be stronger than those on the eastern boundary.

As it travels poleward, warm water transported by the strong warm water current undergoes evaporative cooling. The cooling is wind driven: wind moving over the water cools it and also causes evaporation, leaving a saltier brine. In this process, the water increases in salinity and density, and decreases in temperature. Once sea ice forms, salts are left out of the ice, a process known as brine exclusion. These two processes produce water that is denser and colder (or, more precisely, water that is still liquid at a lower temperature). The water across the northern Atlantic ocean becomes so dense that it begins to sink down through less salty and less dense water. This downdraft of heavy, cold and dense water becomes a part of the North Atlantic Deep Water, a southgoing stream.

MANTLE CONVECTION

Mantle convection is the slow creeping motion of Earth's rocky mantle caused by convection currents carrying heat from the interior of the earth to the surface. It is the driving force that causes tectonic plates to move around the Earth's surface.

The Earth's surface is divided into a number of tectonic plates that are continuously being created and consumed at their opposite plate boundaries. Creation (accretion) occurs as mantle is added to the growing edges of a plate. This hot added material cools down by conduction and convection of heat. At the consumption edges of the plate, the material has thermally contracted to become dense, and it sinks under its own weight in the process of subduction at an ocean trench.

This subducted material sinks to some depth in the Earth's interior where it is prohibited from sinking further. The subducted oceanic crust triggers volcanism.

Stack Effect and Chimney Effect

The Stack effect or chimney effect is the movement of air into and out of buildings, chimneys, flue gas stacks, or other containers due to buoyancy. Buoyancy occurs due to a difference in indoor-to-outdoor air density resulting from temperature and moisture differences. The greater the thermal difference and the height of the structure, the greater the buoyancy force, and thus the stack effect. The stack effect helps drive natural ventilation and infiltration. Some cooling towers operate on this principle; similarly the solar updraft tower is a proposed device to generate electricity based on the stack effect.

STELLAR PHYSICS

The convection zone of a star is the range of radii in which energy is transported primarily by convection. Granules on the photosphere of the Sun are the visible tops of convection cells in the photosphere, caused by convection of plasma in the photosphere. The rising part of the granules is located in the center where the plasma is hotter. The outer edge of the granules is darker due to the cooler descending plasma. A typical granule has a diameter on the order of 1,000 kilometers and each lasts 8 to 20 minutes before dissipating. Below the photosphere is a layer of much larger "supergranules" up to 30,000 kilometers in diameter, with lifespans of up to 24 hours.

Convection Mechanisms

Convection may happen in fluids at all scales larger than a few atoms. There are a variety of circumstances in which the forces required for natural and forced convection arise, leading to different types of convection. In broad terms, convection arises because of body forces acting within the fluid, such as gravity (buoyancy), or surface forces acting at a boundary of the fluid.

The causes of convection are generally described as one of either "natural" ("free") or "forced", although other mechanisms also exist. However the distinction between natural and forced convection is particularly important for convective heat transfer.

NATURAL AND FREE CONVECTION

Natural convection, or free convection, occurs due to temperature differences which affect the density, and thus relative buoyancy, of the fluid. Heavier (more dense) components will fall, while lighter (less dense) components rise, leading to bulk fluid movement. Natural convection can only occur, therefore, in a gravitational field. A common example of natural convection is the rise of smoke from a fire. It can be seen in a pot of boiling water in which the hot and less-dense water on the bottom layer moves upwards in plumes, and the cool and more dense water near the top of the pot likewise sinks.

Natural convection will be more likely and/or more rapid with a greater variation in density between the two fluids, a larger acceleration due to gravity that drives the convection, and/or a larger distance through the convecting medium. Natural convection will be less likely and/or less rapid with more rapid diffusion (thereby diffusing away the thermal gradient that is causing the convection) and/or a more viscous (sticky) fluid.The onset of natural convection can be determined by the Rayleigh number (Ra).

Note that differences in buoyancy within a fluid can arise for reasons other than temperature variations, in which case the fluid motion is called gravitational convection. However, all types of buoyant convection, including natural convection, do not occur in microgravity environments. All require the presence of an environment which experiences g-force (proper acceleration).

Forced Convection

In forced convection, also called heat advection, fluid movement results from external surface forces such as a fan or pump. Forced convection is typically used to increase the rate of heat exchange. Many types of mixing also utilize forced convection to distribute one substance within another. Forced convection also occurs as a by-product to other processes, such as the action of a propeller in a fluid or aerodynamic heating. Fluid radiator systems, and also heating and cooling of parts of the body by blood circulation, are other familiar examples of forced convection.

Forced convection may happen by natural means, such as when the heat of a fire causes expansion of air and bulk air flow by this means. In microgravity, such flow (which happens in all directions) along with diffusion is the only means by which fires are able to draw in fresh oxygen to maintain themselves. The shock wave that transfers heat and mass out of explosions is also a type of forced convection.

Although forced convection from thermal gas expansion in zero-g does not fuel a fire as well as natural convection in a gravity field, some types of artificial forced convection are far more efficient than free convection, as they are not limited by natural mechanisms. For instance, a convection oven works by forced convection, as a fan which rapidly circulates hot air forces heat into food faster than would naturally happen due to simple heating without the fan.

Buoyant Convection

Gravitational convection is a type of natural convection induced by buoyancy variations resulting from material properties other than temperature. Typically this is caused by a variable composition of the fluid. If the varying property is a concentration gradient, it is known as solutal convection. For example, gravitational convection can be seen in the diffusion of a source of dry salt downward into wet soil due to the buoyancy of fresh water in saline. Variable salinity in water and variable water content in air masses are frequent causes of convection in the oceans and atmosphere which do not involve heat, or else involve additional compositional density factors other than the density changes from thermal expansion.

Similarly, variable composition within the Earth's interior which has not yet achieved maximal stability and minimal energy (in other words, with densest parts deepest) continues to cause a fraction of the convection of fluid rock and molten metal within the Earth's interior.

Gravitational convection, like natural thermal convection, also requires a g-force environment in order to occur.

Granular Convection

Vibration-induced convection occurs in powders and granulated materials in containers subject to vibration where an axis of vibration is parallel to the force of gravity. When the container accelerates upward, the bottom of the container pushes the entire contents upward. In contrast, when the container accelerates downward, the sides of the container push the adjacent material downward by friction, but the material more remote from the sides is less affected. The net result is a slow circulation of particles downward at the sides, and upward in the middle.

If the container contains particles of different sizes, the downward-moving region at the sides is often narrower than the largest particles. Thus, larger particles tend to become sorted to the top of such a mixture. This is one possible explanation of the Brazil nut effect.

Marangoni Effect

The Marangoni effect is the convection of fluid along an interface between dissimilar substances because of variations in surface tension. Surface tension can vary because of inhomogeneous composition of the substances, and/or the temperature-dependence of surface tension forces. In the latter case the effect is known as thermo-capillary convection.

A well-known phenomenon exhibiting this type of convection is the "tears of wine".

Weissenberg Effect

The Weissenberg effect is a phenomenon that occurs when a spinning rod is placed into a solution of liquid polymer.

Entanglements cause the polymer chains to be drawn towards the rod instead of being thrown outward as would happen with an ordinary fluid (*i.e.*, water).

Thermomagnetic Convection

Thermomagnetic convection can occur when an external magnetic field is imposed on a ferrofluid with varying magnetic susceptibility. In the presence of a temperature gradient this results in a nonuniform magnetic body force, which leads to fluid movement. A ferrofluid is a liquid which becomes strongly magnetized in the presence of a magnetic field.

This form of heat transfer can be useful for cases where conventional convection fails to provide adequate heat transfer, e.g., in miniature microscale devices or under reduced gravity conditions.

Capillary Action

Capillary action is a phenomenon where liquid spontaneously rises in a narrow space such as a thin tube, or in porous materials. This effect can cause liquids to flow against the force of gravity. It occurs because of inter-molecular attractive forces between the liquid and solid surrounding surfaces; If the diameter of the tube is sufficiently small, then the combination of surface tension and forces of adhesion between the liquid and container act to lift the liquid.

Combustion

In a zero-gravity environment, there can be no buoyancy forces, and thus no natural (free) convection possible, so flames in many circumstances without gravity smother in their own waste gases. However, flames may be maintained with any type of forced convection (breeze); or (in high oxygen environments in "still" gas environments) entirely from the minimal forced convection that occurs as heat-induced *expansion* (not buoyancy) of gases allows for ventilation of the flame, as waste gases move outward and cool, and fresh high-oxygen gas moves in to take up the low pressure zones created when flame-exhaust water condenses.

THERMAL PROPERTIES AND TREATMENTS

The microstructures of alloys that were allowed to solidify by slow cooling were considered. It should also be known, however, that it is possible to modify the microstructure of an alloy by subjecting it to various thermal treatments. Heat-treating is a term used to describe all of the controlled heating and cooling operations performed on a material in the solid state for the purpose of altering its microstructure and/or properties. The focus of this discussion will be on metals but is should be noted that heat-treatment is also used on ceramics and composites to modify their properties.

The major objectives of the different kinds of thermal treatments are:

- Soften the material for improved workability.
- Increase the strength or hardness of the material.
- Increase the toughness or resistance to fracture of the material.
- Stabilize mechanical or physical properties against changes that might occur during exposure to service environments.
- Insure part dimensional stability.
- Relieve undesirable residual stresses induced during part fabrication.

Different metals respond to treatment at different temperatures. Each metal has a specific chemical composition, so changes in physical and structural properties take place at different, critical temperatures. Even small percentages of elements in the metal composition, such as carbon, will greatly determine the temperature, time, method and rate of cooling that needs to be used in the heat treating process. Depending on the thermal treatment used, the atomic structure and/or microstructure of a material may change due to movement of dislocations, an increase or decrease in solubility of atoms, an increase in grain size, the formation of new grains of the same or different phase, a change in the crystal structure, and others mechanisms.

Since there are so many ways in which metals are heat treated, it is not practical to discuss them all. But, as an example, let's look at how heat treatment is used to strengthen a copper aluminum alloy.

PRECIPITATION HARDENING

In designing alloys for strength, an approach often taken is to develop an alloy with a structure that consists of particles (which impede dislocation movement) dispersed in a ductile matrix. Such a dispersion can be obtained by choosing an alloy that is a single phase at elevated temperature but on cooling will precipitate another phase in the matrix. A thermal process is then developed to produce the desired distribution of precipitate in the matrix. When the alloy is strengthened by this thermal treatment, it is called precipitation strengthening or hardening.

Precipitation hardening consists of three main steps: solution treatment, quenching, and aging. Solution treatment involves heating the alloy to a temperature that allows the alloying atoms (called the solute) to dissolve into the solution. This results in a homogeneous solid solution of one phase. Quenching rapidly cools the solution and freezes the atoms in solution. In more technical terms, the quenching cools the material so fast that the atoms of the alloying elements do not have time to diffuse out of the solution. In the as-quenched condition, the solute is supersaturated meaning that the lattice is overly stressed by the alloying atoms. Aging is the process where the solute particles diffuse out of solution and into clusters that distort and strengthen the material.

The precipitation hardening process for a copper-aluminum alloy. On the right is phase diagram, which is a very useful tool for understanding and controlling polyphase structures. The phase diagram is simply a map showing the structure of phases present as the temperature and overall composition of the alloy are varied. The images on the right in the image show the resulting microstructure at each step in the process.

COMMON HEAT TREATING PROCESSES

A few of the more common terms used in heat treating. It should be noted that not all of the term are applicable to all alloys. Age Hardening is a relatively low-temperature heat treatment process that strengthens a material by causing the precipitation of components or phases of alloy from a super-saturated solid solution condition.

Annealing is a softening process in which metals are heated and then allowed to cool slowly. The purpose of annealing is to soften the material for improve machinability, formability, and sometimes to control magnetic properties. Normallizing is much like annealing, but the cooling process is much faster. This results in increased strength but less ductility in the metal. Its purpose is to refine grain structure, produce more uniform mechanical properties, and sometimes to relieve internal and surface stresses.

Precipitation Heat Treatment is the three step process of solution treating, quenching, and age hardening to increase the strength or hardness of an alloy. Solution Heat Treatment involves heating the material to a temperature that puts all the elements in solid solution and then cooling very rapidly to freeze the atoms in place. Stress Relieving is a low temperature heat treat process that is used to reduce the level of residual stresses in a material. Tempering involves gently heating a hardened metal and allowing it to cool slowly will produce a metal that is still hard but also less brittle. This process is known as tempering.

Quenching is the rapid cooling of a hot material. The medium used to quench the material can vary from forced air, oil, water and others. Many steels are hardened by heating and quenching. Quenching results in a metal that is very hard but also brittle.

HEAT CAPACITY

For one thing, it has an unusually high specific heat, or heat capacity. Heat capacity, you should remember, is the amount of heat or the number of calories required to raise the temperature of one gram of that substance by one degree Celsius. Water's high heat capacity means that is can absorb or lose a relatively large amount of heat without undergoing a large change in temperature. Since many biological functions will not take place outside a narrow range of temperatures, water's ability to absorb and lose heat without a large temperature change provides an organism with a protection against the ill effects of a large external temperature change. Another way to say this is that large amount of water in our bodies stabilizes the temperature of our bodies.

Heat Capacity	*(cal/g°C)*
water	1.0
CCl_4	0.2
diethyl ether	0.6
ethanol	0.6
acetone	0.5
benzene	0.4

Heat of Vapourization

Water also has a very large heat of vaporization. You should remember that the heat of vaporization is the amount of heat necessary to vaporize or evaporate one gram of liquid water. We use this high heat of vaporization to cool off on a hot day. When we perspire, the evaporating water absorbs about 540 calories of heat from the body for each gram of water that evaporates. This transfer of heat provides an effective means of cooling our bodies.

Heat of Vapourization	*(cal/g)*
water	540
CCl_4	50
diethyl ether	90
ethanol	210
acetone	130
benzene	130

6

Gas Laws and Kinetic Theory

GAS LAWS

The early gas laws were developed at the end of the 18th century, when scientists began to realise that relationships between the pressure, volume and temperature of a sample of gas could be obtained which would hold for all gases.

Gases behave in a similar way over a wide variety of conditions because to a good approximation they all have molecules which are widely spaced, and nowadays the equation of state for an ideal gas is derived from kinetic theory. The earlier gas laws are now considered as special cases of the ideal gas equation, with one or more of the variables held constant.

IDEAL GAS LAW

The ideal gas law is the equation of state of a hypothetical ideal gas. It is a good approximation to the behaviour of many gases under many conditions, although it has several limitations. It was first stated by Émile Clapeyron in 1834 as a combination of Boyle's law and Charles's law. It can also be derived from kinetic theory, as was achieved (apparently independently) by August Krönig in 1856 and Rudolf Clausius in 1857.

Equation

The state of an amount of gas is determined by its pressure, volume, and temperature. The modern form of the equation relates these simply in two main forms. The temperature used in the equation of state is an absolute temperature: in the SI system of units, kelvins; in the Imperial system, degrees Rankine.

Common Form

The most frequently introduced form is

$$PV = nRT$$

where P is the pressure of the gas, V is the volume of the gas, n is the amount of substance of gas (also known as number of moles), T is the temperature of the gas and R is the ideal, or universal, gas constant, equal to the product of Boltzmann's constant and Avogadro's constant.

In SI units, n is measured in moles, and T in kelvin. R has the value 8.314 $J{\cdot}K^{-1}{\cdot}mol^{-1}$ or 0.08206 $L{\cdot}atm{\cdot}mol^{-1}{\cdot}K^{-1}$.

Molar Form

How much gas is present could be specified by giving the mass instead of the chemical amount of gas. Therefore, an alternative form of the ideal gas law may be useful. The chemical amount (n) (in moles) is equal to the mass (m) (in grams) divided by the molar mass (M) (in grams per mole):

$$n = \frac{m}{M}$$

By replacing n with m/M, and subsequently introducing density $\rho = m/V$, we get:

$$PV = \frac{m}{M}RT$$

$$P = \rho\frac{R}{M}T$$

Defining the specific gas constant R_{specific} as the ratio R/M,

$$P = \rho R_{\text{specific}} T$$

This form of the ideal gas law is very useful because it links pressure, density, and temperature in a unique formula independent of the quantity of the considered gas. Alternatively, the law may be written in terms of the specific volume v, the reciprocal of density, as

$$Pv = R_{\text{specific}}T$$

It is common, especially in engineering applications, to represent the ideal gas constant by the symbol R. In such cases, the universal gas constant is usually given a different symbol such as R to distinguish it. In any case, the context and/or units of the gas constant should make it clear as to whether the universal or specific gas constant is being referred to.

Statistical Mechanics

In statistical mechanics the following molecular equation is derived from first principles:

$$PV = NkT$$

where P is the absolute pressure of the gas measured in Pascals; V is the volume (in this equation the volume is expressed in meters cubed as pascal times cubic meter equals one Joule); N is the number of particles in the gas; k is Boltzmann's constant relating temperature and energy; and T is the absolute temperature.

The *actual number* of molecules contrasts to the other formulation, which uses n, the *number of moles*. This relation implies that $Nk = nR$, and the consistency of this result with experiment is a good check on the principles of statistical mechanics.

From this we can notice that for an average particle mass of μ times the atomic mass constant m_{u} (*i.e.*, the mass is μ u)

$$N = \frac{m}{\mu m_{\text{u}}}$$

and since $\rho = m/V$, we find that the ideal gas law can be rewritten as:

$$P = \frac{1}{V}\frac{m}{\mu m_{\text{u}}}kT = \frac{k}{\mu m_{\text{u}}}\rho T.$$

In SI units, P is measured in pascals; V in cubic metres; N is a dimensionless number; and T in kelvin. k has the value $1.38 \cdot 10^{-23}$ J·K^{-1} in SI units.

APPLICATIONS TO THERMODYNAMIC PROCESSES

The table below essentially simplifies the ideal gas equation for a particular processes, thus making this equation easier to solve using numerical methods.

A thermodynamic process is defined as a system that moves from state 1 to state 2, where the state number is denoted by subscript. As shown in the first column of the table, basic thermodynamic processes are defined such that one of the gas properties (P, V, T, or S) is constant throughout the process.

For a given thermodynamics process, in order to specify the extent of a particular process, one of the properties ratios (listed under the column labelled "known ratio") must be specified (either directly or indirectly). Also, the property for which the ratio is known must be distinct from the property held constant in the previous column (otherwise the ratio would be unity, and not enough information would be available to simplify the gas law equation).

DEVIATIONS FROM REAL GASES

The equation of state given here applies only to an ideal gas, or as an approximation to a real gas that behaves sufficiently like an ideal gas. There are in fact many different forms of the equation of state for different gases. Since it neglects both molecular size and intermolecular attractions, the ideal gas law is most accurate for monatomic gases at high temperatures and low pressures.

The neglect of molecular size becomes less important for lower densities, *i.e.* for larger volumes at lower pressures, because the average distance between adjacent molecules becomes much larger than the molecular size. The relative importance of intermolecular attractions diminishes with increasing thermal kinetic energy, *i.e.*, with increasing temperatures. More detailed *equations of state*, such as the van der Waals equation, allow deviations from ideality caused by molecular size and intermolecular forces to be taken into account.

A residual property is defined as the difference between a real gas property and an ideal gas property, both considered at the same pressure, temperature, and composition.

Derivations

Empirical

The ideal gas law can be derived from combining two empirical gas laws: the combined gas law and Avogadro's law. The combined gas law states that

$$\frac{PV}{T} = C$$

where C is a constant which is directly proportional to the amount of gas, n (Avogadro's law). The proportionality factor is the universal gas constant, R, *i.e.* $C = nR$.

Hence the ideal gas law;

$$PV = nRT$$

THEORETICAL KINETIC THEORY

The ideal gas law can also be derived from first principles using the kinetic theory of gases, in which several simplifying assumptions are made, chief among which are that the molecules, or atoms, of the gas are point masses, possessing mass but no significant volume, and undergo only elastic collisions with each other and the sides of the container in which both linear momentum and kinetic energy are conserved.

Statistical Mechanics

Let q = (q_x, q_y, q_z) and p = (p_x, p_y, p_z) denote the position vector and momentum vector of a particle of an ideal gas, respectively. Let F denote the net force on that particle. Then the time average momentum of the particle is:

$$\begin{aligned}\langle q\cdot F\rangle &= \left\langle q_x \frac{dp_x}{dt}\right\rangle + \left\langle q_y \frac{dp_y}{dt}\right\rangle + \left\langle q_z \frac{dp_z}{dt}\right\rangle \\ &= -\left\langle q_x \frac{\partial H}{\partial q_x}\right\rangle - \left\langle q_y \frac{\partial H}{\partial q_y}\right\rangle - \left\langle q_z \frac{\partial H}{\partial q_z}\right\rangle = -3k_BT,\end{aligned}$$

where the first equality is Newton's second law, and the second line uses Hamilton's equations and the equipartition theorem. Summing over a system of N particles yields

$$3Nk_BT = -\left\langle \sum_{k=1}^{N} q_k \cdot F_k \right\rangle.$$

By Newton's third law and the ideal gas assumption, the net force on the system is the force applied by the walls of their container, and this force is given by the pressure P of the gas. Hence

$$-\left\langle \sum_{k=1}^{N} q_k \cdot F_k \right\rangle = P\oint_{surface} q\cdot dS,$$

where dS is the infinitesimal area element along the walls of the container. Since the divergence of the position vector q is

$$\nabla\cdot q = \frac{\partial q_x}{\partial q_x} + \frac{\partial q_y}{\partial q_y} + \frac{\partial q_z}{\partial q_z} = 3,$$

the divergence theorem implies that

$$P\oint_{surface} q\cdot dS = P\int_{volume} (\nabla\cdot q)\, dV = 3PV,$$

where dV is an infinitesimal volume within the container and V is the total volume of the container.

Putting these equalities together yields

$$3Nk_BT = -\left\langle \sum_{k=1}^{N} q_k \cdot F_k \right\rangle = 3PV,$$

which immediately implies the ideal gas law for N particles:

$$PV = Nk_BT = nRT,$$

where $n = N/N_A$ is the number of moles of gas and $R = N_A k_B$ is the gas constant.

THE IDEAL GAS EQUATION

Gases can described in terms of four variables: pressure (P), volume (V), temperature (T), and the amount of gas (n). There are five relationships between pairs of these variables in which two of the variables were allowed to change while the other two were held constant.

	P	**∝**	**n**	***(T and V constant)***
Boyle's law:	P	∝	$1/V$	(T and n constant)
Amontons' law:	P	∝	T	(V and n constant)
Charles' law:	V	∝	T	(P and n constant)
Avogadro's hypothesis:	V	∝	n	(P and T constant)

Each of these relationships is a special case of a more general relationship known as the ideal gas equation.

$$PV = nRT$$

In this equation, R is a proportionality constant known as the *ideal gas constant* and T is the absolute temperature. The value of R depends on the units used to express the four variables P, V, n, and T. By convention, most chemists use the following set of units.

P: atmospheres

T: kelvin

V: liters

n: moles.

ABSOLUTE ZERO OF THEORETICAL TEMPERATURE

Absolute zero is the theoretical temperature at which entropy reaches its minimum value. The laws of thermodynamics state that absolute zero cannot be reached using only thermodynamic means. A system at absolute zero still possesses quantum mechanical zero-point energy, the energy of its ground state. The kinetic energy of the ground state cannot be removed. However, in the classical interpretation it is zero and the thermal energy of matter vanishes.

The zero point of any thermodynamic temperature scale, such as Kelvin or Rankine, is set at absolute zero. By international agreement, absolute zero is defined as 0K on the Kelvin scale and as –273.15° on the Celsius scale. This equates to –459.67° on the Fahrenheit scale and 0 R on the Rankine scale. Scientists have achieved temperatures very close to absolute zero, where matter exhibits quantum effects such as superconductivity and superfluidity.

History

One of the first to discuss the possibility of an absolute minimal temperature was Robert Boyle. His 1665 *New Experiments and Observations touching Cold,* articulated the dispute known as the *primum frigidum*. The concept was well known among naturalists of the time. Some contended an absolute minimum temperature occurred within earth (as one of the four so-called "elements"), others within water, others air, and some more recently within nitre. But all of them seemed to agree that, "There is some body or other that is of its own nature supremely cold and by participation of which all other bodies obtain that quality."

Limit to the "Degree of Cold"

The question whether there is a limit to the degree of cold possible, and, if so, where the zero must be placed, was first addressed by the French physicist Guillaume Amontons in 1702, in connection with his improvements in the air thermometer. In his instrument, temperatures were indicated by the height at which a column of mercury was sustained by a certain mass of air, the volume, or "spring", of which varied with the heat to which it was exposed. Amontons therefore argued that the zero of his thermometer would be that temperature at which the spring of the air in it was reduced to nothing. On the scale he used, the boiling-point of water was marked at +73 and the melting-point of ice at 51, so that the zero of his scale was equivalent to about "240 on the Celsius scale. This close approximation to the modern value of "273.15 °C for the zero of the air-thermometer was further improved upon in 1779 by Johann Heinrich Lambert, who observed that "270 °C might be regarded as absolute cold.

Values of this order for the absolute zero were not, however, universally accepted about this period. Pierre-Simon Laplace and Antoine Lavoisier, in their 1780 treatise on heat, arrived at values ranging from 1,500 to 3,000 below the freezing-point of water, and thought that in any case it must be at least 600 below. John Dalton in his *Chemical Philosophy* gave ten calculations of this value, and finally adopted "3000 °C as the natural zero of temperature.

Lord Kelvin's Work

After James Prescott Joule had determined the mechanical equivalent of heat, Lord Kelvin approached the question from an entirely different point of view, and in 1848 devised a scale of absolute temperature which was independent of the properties of any particular substance and was based solely on the fundamental laws of thermodynamics. It followed from the principles on which this scale was constructed that its zero was placed at "273.15 °C, at almost precisely the same point as the zero of the air-thermometer.

Very Low Temperatures

The average temperature of the universe due to cosmic microwave background radiation today is 2.73 K.

Absolute zero cannot be achieved, although it is possible to reach temperatures close to it through the use of cryocoolers, dilution refrigerators, and nuclear adiabatic demagnetization. The use of laser cooling has produced temperatures less than a billionth of a kelvin. At very low temperatures in the vicinity of absolute zero, matter exhibits many unusual properties, including superconductivity, superfluidity, and Bose–Einstein condensation. To study such phenomena, scientists have worked to obtain even lower temperatures.

- The current world record was set in 1999 at 100 picokelvins (pK), or 0.000 000 000 1 of a kelvin, by cooling the nuclear spins in a piece of rhodium metal.

- In November 2000, nuclear spin temperatures below 100 pK were reported for an experiment at the Helsinki University of Technology's Low Temperature Lab. However, this was the temperature of one particular degree of freedom – a quantum property called nuclear spin – not the overall average thermodynamic temperature for all possible degrees in freedom.
- In February 2003, the Boomerang Nebula was observed to have been releasing gases at a speed of 500,000 km/h (over 300,000 mph) for the last 1,500 years. This has cooled it down to approximately 1 K, as deduced by astronomical observation, which is the lowest natural temperature ever recorded.
- In May 2005, the European Space Agency proposed research in space to achieve femto-kelvin temperatures.
- In May 2006, the Institute of Quantum Optics at the University of Hanover gave details of technologies and benefits of femto-kelvin research in space.

Thermodynamics Near Absolute Zero

At temperatures near 0 K, nearly all molecular motion ceases and, when entropy = S, $\Delta S = 0$ for any adiabatic process. Pure substances can (ideally) form perfect crystals as $T \rightarrow 0$. Max Planck's strong form of the third law of thermodynamics states the entropy of a perfect crystal vanishes at absolute zero. The original Nernst *heat theorem* makes the weaker and less controversial claim that the entropy change for any isothermal process approaches zero as $T \rightarrow 0$:

$$\lim_{T \to 0} \Delta S = 0$$

The implication is that the entropy of a perfect crystal simply approaches a constant value.

The Nernst postulate identifies the isotherm T = 0 as coincident with the adiabat S = 0, although other isotherms and adiabats are distinct. As no two adiabats intersect, no other adiabat can intersect the T = 0 isotherm. Consequently no adiabatic process initiated at nonzero temperature can lead to zero temperature.

An even stronger assertion is that It is impossible by any procedure to reduce the temperature of a system to zero in a finite number of operations.

A perfect crystal is one in which the internal lattice structure extends uninterrupted in all directions. The perfect order can be represented by translational symmetry along three (not usually orthogonal) axes. Every lattice element of the structure is in its proper place, whether it is a single atom or a molecular grouping. For substances which have two (or more) stable crystalline forms, such as diamond and graphite for carbon, there is a kind of "chemical degeneracy". The question remains whether both can have zero entropy at $T = 0$ even though each is perfectly ordered.

Perfect crystals never occur in practice; imperfections, and even entire amorphous materials, simply get "frozen in" at low temperatures, so transitions to more stable states do not occur.

Using the Debye model, the specific heat and entropy of a pure crystal are proportional to T^3, while the enthalpy and chemical potential are proportional to T^4. These quantities drop towards their $T = 0$ limiting values and approach with *zero* slopes. For the specific heats at least, the limiting value itself is definitely zero, as borne out by experiments to below 10 K. Even the less detailed Einstein model shows this curious drop in specific heats. In fact, all specific heats vanish at absolute zero, not just those of crystals. Likewise for the coefficient of thermal expansion. Maxwell's relations show that various other quantities also vanish. These phenomena were unanticipated.

Since the relation between changes in Gibbs free energy (*G*), the enthalpy (*H*) and the entropy is

$$\Delta G = \Delta H - T\Delta S$$

thus, as T decreases, ΔG and ΔH approach each other (so long as ΔS is bounded). Experimentally, it is found that all spontaneous processes (including chemical reactions) result in a decrease in G as they proceed towards equilibrium. If ΔS and/or T are small, the condition $\Delta G < 0$ may imply that $\Delta H < 0$, which would indicate an exothermic reaction. However, this is not required; endothermic reactions can proceed spontaneously if the $T\Delta S$ term is large enough.

Moreover, the slopes of the derivatives of ΔG and ΔH converge and are equal to zero at $T = 0$. This ensures that ΔG and ΔH are nearly the same over a considerable range of temperatures and justifies the approximate empirical Principle of Thomsen and Berthelot, which states that the equilibrium state to which a system proceeds is the one which evolves the greatest amount of heat, i.e. an actual process is the most exothermic one.

One model that estimates the properties of an electron gas at absolute zero in metals is the Fermi gas. The electrons, being Fermions, have to be in different quantum states, which leads the electrons to get very high typical velocities, even at absolute zero. The maximum energy that an electrons can have at absolute zero is called the Fermi energy. The Fermi temperature is defined as this maximum energy divided by Boltzmann's constant, and is of the order of 80,000 K for typical electron densities found in metals. For temperatures significantly below the Fermi temperature, the electrons behave in almost the same way as at absolute zero. This explains the failure of the classical equipartition theorem for metals that eluded classical physicists in the late 19th century.

Relation with Bose-Einstein Condensates

A Bose-Einstein condensate (BEC) is a state of matter of a dilute gas of weakly interacting bosons confined in an external potential and cooled to temperatures very near to absolute zero. Under such conditions, a large fraction of the bosons occupy the lowest quantum state of the external potential, at which point quantum effects become apparent on a macroscopic scale.

This state of matter was first predicted by Satyendra Nath Bose and Albert Einstein in 1924–25. Bose first sent a paper to

Einstein on the quantum statistics of light quanta (now called photons). Einstein was impressed, translated the paper himself from English to German and submitted it for Bose to the *Zeitschrift für Physik* which published it. Einstein then extended Bose's ideas to material particles (or matter) in two other papers.

Seventy years later, the first gaseous condensate was produced by Eric Cornell and Carl Wieman in 1995 at the University of Colorado at Boulder NIST-JILA lab, using a gas of rubidium atoms cooled to 170 nanokelvin (nK) (1.7×10^{-7} K).

A record cold temperature of 450 ±80 pK in a Bose–Einstein condensate (BEC) of sodium atoms was achieved in 2003 by researchers at MIT. It's noteworthy that this record's peak emittance black-body wavelength of 6,400 kilometers is roughly the radius of Earth.

ABSOLUTE TEMPERATURE SCALES

Absolute, or thermodynamic, temperature is conventionally measured in kelvins (Celsius-scaled increments) and in the Rankine scale (Fahrenheit-scaled increments) with increasing rarity. Absolute temperature measurement is uniquely determined by a multiplicative constant which specifies the size of the "degree", so the *ratios* of two absolute temperatures, T_2/T_1, are the same in all scales. The most transparent definition of this standard comes from the Maxwell–Boltzmann distribution. It can also be found in Fermi–Dirac statistics (for particles of half-integer spin) and Bose–Einstein statistics (for particles of integer spin). All of these define the relative numbers of particles in a system as decreasing exponential functions of energy (at the particle level) over kT, with k representing the Boltzmann constant and T representing the temperature observed at the macroscopic level.

Negative Temperatures

Temperatures that are expressed as negative numbers on the familiar Celsius or Fahrenheit scales are simply colder than the zero points of those scales. Certain systems can achieve truly negative temperatures; that is, their thermodynamic temperature (expressed in kelvin) can be of a negative quantity. A system with a truly negative temperature is not colder than absolute zero. Rather, a system with a negative temperature is hotter than *any* system with a positive temperature in the sense that if a negative-temperature system and a positive-temperature system come in contact, heat will flow from the negative-to the positive-temperature system.

Most familiar systems cannot achieve negative temperatures because adding energy always increases their entropy. However, some systems have a maximum amount of energy that they can hold, and as they approach that maximum energy their entropy actually begins to decrease. Because temperature is defined by the relationship between energy and entropy, such a system's temperature becomes negative, even though energy is being added. As a result, the Boltzmann factor for states of systems at negative temperature increases rather than decreases with increasing state energy. Therefore no complete system, *i.e.* including the electromagnetic modes, can have negative temperatures, since there is no highest energy state, so that the sum of the probabilities of the states would diverge for negative temperatures. However, for quasi-equilibrium systems (*e.g.* spins out of equilibrium with the electromagnetic field) this argument does not apply, and negative effective temperatures are attainable.

DALTON'S LAW OF PARTIAL PRESSURES

The atmosphere as 78.084% N_2, 20.946% O_2, 0.934% Ar, and 0.033% CO_2 by volume when the water vapour has been removed. What image does this description evoke in your mind? Do you believe that only 20.463% of the room in which you are sitting contains O_2? Or do you believe that the atmosphere in your room is a more or less homogeneous mixture of these gases?

Gases expand to fill their containers. The volume of O_2 in your room is therefore the same as the volume of N_2. (Both gases expand to fill the room.) When we describe the atmosphere as 20.946% O_2 by volume, we mean that the volume of the atmosphere would shrink by 20.946% if the O_2 is removed.

What about the pressure of the different gases in your room? Is the pressure of the O_2 in the atmosphere the same as the pressure of the N_2? We can answer this question by rearranging the ideal gas equation as follows.

$$P = n \times \frac{RT}{V}$$

According to this equation, the pressure of a gas is proportional to the number of moles of gas, if the temperature and volume are held constant. Because the temperature and volume of the O_2 and N_2 in the atmosphere are the same, the pressure of each gas must be proportional to the number of the moles of the gas. Because there is more N_2 in the atmosphere than O_2, the contribution to the total pressure of the atmosphere from N_2 is larger than the contribution from O_2.

John Dalton was the first to recognize that the total pressure of a mixture of gases is the sum of the contributions of the individual components of the mixture. By convention, the part of the total pressure of a mixture that results from one component is called the partial pressure of that component. Dalton's law of partial pressures states that the total pressure of a mixture of gases is the sum of the partial pressures of the various components.

$$P_T = P_1 + P_2 + P_3 + \ldots$$

BOYLE'S LAW

Torricelli's experiment did more than just show that air has weight; it also provided a way of creating a vacuum because the space above the column of mercury at the top of a barometer is almost completely empty. (It is free of air or other gases except a negligible amount of mercury vapour.) Torricelli's work with a vacuum soon caught the eye of the British scientist Robert Boyle.

Boyle's most famous experiments with gases dealt with what he called the "spring of air." These experiments were based on the observation that gases are *elastic*. Boyle studied the elasticity of gases in a J-tube similar to the apparatus. By adding mercury to the open end of the tube, he trapped a small volume of air in the sealed end.

Boyle noticed that the product of the pressure times the volume for any measurement in this table was equal to the product of the pressure times the volume for any other measurement, within experimental error.

$$P_1V_1 = P_2V_2$$

This expression, or its equivalent,

$$P \propto \frac{1}{V}$$

is now known as Boyle's Law.

CHARLES'S LAW

Charles's law (also known as the law of volumes) is an experimental gas law which describes how gases tend to expand when heated. It was first published by French natural philosopher Joseph Louis Gay-Lussac in 1802, although he credited the discovery to unpublished work from the 1780s by Jacques Charles. The law was independently discovered by British natural philosopher John Dalton by 1801, although Dalton's description was less thorough than Gay-Lussac's. The basic principles had already been described a century earlier by Guillaume Amontons.

Taylor Buchanan was the first to demonstrate that the law applied generally to all gases, and also to the vapours of volatile liquids if the temperature was more than a few degrees above the boiling point. His statement of the law can be expressed mathematically as:

$$V_{100} - V_0 = kV_0$$

where V_{100} is the volume occupied by a given sample of gas at 100 °C; V_0 is the volume occupied by the same sample of gas at 0 °C; and k is a constant which is the same for all gases at constant pressure. Gay-Lussac's value for k was $^1D_{2.6666}$, remarkably close to the present-day value of $^1D_{2.7315}$.

Volume and temperature are directly proportional, as long as the pressure stays at a constant.

A modern statement of Charles' law is:

At constant pressure, the volume of a given mass of an ideal gas increases or decreases by the same factor as its temperature on the absolute temperature scale (*i.e.* the gas expands as the temperature increases).

which can be written as:

$$V \propto T$$

where V is the volume of the gas; and T is the absolute temperature. The law can also be usefully expressed as follows:

$$\frac{V_1}{T_1} = \frac{V_2}{T_2} \quad \text{or} \quad \frac{V_2}{V_1} = \frac{T_2}{T_1} \quad \text{or} \quad V_1 T_2 = V_2 T_1.$$

The equation shows that, as absolute temperature increases, the volume of the gas also increases in proportion.

CHARLES'S GAS LAW

When a given mass of a gas is heated at constant pressure, the volume V of given mass of a gas is directly proportional to its absolute temperature.

Relation to the Ideal Gas Law

French physicist Émile Clapeyron combined Charles's law with Boyle's law in 1834 to produce a single statement which would become known as the ideal gas law. Claypeyron's original statement was:

$$pV = \frac{p_0 V_0}{267 + t_0}(267 + t)$$

where t is the Celsius temperature; and p_0, V_0 and t_0 are the pressure, volume and temperature of a sample of gas under some standard state. The figure of 267 came directly from Gay-Lussac's work: the modern figure would be 273.15. For any given sample of gas, $p_0V_0/(267+t_0)$ is a constant (Clapeyron denoted this constant R, and it is closely related to the modern gas constant); if the pressure is also constant, the equation simplifies to

$$V \propto (267 + t)$$

as required.

The modern statement of the ideal gas law is:

$$pV = nRT$$

where n is the amount of substance of the gas sample; and R is the gas constant. The amount of substance is constant for any given gas sample so, at constant pressure, the equation rearranges to:

$$V = \frac{nR}{p}T$$

where nR/p is the constant of proportionality.

An ideal gas is *defined* as a gas which obeys the ideal gas law, so Charles's law is only expected to be followed exactly by ideal gases. Nevertheless, it is a good approximation to the behaviour of real gases at relatively high temperatures and relatively low pressures.

Relation to Absolute Zero

Charles' law appears to imply that the volume of a gas will descend to zero at a certain temperature or -273°C. Gay-Lussac was clear in his description that the law was not applicable at low temperatures:

but I may mention that this last conclusion cannot be true except so long as the compressed vapours remain entirely in the elastic state; and this requires that their temperature shall be sufficiently elevated to enable them to resist the pressure which tends to make them assume the liquid state.

Gay-Lussac had no experience of liquid air (first prepared in 1877), although he appears to believe (as did Dalton) that the "permanent gases" such as air and hydrogen could be liquified. Gay-Lussac had also worked with the vapours of volatile liquids in demonstrating Charles's law, and was aware that the law does not apply just above the boiling point of the liquid: However remark that when the temperature of the ether is only a little above its boiling point, its condensation is a little more rapid than that of atmospheric air. This fact is related to a phenomenon which is exhibited by a great many bodies when passing from the liquid to the solid state, but which is no longer sensible at temperatures a few degrees above that at which the transition occurs.

The first mention of a temperature at which the volume of a gas might descend to zero was by William Thomson (later known as Lord Kelvin) in 1848: This is what we might anticipate, when we reflect that infinite cold must correspond to a finite number of degrees of the air-thermometer below zero; since if we push the strict principle of graduation, stated above, sufficiently far, we should arrive at a point corresponding to the volume of air being reduced to nothing, which would be marked as –273° of the scale (–100/.366, if .366 be the coefficient of expansion); and therefore –273° of the air-thermometer is a point which cannot be reached at any finite temperature, however low.

However, the "absolute zero" on the Kelvin temperature scale was originally defined in terms of the second law of thermodynamics, which Thomson himself described in 1852. Thomson did not assume that this was equal to the "zero-volume point" of Charles's law, merely that Charles's law provided the minimum temperature which could be attained. The two can be shown to be equivalent by Ludwig Boltzmann's statistical view of entropy (1870).

Relation to Kinetic Theory

The kinetic theory of gases relates the macroscopic properties of gases, such as pressure and volume, to the microscopic properties of the molecules which make up the gas, particularly the mass and speed of the molecules. In order to derive Charles's law from kinetic theory, it is necessary to have a microscopic definition of temperature: this can be conveniently taken as the temperature being proportional to the average kinetic energy of the gas molecules, E_k:

$$T \propto \overline{E_k}.$$

Under this definition, the demonstration of Charles's law is almost trivial. The kinetic theory equivalent of the ideal gas law relates pV to the average kinetic energy:

$$pV = \frac{2}{3} N \overline{E_k}$$

where N is the number of molecules in the gas sample. If the pressure is constant, the volume is directly proportional to the average kinetic energy (and hence to the temperature) for any given gas sample.

AMONTON'S LAW

Towards the end of the 1600s, the French physicist Guillaume Amontons built a thermometer based on the fact that the pressure of a gas is directly proportional to its temperature. The relationship between the pressure and the temperature of a gas is therefore known as Amontons' law.

$P \propto T$

Amontons' law explains why car manufacturers recommend adjusting the pressure of your tires before you start on a trip. The flexing of the tire as you drive inevitably raises the temperature of the air in the tire. When this happens, the pressure of the gas inside the tires increases.

Amontons' law can be demonstrated with the apparatus, which consists of a pressure gauge connected to a metal sphere of constant volume, which is immersed in solutions that have different temperatures. In 1779 Joseph Lambert proposed a definition for absolute zero on the temperature scale that was based on the straight-line relationship between the temperature and pressure of a gas.

He defined absolute zero as the temperature at which the pressure of a gas becomes zero when a plot of pressure versus temperature for a gas is extrapolated. The pressure of a gas approaches zero when the temperature is about -270°C. When more accurate measurements are made, the pressure of a gas extrapolates to zero when the temperature is -273.15°C. Absolute zero on the Celsius scale is therefore -273.15°C.

The relationship between temperature and pressure can be greatly simplified by converting the temperatures from the Celsius to the Kelvin scale.

$$T_K = T_{°C} + 273.15$$

When this is done, a plot of the temperature versus the pressure of a gas gives a straight line that passes through the origin. Any two points along the line therefore fit the following equation.

$$\frac{P_1}{P_2} = \frac{T_1}{T_2}$$

It is important to remember that this equation is only valid if the temperatures are converted from the Celsius to the Kelvin scale before calculations are done.

GAY-LUSSAC'S LAW

The expression Gay-Lussac's law is used for each of the two relationships named after the French chemist Joseph Louis Gay-Lussac and which concern the properties of gases, though it is more usually applied to his law of combining volumes, the first listed here. One law relates to volumes before and after a chemical reaction while the other concerns the pressure and temperature relationship for a sample of gas.

Law of Combining Volumes

The law of combining volumes states that, when gases react together to form other gases, and all volumes are measured at the same temperature and pressure:

The ratio between the volumes of the reactant gases and the products can be expressed in simple whole numbers.

For example, Gay-Lussac found that 2 volumes of Hydrogen and 1 volume of Oxygen would react to form 2 volume of gaseous water. In addition to Gay-Lussac's results, Amedeo Avogadro theorized that, at the same temperature and pressure, equal volumes of gas contain equal numbers of molecules (Avogadro's law). This hypothesis meant that the previously stated result

2 volumes of Hydrogen + 1 volume of Oxygen = 2 volumes of gaseous water

could also be expressed as

2 molecules of Hydrogen + 1 molecule of Oxygen = 2 molecules of water.

The law of combining gases was published by Joseph Louis Gay-Lussac in 1808. Avogadro's hypothesis, however, was not initially accepted by chemists until the Italian chemist Stanislao Cannizzaro was able to convince the First International Chemical Congress in 1860.

Pressure-temperature Law

Gay-Lussac's name is also associated in physics with another gas law, the so-called pressure law, which states that:

The pressure of a gas of fixed mass and fixed volume is directly proportional to the gas' absolute temperature.

Simply put, if a gas' temperature increases then so does its pressure, if the mass and volume of the gas are held constant. The law has a particularly simple mathematical form if the temperature is measured on an absolute scale, such as in kelvins. The law can then be expressed mathematically as:

$$P \propto T$$

or

$$\frac{P}{T} = k$$

where:

P is the pressure of the gas (measured in ATM).

T is the temperature of the gas (measured in Kelvin).

k is a constant.

This law holds true because temperature is a measure of the average kinetic energy of a substance; as the kinetic energy of a gas increases, its particles collide with the container walls more rapidly, thereby exerting increased pressure.

For comparing the same substance under two different sets of conditions, the law can be written as:

$$\frac{P_1}{T_1} = \frac{P_2}{T_2} \quad \text{or} \quad P_1T_2 = P_2T_1.$$

Amontons' Law of Pressure-Temperature: The pressure law should actually be attributed to Guillaume Amontons, who, between 1700 and 1702, discovered that the pressure of a fixed mass of gas kept at a constant volume is proportional to the temperature. Amontons discovered this while building an "air thermometer". Calling it Gay-Lussac's law is simply incorrect as Gay-Lussac investigated the relationship between volume and temperature (*i.e.* Charles' Law), not pressure and temperature.

Charles' Law was also known as the Law of Charles and Gay-Lussac, because Gay-Lussac published it in 1802 using much of Charles's unpublished data from 1787. However, in recent years the term has fallen out of favour, and Gay-Lussac's name is now generally associated with the law of combining volumes. Amontons' Law, Charles' Law, and Boyle's law form the combined gas law. The three gas laws in combination with Avogadro's Law can be generalized by the ideal gas law.

AVOGADRO'S HYPOTHESIS

Gay-Lussac's law of combining volumes was announced only a few years after John Dalton proposed his atomic theory. The link between these two ideas was first recognized by the Italian physicist Amadeo Avogadro three years later, in 1811. Avogadro argued that Gay-Lussac's law of combining volumes could be explained by assuming that equal volumes of different gases collected under similar conditions contain the same number of particles.

HCl and NH_3 therefore combine in a 1:1 ratio by volume because one molecule of HCl is consumed for every molecule of NH_3 in this reaction and equal volumes of these gases contain the same number of molecules.

$$NH_3 + HCl(g) \rightarrow NH_4Cl(s)$$

Anyone who has blown up a balloon should accept the notion that the volume of a gas is proportional to the number of particles in the gas.

$$V \propto n$$

The more air you add to a balloon, the bigger it gets. Unfortunately this example does not test Avogadro's hypothesis that equal volumes of *different gases* contain the same number of particles.

The best way to probe the validity of this hypothesis is to measure the number of molecules in a given volume of different gases.

A small hole is drilled through the plunger of a 50-mL plastic syringe. The plunger is then pushed into the syringe and the syringe is sealed with a syringe cap.

The plunger is then pulled out of the syringe until the volume reads 50 mL and a nail is inserted through the hole in the plunger so that the plunger is not sucked back into the barrel of the syringe.

The "empty" syringe is then weighed, the syringe is filled with 50 mL of a gas, and the syringe is reweighed. The difference between these measurements is the mass of 50 mL of the gas.

The results of experiments with six gases are given in the table below.

Experimental Data for the Mass of 50-mL Samples of Different Gases

Compound	*Mass of 50 mL of Gas (g)*	*Molecular Weight of Gas*	*Number of Gas Molecules*
H_2	0.005	2.02	1×10^{21}
N_2	0.055	28.01	1.2×10^{21}
O_2	0.061	32.00	1.1×10^{21}
CO_2	0.088	44.01	1.2×10^{21}
C_4H_{10}	0.111	58.12	1.15×10^{21}
CCl_2F_2	0.228	120.91	1.14×10^{21}

The number of molecules in a 50-mL sample of any one of these gases can be calculated from the mass of the sample, the molecular weight of the gas, and the number of molecules in a mole. Consider the following calculation of the number of H_2 molecules in 50 mL of hydrogen gas, for example.

$$0.005\,g\,H_2 \times \frac{1\,\text{mol}\,H_2}{2.02\,g\,H_2} \times \frac{6.02 \times 10^{23}\,\text{molecules}}{1\,\text{mol}\,H_2} = 1 \times 10^{21}\,H_3\,\text{molecules}$$

The last column in the table above summarizes the results obtained when this calculation is repeated for each gas. The number of significant figures in the answer changes from one calculation to the next. But the number of molecules in each sample is the same, within experimental error. We therefore conclude that equal volumes of different gases collected under the same conditions of temperature and pressure do in fact contain the same number of particles.

7

Thermal Properties of Matter

INTRODUCTION

CONCEPT OF HEAT AND TEMPERATURE

Familiar sensations of hotness and coldness are described with adjectives such as hot, warm, cold, cool etc. When we touch an object, we use our temperature sence to ascribe to object a property called temperature. Temperature of a body determines whether it feels hot or cold to the touch. The hotter you feel on touching the body higher is its temperature.

So we can say that Temperature is relative measurement of hotness or coldness of a body. An observation about hot and cold bodies in contact is that, when they both are in contact temperature of cold body increases and that of hot body decreases. This happens because energy is transferred from hot body to cold body when they are in contact and this is a nonmechanical process. This energy which is transferred from one body to another without any mechanical work involved is known as HEAT.

Heat is a form of energy and heat transfer from one body to another takes place by virtue of temperature difference only also heat transfer takes place from body at higher temperature to body at lower temperature. S.I. unit of heat is Joule(J) and that of temperature is Kelvin(K).

Measurement of Temperature

Measurement of temperature can be obtained using a thermometer. Construction of thermometers generally require a measurable property of a substance which monotonically changes with temperature.

Examples of some common type of thermometers:

- *Mercury in a glass thermometer.* The height of mercury in the tube is taken as thermometric parameter.
- *Constant Volume gas thermometer.* Gas in bulb is maintained at constant volume. The mean pressure of gas is taken as thermomtric parameter.
- *Constant Pressure gas thermometer.* Gas in bulb is maintaned at constant pressure. Volume of gas is taken as thermomtric parameter.
- *Resistance therometer.* Electric resistance of a metal wire increases monitonically with the temperature and may be used to define temperature scale. Such thermometers are resistance theromometers.

Thermometers are calibrated to assign a numerical value to any given temperature. Definition of any standard scale needs two fixed reference points and these points can be correlated to physical phenomenon reproducible at the same temperature. Two such standard points are freezing and boiling points of water at same pressure. Two such familiar scales used for measurement of temperature are Celsius and Fahrenheit scale. Temperature in Celsius is measured in degree.

Fahrenheit scale has a smaller degree then Celsius scale and a different zero of temperature.

Relation between Celsius and Fahrenheit scale is

$$T_F = 9/5\ T_C + 32°.$$

where,

T_F - Fahrenheit Temperature.

T_C - Celsius Temperature.

Letters C & F are used to distinguish measurements on two scale thus

0° C = 32° F

this means that 0° C on Celsius scale measures the same temperature as 32° F on the Fahrenheit scale.

On Fahrenheit scale melting point of ice and boiling point

of water have values 32° F and 212° F and that on Celsius scale are 0° C and 100° C.

If we now talk of Kelvin scale, the melting point of ice and boiling point of water in the scale are 273.15 K and 373.15 K respectively.

Size of a degree in celsius and kelvin scale are same.

Relation between Celsius and kelvin scale is

$$T_C = T_K - 273.15\ K$$

where,

T_K - Temperature in Kelvin

T_C - Temperature in celsius

Another modern fixed point of temperature is the triple point of water.

Three phases of water i.e, ice, water, water vapour co-exist at this value of temperature and pressure where

$$T_{tr} = 273.16\ K$$

$$P_{tr} = 0.46\ \text{cm of HG.}$$

where,

T_{tr} & P_{tr} are triple point temperature and pressure.

Now if P_{tr} is pressure of an ideal gas thermometer at triple point temperature T_{tr} and if P is pressure at some other temperature T then corresponding temperature is

$$T = P(T_{tr}/P_{tr})$$

provided T_{tr} & P_{tr} are low.

Electric resistance of metal wire increase monitonically with temperature and may be used to define the temperature scale

If R_0 & R_{100} are resistance of metal wire at ice and steam point respectively then temperature t can be defined corresponding to resistance R_T as follows;

$$T = \frac{(R_t - R_0) \times 100}{R_{100} - R_0}$$

A platinum wire is oftently used to construct a thermometer which is known as platinum resistance thermometer.

Gas thermometer can also define Celsius scale.

If P_0 is pressure of gas at ice point and P_{1000} is pressure of gas at steam point then temperature T corresponding to a pressure P of gas is defined by

$$T = \frac{(P - P_0) \times 100}{P_{100} - P_0}$$

Absolute Temperature

In gas thermometer different gases are used for measuring high temperatures and temperature reading are found to be independent of the nature of the gas used

Graphs between pressure and temperature for different gases are plotted below;

It is found that when graph were extrapolated for temperature below 0° C, pressure comes out to be zero at -273° C and this is the lowest temperature.

Lord kelvin suggested that instead of 0° C which is the melting point of ice,- 273° C should be regarded as the zero of the temperature scale. Such a scale of temperature is absolute scale of temperature and -273.15° C as absolute zero of this new scale and is denoted as 0K and steam point in this scale correspond to 373.15 K

Ideal Gas Equation

Pressure of all the gases changes with the temperature in a similar fashion for low temperature. Also many properties of gases are common at low pressure. The pressure, volume and temperature in kelvin of such gases obey the equation

$$PV = nRT$$

where n is amount of gas in number of moles and is given as, n = [Total no of molecules in given mass of gas]/[Avagadro No. (N_A)]

$$N_A = 6.023 \times 10^{23}$$

R is universal gas constant and its value is R = 8.316 J/mol-K

Equation above is known as ideal gas equation and a gas obeying this equation is known as ideal gas.

Thermal Expansion

Most of the solid material expand when heated.

Increase in dimension of a body due to increase in its temperature is called thermal expansion.

For small change in temperature ΔT of a rod of length L, the fractional change in length $\Delta L/L$ is directly proportional to ΔT;

$$DL/L = \alpha_L \Delta T$$

or,

$$DL = \alpha_L L \Delta T$$

Constant α_L characterizes the thermal expansion properties of a particular material and it is known as coefficient of linear expansion.For materials having no preferential direction, every linear dimension changes according to equation above and L could equally well represent the thickness of the rod, side length of the square sheet etc.

Normally metals expand more and have high value of α.

Again consider the initial surface area A of any surface and A′ is the area of the solid when the temperature of the body changes by ΔT then increase in surface area is given by

$$\Delta A = \alpha_A A \Delta T$$

where α_A is the coefficient of area expansion.

Similary we can define coefficient of volume expansion as fractional change in volume $\Delta V/V$ of a substance for a temperature change ΔT as;

$$\alpha_V = \frac{\Delta V}{V \Delta T}$$

K^{-1} is the unit of these coefficients of expansions.

These three coefficient are not strictly constant for a substance and there value is depends on temperature range in which they are being measured. As an example, that coefficient of volume expansion increase with temperature and takes a constant value above 500K.

Relation between volume and linear coefficient of expansion for solid material:

Consider a solid paraboloid with dimension L_1, L_2 and L_3 then its volume is

$$V = L_1L_2L_3$$

When temperature increase by a amount ΔT then each linear dimension changes and then new volume is

$$V+\Delta V = L_1L_2L_3(1+\alpha_L\Delta T)^3$$
$$= V(1+\alpha_L\Delta T)^3$$
$$= V(1+3\alpha_L\Delta T+3\alpha_L^2(\Delta T)^2+\alpha_L^3(\Delta T)^3)$$

if ΔT is small then higher order of ΔT can be neglected. Thus we find

$$V+\Delta V = V(1+3\alpha_L\Delta T)$$

or,

$$\Delta V = 3\alpha_L V_0\Delta T$$

Comparing this with equation (5) we find

$$\alpha_V = 3\alpha_L$$

Thermal Stress

If we fix the ends of a rod rigidly so that it can not expand or contract then with change in temperature, tensile or compressive stress known as thermal stresses will set up in the rod.

To compute the thermal stress, consider a rod of length L and crossectional area A with its both end rigidly fixed and temperature is then reduced by an amount ΔT.

The fractional change in rod if the rod is free to contract would be

$$\Delta L/L = \alpha\Delta T$$

where ΔL and ΔT both are negative.

As we have fixed the ends of the rod, so it is not free to contract and this causes an increase in tension so as to produce an equal and opposite fractional change in length.

From the definition of Young Modulus

$$Y = \frac{F/A}{\Delta L/L}$$

$$\Delta L/L = \frac{F}{AY}$$

where ΔL is positive

Tensile forces is determined by the requirement that total fractional changes in length, Thermal expansion plus elastic strain must be zero.

$$\alpha\Delta T + F/AY = 0$$

$$F = -AY\alpha\Delta T$$

Thus tensile stress in rod is

$$F/A = -Y\alpha\Delta T$$

Hence F/A is positive in case of decrease in temperature since change in temperature becomes negative.

In case where change in temperature tends to increase in temperature of the body then F and F/A becomes negative, corresponding development of to compressive force and strength.

Finally stress which is positive with decrease in temperature is Tensile stree and stress which is negative with increase in temperature is Compressive stress.

Specific Heat Capacity

If a system undergoes a change of temperature from T to T+ΔT during the transfer of ΔQ amount of heat then heat capacity c of the system is defined as the ratio of

$$c = \frac{\Delta Q}{\Delta T}$$

$$c = \frac{\Delta Q}{m\Delta T}$$

Thus Heat capacity per unit mass of a substance is its specific heat capacity.

where,

m - mass of the substance

ΔQ - Heat absorbed or rejected by the substance

ΔT - Change in Temperature

Specific heat capacity depends on the nature of substance.

It is constant characteristics of the substance and is independent of the amount of substance.

It also depends on the temperature of the substance.

Its unit is J Kg^{-1} K^{-1}

If the amount of substance is specified in terms of no of moles n instead of mass m then the heat capacity per mole of the substance is

$$C = \frac{\Delta Q}{n\Delta T}$$

and is known as Molar Specific Heat capacity.

It is constant characteristics of the substance and independent of the amount of substance. It depends on the nature of the substance, temperature and amount of heat supplied

Its unit is J mol^{-1} K^{-1}

In case of gases, when a gas is heated, ordinary there is change in volume as well as pressure in addition to change in temperature. For simplicity either volume or pressure can be kept constant. Thus gas have two specific heat capacities

- Specific heat capacity at constant volume C_V
- Specific heat capacity at constant pressure C_P.

Calorimetery

Calorimetery means measurement of Heat. Calorimeter is the device used to measure heat and it is cylinderical vessel made of copper and provided by a stirrer and a lid.

This vessel is kept in a wooden block to isolate it thermally from surroundings. A thermometer is used to measure the temperature of the content in the calorimeter. When bodies at different temperature are mixed in a calorimeter, they exchange heat with each other.

Bodies at higher temperature loose heat while bodies at low temperature gain heat. Contents of the calorimeter is continuously stirred to keep temperature of contents uniform Thus principle of calorimetery states that the total heat given by hot objects is equal to the total heat received by cold objects.

Change of Phases

There are three phases of matter i.e, Solid, Liquid and Gas. Substance for example, H_2O exists in solid phase as Ice, in liquid phase as Water and in gas state as Steam. Transition from one phase to another phase are accompanied by absorption or liberation of heat and usually by change in volume even at constant T. Change of phase from solid to liquid is called melting, from liquid to solid is called fusion and from liquid to gas is called vaporisation Once the temperature for phase change is reached (e.g. melting or boiling temperature) no further temperature change occurs until all the substance has undergone phase change. Temperature at which solid and liquid phase are in thermal equilibrium with each other. Boiling point:- Temperature at which liquid and vapour phase are in thermal equilibrium with each other. Change of phase from solid state to Vapour state without passing through liquid state is called sublimation for e.g. Dry Ice and Iodine sublimes.

Latent Heat

The amount of heat per unit mass that must be transferred as heat when a sample completely undergoes phase change is called latent Heat of the substance for the process.Thus when a sample of mass m completely undergoes phase change, the total energy transferred is

$$Q = Lm$$

where,

L- Latent heat and is characteristics of a substance

Its unit is JKg^{-1}.

Latent Heat for a solid liquid change is called Latent Heat of Fusion L_f. Latent Heat for a liquid gas change is called Latent Heat of Vaporisation L_v.

HEAT ENERGY

Heat energy (or just *heat*) is a form of energy which transfers among particles in a substance (or system) by means of kinetic energy of those particle. In other words, under kinetic theory, the heat is transferred by particles bouncing into each other.

UNITS OF HEAT

As a form of energy, the SI unit for heat is the joule (J), though heat is frequently also measured in the calorie (cal), which is defined as "the amount of heat required to raise the temperature of one gram of water from 14.5 degrees Celsius to 15.5 degrees Celsius." Heat is also sometimes measured in "British thermal units" or Btu.

Specific Hat Capacity

Conversion of macroscopic energy to microscopic kinetic energy thus tends to raise the temperature, while the reverse conversion lowers it. It is easy to show experimentally that the amount of heating needed to change the temperature of a body by some amount is proportional to the amount of matter in the body. Thus, it is natural to write

$$\Delta Q = MC\Delta T$$

where M the mass of material, ΔQ s the amount of energy transferred to the material, and ΔT is the change of the material's temperature. The quantity C is called the specific heat of the material in question and is the amount of energy needed to raise the temperature of a unit mass of material one degree in temperature. C varies with the type of material.

Specific heats of common materials

Material	C ($Jkg^{-1}K^{-1}$)
brass	385
glass	669
ice	2092
steel	448
methyl alcohol	2510
glycerine	2427
water	4184

DISTINCTION OF THERMAL ENERGY AND HEAT

In engineering and technology, and particularly in fields that deal with civil energy use and conservation in building construction, heating systems, and power generation, *heat* and *thermal energy* are often indiscriminately used interchangeably. In thermodynamics, heat must always be defined as energy in exchange between two systems, or a single system and its surroundings.

According to the zeroth law of thermodynamics, heat is exchanged *between* thermodynamic systems in thermal contact only if their temperatures are different, as this is the condition when the net exchange of thermal energy is non-zero. For the purpose of distinction, a system is defined to be enclosed by a well-characterized boundary.

If heat traverses the boundary in direction *into* the system, the internal energy change is considered to be a positive quantity, while *exiting* the system, it is negative. As a process variable, heat is never a property of the system, nor is it *contained* within the boundary of the system.

In contrast to heat, thermal energy exists on both sides of a boundary.

It is the statistical mean of the microscopic fluctuations of the kinetic energy of the systems' particles, and it is the source and the effect of the transfer of heat across a system boundary. Statistically, thermal energy is always exchanged between systems, even when the temperatures on both sides is the same, *i.e.* the systems are in thermal equilibrium. However, at equilibrium, the *net* exchange of thermal energy is zero, and therefore there is no heat.

Thermal energy may be increased in a system by other means than heat, for example when mechanical or electrical work is performed on the system.

No qualitative difference exists between the thermal energy added by other means. Thermal energy is a state function. There is also no need in classical thermodynamics to characterize the thermal energy in terms of atomic or molecular behaviour. A change in thermal energy induced in a system is the product of the change in entropy and the temperature of the system.

Heat exchanged across a boundary may cause changes other than a change in thermal energy. For example, it may cause phase transitions, such as melting or evaporation, which are changes in the configuration of a material. Since such an energy exchange is not observable by a change in temperature, it is called a latent heat and represents a change in the potential energy of the system. Rather than being itself the thermal energy involved in a transfer, heat is sometimes also understood as the process of that transfer, *i.e. heat* functions as a verb. Today's narrow definition of *heat* in physics contrasts with its use in common language, in some engineering disciplines, and in the historical scientific development of thermodynamics in the caloric theory of heat. The phenomenon of *heat* in these instances is today properly identified as the entropy.

BASIC IDEAS OF KINETIC THEORY

The zeroth law of thermodynamics gives us a macroscopic (large scale) definition of the concept of the temperature of a body. The kinetic theory of matter can be used to give a microscopic definition of temperature. The *basic* ideas of the kinetic theory are;

- All matter consists of particles (atoms or molecules) in motion
- As the temperature increases, the average speed of the movement increases.

According to this theory, the temperature of a body is a measure of the average kinetic energy of it particles. This theory can also be used to explain the differences between the different states (or phases) of matter.

Solids

The particles vibrate around fixed positions. They are close together and so attract each other strongly. This is why solids maintain their shape.

Liquids

The particles are still relatively close together but now have enough energy to "change places" with each other. This is why liquids can flow.

Gases

Average distance between particles typically 10 times greater than in solids and liquids. The particles now move freely at random, occupying all the space available to them.

CHANGE OF STATE AND KINETIC THEORY

The kinetic theory of matter gives a clear explanation of the internal processes involved at the particle level when matter undergoes a change of state.

Process of Heating

Theoretically, heating a solid to higher and higher temperatures changes its phase to a liquid, and finally to a gas.

Fusion (Solid to Liquid)

A solid consists of low kinetic energy vibrating particles locked into position by interparticle attractive forces. When heat is applied, energy is absorbed and the particles start vibrating more vigorously.

Finally, the vibrations become energetic enough to overcome the attractive forces, and the particles start sliding out of their positions to flow about. The solid is now melting into a liquid.

Vaporisation (Liquid to Gas)

On further application of heat to the liquid, the particles move around more energetically within the volume of the liquid. Finally, they become energetic enough to start escaping from the surface of the liquid, overcoming the backward pull by their neighbours in the volume of the liquid.

The process of boiling has begun, wherein the liquid converts to gas as particles escape to move around independently without any constraints.

Evaporation (Liquid to Gas)

According to the kinetic theory, the temperature is a measure of the average kinetic energy possessed by the particles of matter. This means that in any sample of matter, there will be particles with higher kinetic energy than average, balanced by those with lower energy than average.

So, even in a liquid whose temperature is not high enough for boiling to occur, there will be some particles with sufficient kinetic energy to break through the surface of the liquid overcoming the backward pull of others. They slowly escape as gas particles, and the process is called evaporation.

Process of Cooling

Generally, cooling a gas changes its phase to a liquid, and finally to a solid.

Condensation (Gas to Liquid)

When a gas is cooled (*i.e.* heat is removed) progressively, the free moving particles start losing kinetic energy and slowing down. Finally, the forces of attraction between the lower energy particles colliding with each other are strong enough to hold them together, and the gas begins to condense into liquid.

Solidification (Liquid to Solid)

The particles still have energy enough to slide about within the volume of the liquid, but further cooling lowers this energy further.

Finally, the mutual attractive forces overcome the low kinetic energies of the particles and lock them into fixed positions, where they continue to vibrate as the liquid freezes to solid.

CHANGE OF STATE : MELTING AND BOILING

A material will change from one state to another at specific combinations of temperature and surrounding pressure. Typically, the pressure is atmospheric pressure, so temperature is the determining factor to the change in state in those cases. Names such as boiling and freezing are given to the various changes in states of matter.

The temperature of a material will increase until it reaches the point where the change takes place. It will stay at that temperature until that change is completed.

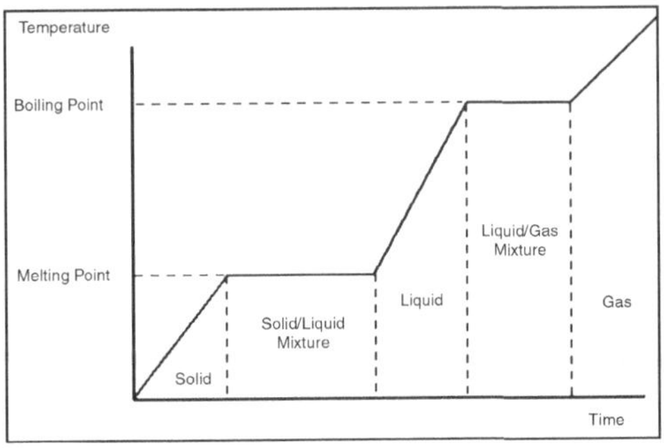

The graph shows the change in temperature of a substance as it is heated steadily. It starts off as a solid, melts (changes to a liquid) and finally boils (changes to a gas). The diagrams represent the arrangement of molecules in the substance at various stages.

Notice:

(a) The molecules become more disordered as these changes take place

(b) There is no temperature change WHILE the substance is changing from a solid to a liquid or from a liquid to a gas

Arrangement of the Molecules

Changes in States Matter

The states of matter are solid, liquid, gas and plasma. Since there is some debate on whether plasma should be classified as a state of matter and since it is not commonly experienced, we will not discuss its properties here.

Names of Changes

Each change in the state of matter has a specific name.

Start from:	*Change to:*	*Name*
solid	liquid	melting
liquid	solid	freezing
liquid	gas	boiling
gas	liquid	condensation
solid	gas	
(skipping liquid phase)	sublimation	
gas	solid	
(skipping liquid phase)	deposition	

Order of Changes

When heat is applied to a material, its change in state typically goes from solid to liquid to gas. There are some exceptions where the material will go directly from a solid to a gas. When a material is cooled, its change in state typically goes from gas to liquid to solid. There are some exceptions where the material will go directly from a gas to a solid.

CHANGE IN TEMPERATURE

When a material reaches the temperature at which a change in state occurs, the temperature will remain the same until all the energy is used to change the state.

Melting

When a solid is heated, its temperature rises until it reaches its melting point. Any additional heat added to the material will not raise the temperature until all of the material is melted.

Thus, if you heat some ice, its temperature will rise until it reaches 0° C (32° F). Then the ice will stay at that temperature until all the ice is melted. The heat energy is used to melt the ice and not to raise the temperature. After the ice is melted, the temperature of the water will continue to rise as more heat is applied.

Boiling

When a liquid is heated, its temperature rises until it reaches its boiling point. The temperature will then remain at that point until all of the liquid is boiled away.

For example, the temperature of a pot of water will increase until it reaches 100° C (212° F). It will stay there until all the water is boiled away. The temperature of the steam can then be increased.

Cooling

Likewise, when a gas is cooled, its temperature will drop until it reaches the condensation point. Any additional cooling or heat loss will not lower the temperature until all of the gas is condensed into the liquid state.

Then the temperature of the liquid will continue to drop as more cooling is applied. Once the liquid reaches the freezing point, the temperature will remain at that point until all of the liquid is solidified. Then the temperature of the solid can continue to decrease.

BOILING AND FREEZING TEMPERATURES

The boiling and freezing temperatures of some common materials at normal atmospheric pressure are:

Material	*Boiling (°C)- becomes a gas*	*Freezing (°C)- becomes a solid*
H_2O (water)	100° C	0°C
Fe (iron)	2750° C	1535°C
O (oxygen)	-183° C	-218°C
Hg (mercury)	357° C	-39°C
Ethyl Alcohol	78° C	-114°C

THE CHANGING STATES OF SOLIDS, LIQUIDS, AND GASES

When a substance goes from one state of matter — solid, liquid, or gas—to another state of matter, the process is a *change of state*. Some rather interesting things occur during this process.

MELTING POINT AS A CHEMISTRY CONCEPT

If you measure the temperature of a chunk of ice, you may find it to be –5° Celsius or so. If you take temperature readings while heating the ice in a pot on your stove, you find that the temperature of the ice begins to rise as the heat from the stove causes the ice particles to begin vibrating faster and faster.

After a while, some of the particles move so fast that they break free of the crystal lattice (which keeps a solid *solid*), and the lattice eventually breaks apart. The solid begins to go from a solid state to a liquid state — a process called *melting*. The temperature at which melting occurs is the *melting point* (*mp*) of the substance. The melting point for ice is 32° Fahrenheit, or 0° Celsius.

If you watch the temperature of ice as it melts, you see that the temperature remains steady at 0°C until all the ice has melted. During changes of state (*phase changes*), the temperature remains constant even though the liquid contains more energy than the ice (because the particles in liquids move faster than the particles in solids).

Boiling Point of Water

If you heat a pot of cool water, the temperature of the water rises and the particles move faster and faster as they absorb the heat. The temperature rises until the water reaches the next change of state – *boiling*. As the particles move faster and faster, they begin to break the attractive forces between each other and move freely as steam – a gas.

The process by which a substance moves from the liquid state to the gaseous state is called *boiling*. The temperature at which a liquid begins to boil is called the *boiling point* (*bp*). The bp is dependent on atmospheric pressure, but for water at sea level, it's 212°F, or 100°C. The temperature of the boiling water will remain constant until all the water has been converted to steam.

You can summarize the process of water changing from a solid to a liquid to a gas in this way:

ice!water!steam

Because the basic particle in ice, water, and steam is the water molecule, the same process can also be shown as:

$$H_2O(s) \rightarrow H_2O(l) \rightarrow H_2O(g)$$

Here the *(s)* stands for solid, the *(l)* stands for liquid, and the *(g)* stands for gas. Unlike water, most chemical substances don't have different names for the solid, liquid, and gas forms.

FREEZING POINT OF A SUBSTANCE

If you cool a gaseous substance, you can watch the phase changes that occur. The phase changes are:

- Condensation – going from a gas to a liquid
- Freezing – going from a liquid to a solid

The gas particles have a high amount of energy, but as they're cooled, that energy is reduced. The attractive forces now have a chance to draw the particles closer together, forming a liquid. This process is called condensation. The particles are now in clumps, but as more energy is removed by cooling, the particles start to align themselves, and a solid is formed. This is known as *freezing*. The temperature at which this occurs is called the *freezing point* (*fp*) of the substance. You can represent water changing states from a gas to a solid like this:

$$H_2O(g) \rightarrow H_2O(l) \rightarrow H_2O(s)$$

SUBLIMATION

Most substances go through the logical progression from solid to liquid to gas as they're heated — or *vice versa* as they're cooled. But a few substances go directly from the solid to the gaseous state without ever becoming a liquid. Scientists call this process sublimation. Dry ice — solid carbon dioxide — is the classic example of sublimation. You can see dry ice particles becoming smaller as the solid begins to turn into a gas, but no liquid is formed during this phase change.

The process of sublimation is represented as:

$$CO_2(s) \rightarrow CO_2(g)$$

In addition to dry ice, mothballs and certain solid air fresheners also go through the process of sublimation. The reverse of sublimation is deposition — going directly from a gaseous state to a solid state.

EVAPORATION

The molecules in a liquid are in a state of continuous motion, some moving faster than others. In the middle of the liquid they collide with each other but at the surface of the liquid some of them are going fast enough to escape from the liquid altogether.

Of course the molecules need energy to escape and so the hotter the liquid becomes the more evaporation there is. Notice that it is only the surface molecules that evaporate and there are no bubbles of gas formed in the body of liquid

Evaporation is very important in the cooling of surfaces. If we put a drop of methylated spirit on our hand the methylated spirit will soon evaporate and our hand feels cold. The molecules of methylated spirit get the energy they need from our hand, leaving the molecules of the hand with less energy and so colder. The same thing happens when you sweat, only in this case you are losing water from your body by evaporation. The evaporation of perfume is why you can smell it – no evaporation means no perfume molecules in the air and so no smell.

You can show the cooling effect of evaporation by the following simple experiment. Air is pumped through the ether. As the ether evaporates pump into the air bubbles it takes away heat energy from the tube, lowering its temperature. Ice will start to form on the outside of the test tube. Ether is a highly volatile liquid, that means that it evaporates easily and so it is ideal for this experiment.

Evaporation is vital for drying washing. The washing will dry better on a warm, dry day than on a cold day and it will also help if it is windy. The warm dry air can hold a lot of moisture and the wind will move the damp air from near the washing, replacing it with more dry air that can then absorb more moisture.

What Causes Evaporation?

It would be difficult to find a more important process in our weather and climate system than evaporation. Evaporation is the change of water from a liquid to a gas. Water is continuously evaporating from the surface of the Earth, literally pumping more and more water vapour into the atmosphere.

Averaged across the entire Earth, water evaporates from the surface at a rate of about 3 millimetres per day (about 1/8 of an inch). Over the tropical oceans, the value is much larger; over cold surfaces, it is much lower; and over deserts it is almost zero, since there is little or no water to evaporate.

This change of phase (from a liquid to a gas) requires heat, called "latent heat". When water evaporates, it removes heat, lowering the temperature of whatever the water was in contact with. For both water and land surface, most of this heat energy comes from the surface, not from the air.

Evaporative cooling, along with convection, helps keeps the surface of the Earth from getting too hot in the presence of solar heating and the Earth's natural greenhouse effect. Interesting facts: Averaged over the whole Earth, Evaporation Equals Precipitation: The only thing that keeps all of this evaporation from filling up the atmosphere with water vapour is precipitation. Rain and snow are continually forming within clouds and falling back to the surface, completing one element of the Earth's hydrologic cycle. The latent heat of condensation, absorbed when the water evaporated, is released to the atmosphere when the water vapour condenses back into cloud water (or cloud ice). This source of heat helps to drive clouds and most other weather systems. For instance, evaporation from the ocean surface is the primary source of energy for hurricanes.

THEORY OF EVAPORATION

For molecules of a liquid to evaporate, they must be located near the surface, be moving in the proper direction, and have sufficient kinetic energy to overcome liquid-phase intermolecular forces. Only a small proportion of the molecules meet these criteria, so the rate of evaporation is limited. Since the kinetic energy of a molecule is proportional to its temperature, evaporation proceeds more quickly at higher temperatures.

As the faster-moving molecules escape, the remaining molecules have lower average kinetic energy, and the temperature of the liquid, thus, decreases. This phenomenon is also called evaporative cooling. This is why evaporating sweat cools the human body. Evaporation also tends to proceed more quickly with higher flow rates between the gaseous and liquid phase and in liquids with higher vapour pressure.

For example, laundry on a clothes line will dry (by evaporation) more rapidly on a windy day than on a still day. Three key parts to evaporation are heat, atmospheric pressure (determines the per cent humidity) and air movement.

On a molecular level, there is no strict boundary between the liquid state and the vapour state. Instead, there is a

Knudsen layer, where the phase is undetermined. Because this layer is only a few molecules thick, at a macroscopic scale a clear phase transition interface can be seen.

Liquids that do not evaporate visibly at a given temperature in a given gas (*e.g.*, cooking oil at room temperature) have molecules that do not tend to transfer energy to each other in a pattern sufficient to frequently give a molecule the heat energy necessary to turn into vapour. However, these liquids *are* evaporating. It is just that the process is much slower and thus significantly less visible.

Evaporative Equilibrium

If evaporation takes place in a closed vessel, the escaping molecules accumulate as a vapour above the liquid. Many of the molecules return to the liquid, with returning molecules becoming more frequent as the density and pressure of the vapour increases.

When the process of escape and return reaches an equilibrium, the vapour is said to be "saturated," and no further change in either vapour pressure and density or liquid temperature will occur. For a system consisting of vapour and liquid of a pure substance, this equilibrium state is directly related to the vapour pressure of the substance, as given by the Clausius-Clapeyron relation:

$$\ln\left(\frac{P_2}{P_1}\right) = -\frac{\Delta H_{vap}}{R}\left(\frac{1}{T_2} - \frac{1}{T_1}\right)$$

where P_1, P_2 are the vapour pressures at temperatures T_1, T_2 respectively, ΔH_{vap} is the enthalpy of vaporization, and R is the universal gas constant. The rate of evaporation in an open system is related to the vapour pressure found in a closed system. If a liquid is heated, when the vapour pressure reaches the ambient pressure the liquid will boil.

The ability for a molecule of a liquid to evaporate is based largely on the amount of kinetic energy an individual particle may possess. Even at lower temperatures, individual molecules of a liquid can evaporate if they have more than the minimum amount of kinetic energy required for vaporization.

Factors Influencing the Rate of Evaporation

Concentration of the substance evaporating in the air.

If the air already has a high concentration of the substance evaporating, then the given substance will evaporate more slowly.

Concentration of other substances in the air

If the air is already saturated with other substances, it can have a lower capacity for the substance evaporating.

Flow rate of air

This is in part related to the concentration points above. If fresh air is moving over the substance all the time, then the concentration of the substance in the air is less likely to go up with time, thus encouraging faster evaporation. This is the result of the boundary layer at the evaporation surface decreasing with flow velocity, decreasing the diffusion distance in the stagnant layer.

Inter-molecular forces

The stronger the forces keeping the molecules together in the liquid state, the more energy one must get to escape. This is characterized by the enthalpy of vaporization.

Pressure

Evaporation happens faster if there is less exertion on the surface keeping the molecules from launching themselves.

Surface area

A substance that has a larger surface area will evaporate faster, as there are more surface molecules that are able to escape.

Temperature of the substance

If the substance is hotter, then its molecules have a higher average kinetic energy, and evaporation will be faster.

Density

The higher the density the slower a liquid evaporates.

In the US, the National Weather Service measures the actual rate of evaporation from a standardized "pan" open water surface outdoors, at various locations nationwide. Others do likewise around the world. The US data is collected and compiled into an annual evaporation map. The measurements range from under 30 to over 120 inches (3,000 mm) per year.

Applications

- When clothes are hung on a laundry line, even though the ambient temperature is below the boiling point of water, water evaporates. This is accelerated by factors such as low humidity, heat (from the sun), and wind. In a clothes dryer, hot air is blown through the clothes, allowing water to evaporate very rapidly.
- The Matki/Matka, a traditional Indian porous clay container used for storing and cooling water and other liquids.
- The botijo, a traditional Spanish porous clay container designed to cool the contained water by evaporation.
- Evaporative coolers, which can significantly cool a building by simply blowing dry air over a filter saturated with water.

Combustion Vapourization

Fuel droplets vaporize as they receive heat by mixing with the hot gases in the combustion chamber. Heat (energy) can also be received by radiation from any hot refractory wall of the combustion chamber.

Pre-combustion Vaporization

The catalytic cracking of long hydro-carbon chains into the shortest molecular chains possible, vastly improves gasoline mileage and provides reduced pollutant emissions once the fuel vapour is at its optimum ratio with air. The chemically correct air/fuel mixture for total burning of gasoline has been determined to be 15 parts air to one part gasoline or 15/1 by weight.

Changing this to a volume ratio yields 8000 parts air to one part gasoline or 8,000/1 by volume. Theoretically, a homogenous mixture can yield gas mileage in excess of 300 miles per gallon, however the actual fuel mileage is highly dependent on the weight of the vehicle.

Evaporation and Boiling

In evaporation high energy molecules leave the surface

of the liquid. These then escape into the surrounding air. However when the liquid boils bubbles of gas from within the body of the liquid and these then rise to the surface.

These bubbles expand as they rise to the surface an increase of external pressure will prevent boiling until a higher temperature is reached. (This was used in the pressure cooker).

The Effect of Pressure and Impurities on Freezing

The effect is known as regulation. This explains why snowballs can be made. When the snow is compressed the pressure between the snow crystals causes melting and refreezing takes place when the pressure is removed. Gentle pressure with the hands may result in a local pressure of 100 atmospheres where the crystals touch and this will lower the freezing point by about 0.75 °C. This is not enough to melt the snow if the external temperature is - 1.0 °C, however, which is why snowballs cannot be made on a very cold day. The enormous pressure at the base of a glacier will cause melting of the ice.

The famous experiment with a wire cutting through a block of ice. This can be explained by regulation. The experiment will not work if thin string is used rather than a copper wire because although the string will cut into the block the ice will not re-freeze over it. This is because the latent heat cannot be conducted away through the string as efficiently as it can through the copper wire.

When salt is added to an ice-water mixture at the freezing point of the mixture is lowered and when it is added to boiling water the boiling point is raised.

VAPOUR PRESSURE AND BOILING

As the temperature of the water increases, its vapour pressure increases. When the vapour pressure equals the atmospheric pressure on the liquid, the liquid will boil. At high altitudes, the boiling point of liquids is lower than at sea level. In Denver, Colorado, water will boil at about 94°C. Do not confuse boiling with cooking. Cooking pasta in Denver is a slower process because the water is at a lower temperature. Also, realise that water boiling rapidly is no hotter than water boiling slowly. The temperature of the water remains constant during the boiling process. And, the temperature of a boiling liquid never rises above its boiling point. No matter how much heat is applied, the liquid only boils *faster*, not *hotter*.

There are fundamental differences between evaporation and boiling. Evaporation occurs at temperatures lower than the boiling point of the liquid. Also, evaporation occurs at the surface of the liquid, whereas in boiling, bubbles of vapour arise inside the body of the liquid. For a bubble to form, the pressure of the atmosphere on the surface of the liquid must be overcome.

HIGH PRESSURE BOILING

We just saw that in Denver, where atmospheric pressure is less, water will boil at a lower temperature. In contrast, at higher atmospheric pressures, a liquid's boiling point increases. This is because the particles in a liquid need more kinetic energy to escape. Pressure cookers reduce cooking time because at high pressure water boils well above 100° C. An autoclave is similar to a pressure cooker. It is commonly used to sterilize medical instruments. Autoclaves are usually set at 120° C and 1520 mmHg (2 atm) for 15 minutes. The high pressure keeps water at a high enough temperature to kill bacteria and their spores.

DIFFERENCE BETWEEN EVAPORATION AND BOILING

Evaporation occurs on the surface of liquid and it is a vaporization of liquid. It is a state of transition from liquid to gaseous state. The process occurs slowly and cannot be seen as well. It occurs when there is exposure of water to air and water molecules change into vapour and these vapours rise up and form clouds. Boiling occurs on the entire mass of liquid and it is the vaporization of liquid. It occurs rapidly. It happens when the vapour pressure of the liquid is equal to the pressure exerted by the environmental pressure on liquid. It is a state of phase transition. The boiling occurs in three different stages: nucleate boiling, transition boiling and film boiling. There are no such stages for evaporation.

Boiling occurs when the temperature of the liquid is greater than the boiling point of the substance. Evaporation can occur at any temperature. It occurs as long as the substance $\rightarrow$ remains $\rightarrow$ liquid at a particular temperature.

According to Greg Bradburn, evaporation occurs when there is an increased energy present and occurs rapidly. It occurs from the bottom of the container when allowed to boil. The bubbles form at the bottom of the container and then rise on top of the container. In boiling, bubbles do not form at the bottom and rise to the surface. Evaporation occurs at room temperature and therefore, occurs at a slower rate when compared to boiling.

In boiling, there is formation of bubbles as it is a complex physical process and these bubbles are formed on a heated liquid. There is cavitation and acoustic effects seen in boiling. There is no such bubbles formed in evaporation and there is no cavitation and acoustic effect present in evaporation.

The microscopic difference between evaporation and boiling is as follows:

In boiling, the motion of particles is increased and this force separates the particles apart from each other. The temperature is uniform and the boiling also occurs throughout. In evaporation the movement of the particles is not the same. Few particles move at slower speed and few particles move at an increased speed. The surface particles are held in place by the particles beneath the surface layer and the particles in the middle layer is held by the forces acting on the sides of the container. The particles on the surface can break easily from the liquid.

The main difference between evaporation and boiling are:

- Evaporation takes place at all temperatures, while boiling occurs at a particular temperature.
- Evaporation takes place from the surface, whereas the entire liquid boils.
- Evaporation can occur using the internal energy of the system, while boiling requires an external source of heat.
- Evaporation produces cooling but boiling does not.
- Evaporation is a slow process while boiling is a rapid process.

CHANGE OF STATE AND LATENT HEAT

When a substance changes from one state to another energy is either absorbed or liberated. This heat energy is called the latent heat, and part of it is the energy used to overcome the forces of attraction between the molecules.

It is clearly useful to know the energy required to change the state of unit mass of the substance. This is known as the specific latent heat and is defined as follows:

The specific latent heat is the energy required to change the state of 1 kg of the substance

Any material has two specific latent heats:

The specific latent heat fusion is the heat energy needed to change 1 kg of the material in its solid state at its melting point to 1 kg of the material in its liquid state, and that released when 1 kg of the liquid changes to 1 kg of solid

The specific latent heat of vaporisation of a liquid is the heat energy needed to change 1 kg of the material in its liquid state at its boiling point to 1 kg of the material in its gaseous state, and that released when 1 kg of vapour changes to 1 kg of liquid. It is important to realise that no temperature change occurs during the change of state. The temperature will only rise or fall when the entire specimen has changed from one state to the other.

Some examples of specific latent heats are given in the following table:

Material	*Specific latent heat of fusion(Jkg^{-1})*
Aluminium	390000
Benzene	400000
Copper	210000
Ethanol	850000
Iron	270000
Ether	350000
Lead	2600
Turpentine	270000
Mercury	1300
Water	2260000
Naphthalene	150000
Solder	70000
Water	330000

Generally the specific latent heats of vaporisation are greater than the specific latent heats of fusion. The change of state from a liquid to a gas results in a large increase of volume and therefore a large amount of work has to be done against the surrounding atmosphere.

In general energy is needed to;

- Change the state of the material at a constant temperature (and pressure), and
- To do external work if there is a change of volume during the change of state.

This external work is usually positive, although there are exceptions. Ice contracts when it melts, the volume of a sample of water being a minimum at 4 °C, and therefore the external work done on melting is negative.

If a volatile liquid is allowed to evaporate from the surface of an object then its latent heat of vaporisation may be used to cool the object: the heat energy needed to evaporate the liquid is drawn from the object itself and so its temperature falls.

Change of state occurs when the heat gained by (or lost from) a body is not accompanied by a rise (or drop) in its temperature. Latent heat is defined as the heat gained or lost by a body during a change of state when it does not result in any change in temperature.

It is also referred to as hidden heat. It is given by the product of the mass of that body and its specific latent heat.

Latent heat = Mass × Specific latent heat

Specific latent heat of fusion is defined as the amount of heat required to change a unit mass of a solid at its melting point into a liquid, without changing its temperature. Specific latent heat of vaporization is defined as the amount of heat required to change a unit mass of a liquid at its boiling point into a gas (vapour), without changing its temperature.

Fusion or melting is the process by which a solid changes into the liquid state at a certain fixed temperature by the absorption of heat energy.The fusion point or melting point is the fixed temperature at which a solid starts changing into the liquid state.

Solidification or freezing is the process by which a liquid changes into the solid state at a certain fixed temperature by the liberation of heat energy. The solidification point or freezing point is the fixed temperature at which a liquid starts changing into the solid state.

Melting point and freezing point are the same temperature and have the same numerical value. For instance, the melting point of ice is 0°C and the freezing point of water is also 0°C.

Vaporization or boiling is the process by which a liquid changes into the gaseous state at a certain fixed temperature by the absorption of heat energy. The vaporization point or boiling point is the fixed temperature at which a liquid changes into the gaseous state.

Liquefaction or condensing is the process by which a gas changes into the liquid state at a certain fixed temperature by the liberation of heat energy. The liquefaction point or condensing point is the fixed temperature at which a gas changes into the liquid state. Boiling point and condensing point are the same temperature and have the same numerical value. For instance, the boiling point of water is 100°C and the condensing point of steam is also 100°C.

Increase in pressure results in a decrease in the freezing point of a substance. For example, the freezing point of water drops below 0°C with an increase in pressure.

Increase in pressure results in an increase in the boiling point of a substance. For example, water boils above 100°C at high pressures.

Addition of solutes results in a decrease in the freezing point of a substance. For example, when salt [a solute] is added to water to form salt water, its freezing point falls below 0°C.

Addition of solutes results in an increase in the boiling point of a substance. For example, when salt [a solute] is added to water to form salt water, its boiling point becomes greater than 100°C.

PRESSURE

The pressure between two solid surfaces depends on:

- The force exerted at right angles between the two surfaces
- The area of contact of the two surfaces.

Pressure = Force/Area (units Pascal where 1 Pascal (Pa) = 1 Nm^{-2})

Examples of high pressure: pencil point, drawing pin point, S hook and coin, running spikes, stiletto heels

Examples of low pressure: large tractor tyres for use in boggy fields, drawing pin head, snow shoes, caterpillar tracks, buildings built on a concrete raft, lying down on quicksand or using a ladder on ice to increase surface area and so reduce pressure, ladder across weak roofs. One of the simplest and best demonstrations to show that the pressure depends on the area of contact is to hold a sharpened pencil between you thumb and forefinger and press. The end with the point digs into your finger while the base in contact with your thumb does not hurt at all. The force is the same but the areas of contact are different!

Stick Slip Motion

When one solid metal object is placed on top of another they do not touch over the whole of their surfaces but only at a small number of points. This is because they are not really totally smooth. This means that the whole weight of the top object will be supported on the very small area of the top of these points. The pressure there will be large and so the two metals are "cold welded" together. If the top surface is pulled sideways it will not move until these welds are broken. When it does it will jerk forward and the welds will then reform. Pulling again will break these new welds and so on. A stick-slip motion results.

TYPES OF PRESSURE

Fluid Pressure

Fluid pressure is the pressure at some point within a fluid, such as water or air.

Fluid pressure occurs in one of two situations:

- An open condition, called "open channel flow"
- The ocean, or
- Swimming pool, or

- The atmosphere.
- A closed condition, called closed conduits
- Water line, or
- Gas line.

Pressure in open conditions usually can be approximated as the pressure in "static" or non-moving conditions (even in the ocean where there are waves and currents), because the motions create only negligible changes in the pressure. Such conditions conform with principles of fluid statics. The pressure at any given point of a non-moving (static) fluid is called the hydrostatic pressure.

Closed bodies of fluid are either "static", when the fluid is not moving, or "dynamic", when the fluid can move as in either a pipe or by compressing an air gap in a closed container. The pressure in closed conditions conforms with the principles of fluid dynamics.

The concepts of fluid pressure are predominantly attributed to the discoveries of Blaise Pascal and Daniel Bernoulli.

Bernoulli's equation can be used in almost any situation to determine the pressure at any point in a fluid. The equation makes some assumptions about the fluid, such as the fluid being ideal and incompressible. An ideal fluid is a fluid in which there is no friction, it is inviscid, zero viscosity. The equation is written between any two points in a system that contain the same fluid.

$$\frac{p}{\gamma}+\frac{v^2}{2g}+z=\frac{p}{\gamma}+\frac{v^2}{2g}+z$$

where:

p = pressure of the fluid

$\gamma = \rho g$ = density·acceleration of gravity = specific weight of the fluid.

v = velocity of the fluid

g = acceleration of gravity

z = elevation

$\frac{p}{\gamma}$ = pressure head

$\frac{v^2}{2g}$ = velocity head

EXPLOSION OR DEFLAGRATION PRESSURES

Explosion or deflagration pressures are the result of the ignition of explosive gases, mists, dust/air suspensions, in unconfined and confined spaces.

Negative Pressures

While pressures are, in general, positive, there are several situations in which negative pressures may be encountered:

- When dealing in relative (gauge) pressures. For instance, an absolute pressure of 80 kPa may be described as a gauge pressure of "21 kPa (*i.e.*, 21 kPa below an atmospheric pressure of 101 kPa).
- When attractive forces (*e.g.*, van der Waals forces) between the particles of a fluid exceed repulsive forces. Such scenarios are generally unstable since the particles will move closer together until repulsive forces balance attractive forces. Negative pressure exists in the transpiration pull of plants, and is used to suction water even higher than the ten meters that it rises in a pure vacuum.
- The Casimir effect can create a small attractive force due to interactions with vacuum energy; this force is sometimes termed "vacuum pressure" (not to be confused with the negative *gauge pressure* of a vacuum).
- Depending on how the orientation of a surface is chosen, the same distribution of forces may be described either as a positive pressure along one surface normal, or as a negative pressure acting along the opposite surface normal.
- In the cosmological constant.

Stagnation Pressure

Stagnation pressure is the pressure a fluid exerts when it is forced to stop moving. Consequently, although a fluid moving at higher speed will have a lower static pressure, it may have a higher stagnation pressure when forced to a standstill. Static pressure and stagnation pressure are related by the Mach number of the fluid. In addition, there can be differences in pressure due to differences in the elevation (height) of the fluid. The pressure of a moving fluid can be measured using a Pitot tube, or one of its variations such as a Kiel probe or Cobra probe, connected to a manometer. Depending on where the inlet holes are located on the probe, it can measure static pressures or stagnation pressures.

Surface Pressure

There is a two-dimensional analog of pressure – the lateral force per unit length applied on a line perpendicular to the force.

Surface pressure is denoted by π and shares many similar properties with three-dimensional pressure. Properties of surface chemicals can be investigated by measuring pressure/area isotherms, as the two-dimensional analog of Boyle's law, $\pi A = k$, at constant temperature.

$$\pi = \frac{F}{l}.$$

PRESSURE OF AN IDEAL GAS

In an ideal gas, molecules have no volume and do not interact. Pressure varies linearly with temperature, volume, and quantity according to the ideal gas law,

$$P = \frac{nRT}{V}$$

where:

P is the absolute pressure of the gas

n is the amount of substance

T is the absolute temperature

V is the volume

R is the ideal gas constant.

Real gases exhibit a more complex dependence on the variables of state.

Vapour Pressure

Vapour pressure is the pressure of a vapour in thermodynamic equilibrium with its condensed phases in a closed system. All liquids and solids have a tendency to evaporate into a gaseous form, and all gases have a tendency to condense back to their liquid or solid form. The atmospheric pressure boiling point of a liquid (also known as the normal boiling point) is the temperature at which the vapour pressure equals the ambient atmospheric pressure. With any incremental increase in that temperature, the vapour pressure becomes sufficient to overcome atmospheric pressure and lift the liquid to form vapour bubbles inside the bulk of the substance. Bubble formation deeper in the liquid requires a higher pressure, and therefore higher temperature, because the fluid pressure increases above the atmospheric pressure as the depth increases.

The vapour pressure that a single component in a mixture contributes to the total pressure in the system is called partial vapour pressure.

Liquid Pressure or Pressure at Depth

Used with liquid columns of constant density or at a depth within a substance (example: pressure at 20 km depth in the Earth).

$$P = \rho g h$$

where:
P is Pressure
g is gravity at the surface of overlaying material
ρ is density of liquid or overlaying material
h is height of liquid or depth within a substance

DERIVATION OF THE KINETIC THEORY FORMULA

Remember that what follows applies to ideal gases only; the assumptions that we make certainly do not all apply to solids and liquids.

This proof was originally proposed by Maxwell in 1860. He considered a gas to be a collection of molecules and made the following assumptions about these molecules:

- Molecules behave as if they were hard, smooth, elastic spheres
- Molecules are in continuous random motion;
- The average kinetic energy of the molecules is proportional to the absolute temperature of the gas;
- The molecules do not exert any appreciable attraction on each other
- The volume of the molecules is infinitesimal when compared with the volume of the gas
- The time spent in collisions is small compared with the time between collisions.

Consider a volume of gas V enclosed by a cubical box of sides L. Let the box contain N molecules of gas each of mass m, and let the density of the gas be r. Let the velocities of the molecules be u_1, u_2, u_3... u_N.

Consider a molecule moving in the x-direction towards face A with velocity u_1. On collision with face A the molecule will experience a change of momentum equal to $2mu_1$.

It will then travel back across the box, collide with the opposite face and hit face A again after a time t, where $t = 2L/u_1$.

The number of impacts per second on face A will therefore be $1/t = u_1/2L$.

Therefore rate of change of momentum = $[mu_1^2]/L$ = force on face A due to one molecule.

But the area of face A = L^2, so pressure on face A = $[mu_1^2]/L^3$

But there are N molecules in the box and if they were all travelling along the x-direction then total pressure on face A = $[m/L^3](u_1^2 + u_2^2 + ... + u_N^2)$

But on average only one-third of the molecules will be travelling along the x-direction.

Therefore: pressure = $1/3\ [m/L^3](u_1^2 + u_2^2 + ... + u_N^2)$

If we rewrite $Nc^2 = [u_1^2 + u_2^2 + ... + u_N^2]$ where c is the mean square velocity of the molecules:

pressure = $1/3\ [m/L^3]Nc^2$ But L^3 is the volume of the gas and therefore:

Pressure (P) = $1/3\ [m/V]Nc^2$ and so $PV = 1/3\ [mNc^2]$

and this is the kinetic theory equation.

Now the total mass of the gas M = mN, and since r = M/V we can write

Pressure (P) = $1/3[\rho c^2]$

The root mean square velocity or r.m.s. velocity is written as $c_{r.m.s.}$ and is given by the equation: r.m.s. velocity

$$= c_{r.m.s.} = [c^2]^{1/2} = [u_1^2 + u_2^2 + \ldots + u_N^2]^{1/2}/N$$

We can use this equation to calculate the root mean square velocity of gas molecules at any given temperature and pressure.

THE KINETIC MOLECULAR THEORY

The Kinetic Molecular Theory Postulates

The experimental observations about the behaviour of gases discussed so far can be explained with a simple theoretical model known as the kinetic molecular theory. This theory is based on the following postulates, or assumptions.

- Gases are composed of a large number of particles that behave like hard, spherical objects in a state of constant, random motion.
- These particles move in a straight line until they collide with another particle or the walls of the container.
- These particles are much smaller than the distance between particles. Most of the volume of a gas is therefore empty space.
- There is no force of attraction between gas particles or between the particles and the walls of the container.
- Collisions between gas particles or collisions with the walls of the container are perfectly elastic. None of the energy of a gas particle is lost when it collides with another particle or with the walls of the container.
- The average kinetic energy of a collection of gas particles depends on the temperature of the gas and nothing else.

The assumptions behind the kinetic molecular theory can be illustrated with the apparatus, which consists of a glass plate surrounded by walls mounted on top of three vibrating motors. A handful of steel ball bearings are placed on top of the glass plate to represent the gas particles.

The glass plate vibrates, which makes the ball bearings move in a constant, random fashion. Each ball moves in a straight line until it collides with another ball or with the walls of the container. Although collisions are frequent, the average distance between the ball bearings is much larger than the diameter of the balls. There is no force of attraction between the individual ball bearings or between the ball bearings and the walls of the container.

The collisions that occur in this apparatus are very different from those that occur when a rubber ball is dropped on the floor. Collisions between the rubber ball and the floor are *inelastic.*

A portion of the energy of the ball is lost each time it hits the floor, until it eventually rolls to a stop. In this apparatus, the collisions are perfectly *elastic.* The balls have just as much energy after a collision as before.

Any object in motion has a kinetic energy that is defined as one-half of the product of its mass times its velocity squared.

$$KE = {}^1/_2\, mv^2$$

At any time, some of the ball bearings on this apparatus are moving faster than others, but the system can be described by an *average kinetic energy*. When we increase the "temperature" of the system by increasing the voltage to the motors, we find that the average kinetic energy of the ball bearings increases.

USE OF THE KINETIC THEORY FORMULA

BOYLE'S LAW

We have PV = 1/3 [mNc^2] but c^2 is proportional to the absolute temperature T.

For a given mass of gas at constant temperature 1/3 [mNc^2] is constant and therefore PV is constant and this is Boyle's law. The Ideal Gas equation for n moles of gas is PV = nRT and so for one mole of gas we have PV = RT, where R is the gas constant. But in one mole of gas there are L molecules where L is the Avogadro constant (6.02×10^{23}) and therefore:

$$PV = (1/3)[mLc^2] = RT$$

Therefore: $1/3\ [mc^2] = RT/L = kT$

and the quantity k (= R/L) is known as Boltzmann's constant (k).

The equation for one molecule may therefore be rewritten as:

$$(1/3)[mc^2] = kT$$

However the mean kinetic energy of a molecule in the gas is $\frac{1}{2}mc^2$ and so:

Mean kinetic energy of a molecule in an ideal gas = $(1/2)mc^2 = (3/2)kT$

You should be able to see from this formula that the mean kinetic energy of a molecule in an ideal gas is proportional to the absolute temperature (T) of the gas.

CHARLES'S LAW

The total mass of gas is mN = M, therefore:

$$PV = 1/3\ [Mc^2]$$

But if the temperature of the gas is changed from T_1 to T_2 with a resulting change in volume from V_1 to V_2, the pressure being kept constant:

$$PV_1 = 1/3\ [Mc_1^2] \text{ and } PV_2 = 1/3\ [Mc_2^2]$$

Therefore:

$$PV_1/PV_2 = [Mc_1^2]/[Mc_2^2] \text{ and so } V_1/V_2 = [c_1^2]/[c_2^2]$$

But kinetic energy = $\frac{1}{2}$ mc^2 and therefore: V_1/V_2 = [kinetic energy$_1$]/[kinetic energy$_2$]

Now one of the assumptions of the kinetic theory is that the kinetic energy of the molecules is directly proportional to the absolute temperature of the gas (T) and therefore:

$$V_1/V_2 = [c_1^2]/[c_2^2] = T_1/T2$$

So the volume is directly proportional to the absolute temperature, and this is Charles's law.

AVOGADRO'S LAW

Maxwell showed that the average kinetic energies of molecules are equal at the same temperature, that is:

$\frac{1}{2} [m_1c_1^2] = kT = \frac{1}{2} [m_2c_2^2]$ and so $[m_1c_12] = [m_2c_2^2]$

But $P_1V_1 = 1/3 [m_1N_1c_1^2]$ and $P_2V_2 = 1/3 [m_2N_2c_2^2]$

Now if $P_1 = P_2$ and $V_1 = V_2$, $[m_1N_1c_1^2] = [m_2N_2c_2^2]$ and therefore:

$$N_1 = N_2$$

and this is Avogadro's law (equal volumes of all gases at the same temperature and pressure contain equal numbers of molecules).

DALTON'S LAW OF PARTIAL PRESSURES

For a mixture of gases:

$$PV = 1/3 ([m_1N_1c_1^2] + 1/3 [m_2N_2c_2^2] + ...)$$

$$P = 1/3 ([m_1N_1c_1^2]/V + 1/3 [m_2N_2c_2^2]/V + ...)$$

$$= P_1 + P_2 + ...$$

where P_1, P_2 ... are the partial pressures of the gases, and this is Dalton's law (the sum of the partial pressures of all the gases occupying a given volume is equal to the total pressure).

$$P = P_1 + P_2 + ...$$

GRAHAM'S LAW OF DIFFUSION

The rate of diffusion of a gas is directly proportional to the mean velocity of the gas molecules, and this is also proportional to $[c^2]^{1/2}$.

Rate of diffusion of gas A/Rate of diffusion of gas

$$= u_A/u_B = [c_A^2/c_B^2]^{1/2} = [r_B/[r_A]^{1/2}$$

This is Graham's law (the rate of diffusion of a gas varies inversely as the square root of the density of the gas). The difference in mass and hence in the diffusion rates of the two isotopes of uranium (238U and ^{238}U) is used in the nuclear industry to separate them, although the differences are small, and so a series of diffusion processes have to be used to obtain sufficient purity.

KINETIC MOLECULAR THEORY OF GASES

The kinetic theory of gases is a topic that can explain many everyday observations. Have you ever wondered why water boils faster at higher altitudes? Or why inflatable pool toys seem flat after sitting in a cold garage? How about why you can smell a candle all throughout the house? All of these phenomena and many more can be explained by the kinetic theory of gases.

The kinetic theory of gases (also known as kinetic-molecular theory) is a law that explains the behaviour of a hypothetical ideal gas. According to this theory, gases are made up of tiny particles in random, straight line motion. They move rapidly and continuously and make collisions with each other and the walls. This was the first theory to describe gas pressure in terms of collisions with the walls of the container, rather than from static forces that push the molecules apart. Kinetic theory also explains how the different sizes of the particles in a gas can give them different, individual speeds.

Postulates

Kinetic theory makes many assumptions in order to explain the reasons gases act the way they do. According to kinetic theory:

- Gases consist of particles in constant, random motion. They continue in a straight line until they collide with something—usually each other or the walls of their container.
- Particles are point masses with no volume. The particles are so small compared to the space between them, that we do not consider their size in ideal gases.
- No molecular forces are at work. This means that there is no attraction or repulsion between the particles.
- Gas pressure is due to the molecules colliding with the walls of the container. All of these collisions are perfectly elastic, meaning that there is no change in energy of either the particles or the wall upon collision. No energy is lost or gained from collisions.
- The time it takes to collide is negligible compared with the time between collisions.
- The kinetic energy of a gas is a measure of its Kelvin temperature. Individual gas molecules have different

speeds, but the temperature and kinetic energy of the gas refer to the average of these speeds.

- The average kinetic energy of a gas particle is directly proportional to the temperature. An increase in temperature increases the speed in which the gas molecules move.
- All gases at a given temperature have the same average kinetic energy.
- Lighter gas molecules move faster than heavier molecules.

THERMAL ENERGY

Keep in mind that the temperature of a gas is actually a measure of its average kinetic energy, and kinetic energy of a particle is related to its velocity according to the following equation:

$$KE = 1/2mv^2$$

where KE represents kinetic energy of a particle, m equals mass, and v^2 is the square of its velocity. As velocity increases so does kinetic energy. Of course the inverse is also true, that as kinetic energy increases so does velocity. You can see from this relationship how a molecule with a higher temperature will be moving faster.

The temperature of the system is the *average* kinetic energy of its particles.

Thermal energy is the total kinetic energy of all the particles in a system. Temperature, thermal energy, and the speed of a molecule are all directly related.

BASIC GAS LAWS

The gas laws are all based on the properties of gases laid down in kinetic theory. In order to further understand of kinetic theory, let us review some of its applications.

BOYLE'S LAW

Boyle's law states that for the pressure and volume of a gas, when one value increases the other decreases, as long as temperature and number of moles remain constant. Boyle's law is summarized by the equation

$$PV = k$$

where P is the pressure of the molecules on the container, V is the volume of the container, and k is a constant. The value of k always stays the same so that P and V vary appropriately. For example, if pressure increases, k must remains constant and thus volume will decrease. This is consistent with the predictions of Boyle's law.

Consider the box full of moving gas molecules. The particles have the same energy (temperature) throughout. As the box gets smaller, they have a smaller distance to travel before they collide with the walls, and thus the time between collisions gets increasingly smaller. In a given amount of time the partials hit the walls more, which results in a greater amount of pressure. The amount of moles is clearly constant, as we are not adding or subtracting particles from the box. Another way of looking at this is that as the pressure increases, it drives the particles together. These compacted particles now occupy less volume. In order to compare a gas where either pressure or volume vary, we can combine the equations $P_1V_1 = k$ and $P_2V_2 = k$. Because k is constant for both values of pressure and volume,

$$P_1V_1 = P_2V_2$$

This equation for Boyle's law is helpful when solving problems.

CHARLES' LAW

Charles' law states that the values for temperature and volume of a gas are directly related. The equation for Charles' law is

$$V/T = k$$

where V is the volume of the container, T is the temperature of the system in Kelvin, and k is the constant. For changes in volume and temperature, k remains the same.

According to Charles' law, gases will expand when heated. The temperature of a gas is really a measure of the average kinetic energy of the particles. As the kinetic energy increases, the particles will move faster and want to make more collisions with the container. But remember that in order for the law to apply, the pressure must remain constant. The only way to do this is by increasing the volume. This idea is illustrated by the comparing the particles in the small and large boxes.

Both particles leave at and return at the same time, but since the red ball travels a longer distance, it must be moving faster and have more energy. You can see that as the temperature and kinetic energy increase, so does the volume. Also note how the pressure remains constant. Both boxes experience the same number of collisions in a given amount of time. For Charles' Law, you can write the combined equation

$$V_1 / T_1 = V_2 / T_2$$

The Pressure Law (Gay-Lussac's Law)

The pressure law states that the values for temperature and pressure of a gas are directly related. As the temperature of a gas increases, so will the average speed and kinetic energy of the particles. This relationship is expressed in the following equation,

$$P/T = k$$

where P is the pressure of the particles on the container, T is the temperature in Kelvins, and k is a constant. At constant volume, this results in more collisions and thereby greater pressure the container. Because the value of k is the same for differing values of pressure and temperature, the pressure law can be written

$$P_1 / T_1 = P_2 / T_2$$

AVOGADRO'S LAW

Avogadro's law states that the volume of a gas is directly related to the number of moles of atoms contained in the gas. The equation for Avogadro's law is

$$V/n = k$$

where V is the volume of the container, n is the amount of gas as measured by the moles of atoms, and k is a constant. Say you have a given amount of particles in a box. If you want to add more particles but you do not want to increase the pressure, you must make the container larger.

GRAHAM'S LAW

Diffusion

Diffusion is a simple process that can be explained by kinetic theory. When you open a bottle of perfume, it can very quickly be smelled on the other side of the room. This is because as the scent particles drift out of the bottle, gas molecules in the air collide with the particles and gradually distribute them throughout the air. Diffusion of a gas is the process where particles of one gas are spread throughout another gas by molecular motion.

But not all gases diffuse at the same rate. The perfume as being composed of all the same molecules. But in reality the perfume would be composed of many different types of molecules: some larger, more dense molecules and other smaller, lighter molecules. Thomas Graham, a Scottish chemist, discovered that lightweight gases diffuse at a much faster rate than heavy gases. Graham's law of diffusion shows the relationship between diffusion and molar mass.

Rate of *f* fusion

$$\alpha \frac{1}{\sqrt{\text{molar mass}}}$$

Consider hydrogen and oxygen. The molar mass of hydrogen is about 1.0 grams/mol and the molar mass of oxygen is about 16 grams/mol. If you insert these values into the equation above, you get that the rate of diffusion for hydrogen is 1 and the rate of diffusion for oxygen is 1/4. This means that hydrogen will diffuse four times faster than oxygen.

Effusion

Effusion is a similar process. Effusion is the process where gas molecules escape from an evacuated container though a small hole. It is assumed that while a molecule is exiting, there are no collisions on that molecule.

Note how the lighter molecules are the first to exit because they have a faster speed. The smaller green molecules exit at a faster rate.

This is where Graham's law of effusion comes in. It tells us the rate at which the molecules of a certain gas exit the container, or effuse. Graham's law of effusion is derived from kinetic theory, consider the equation for the kinetic energy of a gas.

$$KE = 1/2mv^2$$

Because temperature is a measure of the average kinetic energy of a gas, two gases at the same temperature will also have the same kinetic energy. Thus,

$$1/2m_1v_1^2 = 1/2m_2v_2^2$$

Simplify by multiplying both sides by two,

$$m_1v_1^2 = m_2v_2^2$$

By rearranging terms, we get

$$\frac{v_1^2}{v_2^2} = \frac{m_2}{m_1}$$

Taking the square root of both sides gives the equation,

$$\frac{v_1}{v_2} = \sqrt{\frac{m_2}{m_1}}$$

where v_1 is the average velocity of the molecules in gas 1, v_2 is the average velocity of the molecules in gas 2, and m_1 and m_2 are their respective molar masses. According to Graham's law, the molecular speed is directly proportional to the rate of effusion.

You can imagine that molecules that are moving around faster will effuse more quickly, and similarity molecules with smaller velocities effuse slower. Because this is true, we can substitute the rates of effusion into the equation below. This yields Graham's law of effusion.

$$\frac{\text{rate}1}{\text{rate}2} = \sqrt{\frac{m_2}{m_1}}$$

This equation allows us to compare the rates of effusion for two different gases under the same conditions of temperature and pressure. It is important to note that when solving problems for effusion, the gases must contain equal moles of atoms.

REAL GASES

Kinetic theory assumes that all gases behave ideally; however, we know that this is not the case. Obviously real gas particles do occupy space and attract each other. These properties become apparent at low temperatures or high pressures.

Usually the particles have enough kinetic energy that they whiz by each other without being affected by the push or pull of neighbouring molecules. However, at low temperatures the molecules have very little kinetic energy and move around much slower, so there is time for static forces to take hold. At very high pressures, the molecules of a gas become so tightly packed that their volume is significant compared to the overall volume. Also note that before a gas ever reaches absolute zero, it will condense to a liquid.

BROWNIAN MOTION

The ancients such as the philosophers Democritus and Lucretius held that matter was composed of minute particles. They also Maintained that these particles were in a state of continuous random motion within solids, liquids and gases. The theory was therefore called the kinetic theory of matter, after the Greek work kinema-motion. It was not until 1827, however, that actual experimental evidence for these particles existed.

This was provided by the Scottish physicist Robert Brown. He observed a weak solution of milk and later pollen grains in suspension with a high-powered microscope, and saw that the particles of milk and the pollen grains showed a violent and random motion. Brown wrongly attributed what he saw to living organisms, and the true explanation was not given until some thirty years later when the Frenchman Carbonelle proposed that the motion was due to the impacts of the liquid molecules on the milk particles or pollen grains. The motion is now known as Brownian movement.

However the first good explanation of Brownian movement was advanced by the French scientist Desaulx in 1877: "In my way of thinking the phenomenon is a result of thermal molecular motion in the liquid environment (of the particles)."

A simple modern version of Brown's experiment is the smoke cell. A small cell of air is placed under a microscope and illuminated strongly from the side. Some smoke is then blown into it. Through the microscope the particles of smoke can be seen to be in violent random motion just like Brown's pollen grains. This motion is due to the collisions of the (invisible) air molecules with the much larger particles of smoke. Heating the cell makes the smoke particles' motion even more violent due to the increased velocity of the air molecules.

A model of the kinetic theory of gases is shown in the photograph. Small polystyrene beads are held in a plastic tube and vibrated from beneath. The greater the frequency and amplitude of the vibrations the more violent is the motion of the beads.

Placing a small polystyrene ball in the cylinder simulates Brownian motion. The beads collide with the ball which then moves randomly just like the motion of the smoke particles in the smoke cell.

Bibliography

Anatoly, I. Burshtein: *Introduction to Thermodynamics and Kinetic Theory of Matter*, Wiley, London, 1996.

Bailyn, M.: *A Survey of Thermodynamics*, American Institute of Physics Press, New York, 1994.

Bube, R.H. : *Electrons in Solids*, Academic Press, Delhi, 1992.

Carslaw, H. S., and Jaeger, J.C.: *Conduction of Heat in Solids*, Oxford University Press, London, 1959.

Charles Kittel and Herbert Kroemer: *Thermal Physics*. W.H. Freeman and Co., 1980.

Clausius, R.: *The Tragicomical History of Thermodynamics, 1822-1854*, Springer, New York, 1850.

Craig F. Bohren and Bruce A. Albrecht: *Atmospheric Thermodynamics*, Oxford Univ Press, New York, 1998.

Daniel V. Schroeder: *An Introduction to Thermal Physics*. Addison Wesley Longman, 2000.

Fenn, J. B. : *Engines, Energy and Entropy*, W. H. Freeman, 1982.

Glansdorff, P., Prigogine, I.: *Thermodynamic Theory of Structure, Stability and Fluctuations*, Wiley, London, 1971.

Jeffrey D. Lewins: *Teaching Thermodynamics*, Plenum, London, 1986.

Levine, S.N. : *Quantum Physics of Electronics*, The Macmillan company, Delhi, 1965.

Mark W. Zemansky and Richard H. Dittman: *Heat and Thermodynamics: An Intermediate Textbook*. McGraw-Hill, London, 1997.

Mills, A. F.: *Basic Heat and Mass Transfer*, Richard D. Erwin, Inc., Chicago, 1995.

Ozisik, M.N.: *"Boundary Value Problems of Heat Conduction,"* Constable and Company, Ltd., London, 1968.

Patankar, S.V.: *Numerical Heat transfer and fluid flow,* Hemisphere Pub. Corp., Washington, 1980.

Planck, M.: *Treatise on Thermodynamics,* Longmans, Green & Co., London. 1903.

Ralph Baierlein: *Atoms and Information Theory: An Introduction to Statistical Mechanics,* Freeman, 1971.

Sinha, S.K. : *Thermal Physics,* A.K. Pub, Delhi, 2009.

Sonamuthu, K. : *Textbook of High Temperature and Superconductors,* Discovery, Delhi, 2010.

Stephen J. Blundell and Katherine M. Blundell: *Concepts in Thermal Physics,* Oxford University Press, Delhi, 2008.

Streetman, B. G. : *Solid State Electronic Devices,* Prentice-Hall, Delhi, 2000.

Tikhonov, R.E., and Arsenin, V.Y.: *Solutions of Ill-Posed Problems,* V.H. Winston & Sons, Washington D.C., 1977.

Vinay Ambegaokar, *Reasoning About Luck: Probability and its uses in Physics,* Cambridge University Press, Cambridge, 1996.

Zemansky, M. and R. Dittman, *Heat and Thermodynamics,* McGraw-Hill, London, 1981.

Index

L

M

O

P

R

S

T

V

W